Role of Universities in Promotion of Intellectual Property

Role of Universities in Promotion of Intellectual Property

K. Raja Mohan Rao

SERIALS PUBLICATIONS
NEW DELHI

First Published - 2006

ISBN : 81-8387-073-2

Published by

SERIALS PUBLICATIONS
4830/24, Prahlad Street, Ansari Road
Darya Ganj, New Delhi-110002 (India)
Phone : 23245225. Fax : 91-11-23272135
E-mail: serials@satyam.net.in

Dedicated to

An inborn intellectual, an innovative thinker, an inspiring teacher, an outstanding researcher, an able administrator, above all, an open minded straightforward human being who always believes in equity

Prof. Sukhdeo Thorat
Chairman
University Grants Commission
New Delhi

CONTENTS

डॉ॰ तिलक आर. केम
सचिव

Dr. Tilak R. Kem
Secretary

कार्यालय PHONE : 23239337
23236288
निवास RES. : 26870109
24671331
फैक्स FAX : 23238858
E-mail : trkem@rediffmail.com

विश्वविद्यालय अनुदान आयोग
बहादुर शाह ज़फर मार्ग, नई दिल्ली-110 002
UNIVERSITY GRANTS COMMISSION
BAHADUR SHAH ZAFAR MARG,
NEW DELHI-110 002

FOREWORD

The impact of the WTO's General Agreement on Trade in Services (GATS) upon the higher education sector has recently attracted a great deal of debate. Since 1995, the Agreement on Trade-Related Aspects of Intellectual Property (TRIPS) has become most important international agreement on Intellectual Property protections, of date.

The global strengthening of IP protection will undoubtedly have an impact on higher education and research. One central justification for the TRIPS agreement is that strong IP protection encourages innovation, technology transfer and creativity in society by ensuring endeavours. However, opponents feel that strengthening of intellectual property rights stifles research and innovation by restricting the availability of knowledge.

In view of this, under the WTO regime, it is essential to create awareness among the public about IPRs through public outreach programmes by including the same in the curriculum at the graduate and the postgraduate level. It is in this setting, a seminar was organized wherein a number of scholarly papers were presented on issues concerning IPR by academics and scientists. I congratulate Dr. K. Raja Mohan Rao, Reader, Department of Economics, Gandhigram Rural Institute – Deemed University on the successful conduct of the seminar and its academic contribution by bringing this book on intellectual Property issues.

I am sure this book will help popularize issues of Intellectual Property Rights and the role of universities in propagating these rights through curriculum, research and public outreach programmes and paves the way for the development and strengthening of the Intellectual Property regime.

(Tilak R. Kem)

PREFACE

Intellectual property is the commercial application of imaginative thought to solving a technical or artistic challenge. It is not the product itself, but the special idea behind it, the way the idea is expressed, and the distinctive way it is named and described. Countries with innovative local industries almost invariably have laws to foster innovation by regulating the copying of inventions, identifying symbols, and creative expressions. These laws encompass four separate and distinct types of intangible property—namely, patents, trademarks, copyrights, and trade secrets, which collectively are referred to as "intellectual property."

Intellectual property shares many of the characteristics associated with real and personal property. For example, intellectual property is an asset, and as such it can be bought, sold, licensed, exchanged, or gratuitously given away like any other form of property. Further, the intellectual property owner has the right to prevent the unauthorized use or sale of the property. The most noticeable difference between intellectual property and other forms of property, however, is that intellectual property is intangible, that is, it cannot be defined or identified by its own physical parameters. It must be expressed in some discernible way to be protectable.

Knowledge has long been seen as a major determinant of economic growth. In the era of modern science, characterized by technical advances in biotechnology and information and communication technologies, it has been argued that knowledge has become the principal source of competitive advantage between and within countries. In the developing world, the development of national technical capacity has proved to be a key determinant of economic growth and poverty reduction. Realising the potential of knowledge as the main creator of wealth in the new knowledge economy, the focus is now on protecting and managing Intellectual Property (IP).

In common parlance, Intellectual Property can be explained as the expression of an idea. Intellectual Property Rights are a package of rights that can be bought or sold or leased. They include copyrights, patents, trademarks, industrial designs, geographical indications, protection of layout design and protection of undisclosed information (Trade secrets) etc.

Over the last several decades, IP has assumed an increasingly important role in regulating international trade and this phenomenon has led to the incorporation of Trade Related Aspects of Intellectual Property Rights (TRIPS) within the frame work of the World Trade Organisation (WTO) which was established w.e.f. 1.1.1995.

The impact of the WTO's General Agreement on Trade in Services (GATS) upon the higher education sector has recently attracted a great deal of debate. Since 1995, the Agreement on Trade–Related Aspects of Intellectual Property Rights (TRIPS) has become a compulsory agreement for the 144 WTO members and, as such, is the most far–reaching international agreement on intellectual property protection as of date.

One central justification for the TRIPS agreement is that strong IP protection encourages innovation, technology transfer and creativity in society by ensuring endeavors. However, opponents feel that strengthening of Intellectual Property Rights stifles research and innovation by restricting the availability of knowledge. The major challenge being faced to-day relates to management of knowledge that is either protected or protectable and is embedded in the various forms of IP.

One of the major impediments to the effective participation of India in international negotiations and consultations on IPR matters is the absence of an articulate and well informed multi–disciplinary group of professionals dealing with IPR matters. The vision of the few copy-right and patent law practitioners is limited to the respective national laws. Since IPRs encompass the whole of human achievement—all innovations, inventions and intellectual (scientific and artistic) creations—the country requires experts in various branches of IPRs with trans–disciplinary expertise spanning science, engineering, medicine, law, economics and management. Protection of national interests also warrants that our engineers, scientists and other professions also have a fair knowledge of IPR laws and practices.

Innovation is the key to sustained economic development and a source of competitive advantage for nations. Indian research and development has to be globally competitive to fuel this innovation process. The university system needs to do truly innovative research. This requires an environment that facilitates the process. Generation of intellectual property, its capture, documentation, protection, valuation and exploitation assumes crucial importance in this context.

In relation to innovations, universities deal mainly with basic and applied research and the most wide spread forms of IP protection in the system pertain to patents for inventions and copyright for computer software and published work. In the case of research work done by university teachers, students and other staff members, protection of inventions presumes significant importance.

Against this background, it is imperative that the Indian academia turn its attention to IPR issues and help to spread IPR awareness. Moreover, the implications of IPR being largely prospective, the younger generation now learning in universities and colleges need to be sensitized to IPR issues. To this end, courses and programmes in IPRs should be designed and incorporated in the curricula of universities and colleges. Though there are many institutions addressing these issues, the Gandhigram Rural Institute (GRI), being a pioneer rural institute with a three dimensional approach viz., teaching, research and extension, would like to take the lead in addressing various issues relating to IPRs with a special focus on the rural sector, because, in India, irrespective of the economic status, innovative and enterprising youth are often misled into giving away their creations etc. due to ignorance and lack of proper education about their rights.

Keeping these facts in mind, the Government of India has come up with a proposal for propagating the importance of IPR education among all concerned. In this direction a proposal was submitted to the Ministry of HRD, Government of India, for establishing a Centre for Studies in Intellectual Property Rights (CIPS) in Gandhigram Rural Institute, Gandhigram. The Government of India sanctioned Rs. 2.00 lakhs for organizing a National Level Seminar. Accordingly the National Seminar on "Role of Universities in Intellectual Property Education, Research and Public Outreach" was organized by me in our university. I am indebted to our beloved Vice-Chancellor Dr. T. Karunakaran, Our former Vice-Chancellor Dr. G. Pankajam, the Chief Guest of the Seminar Professor Dr. M. Ramadass, Member of

Parliament and guests of honour Dr. R. P. Gangurde, Dr. Maya D. Kem, Dr. Devinder Sharma, and Sri. Sudhir Ravindiran for their intellectual support for the seminar. The papers presented in the seminar have been brought out in this book form.

PROCEEDINGS OF THE SEMINAR

Inaugurating the Seminar, Dr. M. Ramadass, Professor of Economics, Pondicherry Central University and currently Member of Parliament (Lok Sabha), in his special address, advocated that every university should have a specialized centre for Intellectual Property studies in order to educate the people about IPRs and their benefits and he also stressed that such centres should be accountable to the people and that an academic audit should be conducted for performance of these centres. Stating that a "larger section of the people, other than scientists and technocrats, mostly in rural areas, has better ideas and knowledge gained through experience on medicinal plants and their uses, weather conditions, forest management, health and agriculture practices," he emphasized that such traditional ideas and culture based knowledge meant for sustainable development should be protected and patented".

While delivering the presidential address, Dr. T. Karunakaran, Vice–Chancellor, Gandhigram Rural Institute, mentioned that traditional wisdom and modern knowledge should be blended to create a suitable technology for the nation's growth and such technology should be patented. Village–centred economy, child–centred education, women–centred homes and innovation–centred India should be created to make it stronger and knowledge–supported.

Dr. R.P. Gangurde, former Secretary, University Grants Commission in his valedictory address, emphasized that universities that confined themselves to teaching and conducting examinations, should focus on patentable research and production to face stiff global competition. They should create new knowledge and research. If these cells failed to produce IP products, the University Grants Commission should deduct grants given for this purpose.

In the keynote address, Dr. Maya D. Kem, Additional Director–General of Foreign Trade, pointed out that universities had to be more open and flexible, adopting a "cafeteria approach".

The Chairman of the Forum for Biotechnology and Food Security, Devinder Sharma, who is a well known journalist and an international food policy analyst, Mr. Sudhir Ravindran, an international attorney and an expert in Intellectual Property Rights, and Mr. Annamalai, Special Correspondent, the *Hindu*, Madurai, delivered special key note papers and mentioned that India should formulate its own patent policies for its traditional products.

During the four academic sessions, as many as 60 scholarly papers were presented and discussed on themes such as the concept, content and context of Intellectual Property Rights issues and strategies for the protection and propagation of IPRs and conservation of Biodiversity and Traditional Knowledge and the importance of TRIPS under the WTO regime.

In the brain storming session, various ideas were generated on the role of universities in identification of areas of research in IPR education and strategies for public outreach programmes.

RECOMMENDATIONS

1. It was unanimously resolved to recommend the setting up of a Centre for Intellectual Property Studies (CIPS) in GRI.
2. The participants in the seminar expressed great concern about the biopiracy being done of Indian species by the developed countries which requires to be prevented by taking appropriate steps by the Government with the help of Universities and Research Organisations.
3. The Participants also expressed their anxiety with regard to the protection of biodiversity and indigenous technology, for which adequate legislation needs to be passed by the Government on a priority basis.
4. Since there is a lack of awareness about Intellectual Property Rights in the WTO Regime, Universities and Colleges and as well as NGOs must be encouraged to disseminate relevant information to the public in this regard. The media is expected to play an important role in this respect.
5. Universities and institutions of higher education must be encouraged to undertake IP education, research and extension. They may be provided special financial assistance for this purpose. Research projects in this area must be provided financial assistance as a special case.
6. Universities must be encouraged to undertake research leading to patentable products and they should produce at least 5

patentable products every year for which incentives may be provided.

At this backdrop, it is my continued hope that this book will prove to be of value to academics, Researchers, Scientists, Industrialists, Practicing Lawyers, Artists, Writers, Administrators, Social Workers, Students and also to general Public.

(K. RAJA MOHAN RAO)

ACKNOWLEDGEMENT

It is my bounden duty to thank our beloved Vice-Chancellor Dr. T. Karunakaran, who was a constant source of inspiration in organizing the national seminar on *Role of Universities in Intellectual Property Education, Research and Public Outreach* and publishing this book. I express my deep sense of gratitude to Dr. T.R. Kem, Secretary, University Grants Commission, New Delhi, *for* his blessings and also for writing the foreword to this book. My heartfelt thanks are due to my well wisher and mentor Dr. R K. Chauhan, Addl. Secretary, U.G.C., for his blessings, guidance and advice from time to time in successfully organizing this seminar. No words will be adequate to express my gratitude to Dr. G. Pankajam, our former vice - chancellor, who was, in fact, responsible for my taking up this venture.

I am grateful to Dr. M. Ramadass, Professor of Economics, Pondicherry Central University and currently Member of Parliament (Lok Shaba), *for* inaugurating the seminar and delivering the inaugural address. I thank Dr. (Mrs.) Maya D. Kern, Additional Director General, Foreign Trade, Ministry of Commerce, Govt. of India, New Delhi, for delivering the keynote address. No words will be adequate to express my gratitude to Dr. R.P. Gangurde, former Addl. Secretary, University Grants Commission, for delivering the valedictory address.

I also thank our Registrar Dr. M. Sundaravadivelu for his constant support and encouragement. I thank Dr. M.A. Jeyaraju, Professor of English, GRI for his assistance throughout this endeavour.

My special thanks are due to the Intellectual Property Rights experts Dr. Devinder Sharma, International Food *Policy* Analyst & Chairman, Forum *for* Biotechnology & Food Security, New Delhi, Sri Sudhir Ravindran, Intellectual Property Attorney & C.E.O., Global Business Solutions, Chennai, Dr. V. G. Dhanakumar, Professor, Indian Institute of Plantation Management, Bangalore, Dr. M.V. Srinivasa Gowda, Professor, University of Agricultural Sciences, Bangalore, Dr.

S.Y. Hariharan, Professor of International Economics, Madurai Kamaraj University, Madurai, Dr. V. Reddappa Reddy, Professor, Sri Krishnadevaraya University, Anantapur, Mr. Ram Jawahar, Examiner of Patents and Designs, Patents Office, Chennai, Sri S. Annamalai, Special Correspondent, the *Hindu*, Dr. B.D. Ranjitha Kumari, Department of Plants Science, Bharathidasan University, Trichy, Dr. A.A. Dange, Professor of Economics, Shivaji University, Koolhapur, and Dr. B.R. Dwaraki, former Registrar, GR!, who addressed the various sessions and shared their knowledge and experience with the participants. I thank the chairpersons of the various academic sessions who conducted the proceedings faithfully. I also thank the participants for their active involvement and contribution to achieve the objectives of the seminar.

I also wish to thank my colleagues in the department. I thank Sri V. Arunachalam, Deputy Registrar, and Sri N. Karunakaran, Finance Officer, of our institute for their administrative support and timely suggestions. I wish to thank my colleagues Dr. A. Arokiasamy, Mr. S. Nehru, Dr. P. Padmanabha Pillai, Dr. V. Rajarathnam, and Dr. B. Tamil Mani and my Research Scholars Mr. M. Sabesh Manikandan, Ms. S. Vaidehi, Ms. S. Nirmala Mary, and Dr. L.K. Velayutham for their assistance in organizing this seminar. My thanks are due to my students Mr. James, Mr. Muthuraman, Mr. Kumar and Mr. Nagarajan and the students of MCA Mr. S. Vijaya Kumar Reddy, Mr. B.K. Hariprasad, Mr. T. Srinivasa Roo, Mr. K.V.N.R. Radha Krishna, Mr. G. Uma Maheswara Rao and Mr. M. Sudarshan, for their logistic support.

Finally, I wish to place on record my sincere gratitude to the Ministry of Human Resource Development, Government of India, for sponsoring the seminar. I would be failing in my duty if I don't thank Sri L.R. Aggarwal, Under Secretary, Department of Secondary Education, B.P. & Copyright Division, IC Unit, Min. of HRD, who was instrumental in obtaining sanction for the seminar. I thank Ws Serials Publications for bringing out this book.

K. RAJA MOHAN RAO

LIST OF CONTRIBUTORS

Annadurai A., Lecturer, Department of Economics, Madras Christian College, Thambaram, Chennai.

Annapoorani R., Reader in Economics, Avinashilingam University, Coimbatore.

Arul Chellakumar J.A., Reader & Head, St. Joseph's College, Tiruchirapalli–2.

Chitra Thennalesswaran, Lecturer in Commerce, Seetha Lakshmi Ramasamy College (Eve.), Tiruchirapalli–1.

Dange A.A., Professor, Department of Economics, Shivaji University, Kolhapur–416004.

Devinder Sharma, International Food and Trade Policy Analyst, New Delhi.

Dhanakumar V.G., Professor of Quality, Extension and Operations Management, Indian Institute of Plantation Management, Jnana Bharathi Campus, PO. Malathali, Bangalore–560 056.

Dwaraki B.R., Retd. Professor of Rural Sociology, Bangalore.

Eric Ndemo Okoyo, Research Fellow, Department of Rural Development, Gandhigram Rural Institute, Gandhigram, India.

Ganesh S., Reader, Department of Agriculture & Animal Husbandry, Gandhigram Rural Institute, Gandhigram–624302.

Gangurde R.P., Former Addl. Secretary, University Grants Commission, New Delhi.

Hariharan S.V., Professor of International Economics, School of Economics, Madurai Kamaraj University, Madurai–625021.

Kannan G.S., Reader, Department of Agriculture & Animal Husbandry, Gandhigram Rural Institute, Gandhigram–624302.

Lakshmi Narasaiah, Special Officer, Professor of Economics, Sri Krishnadevaraya University Post Graduate Centre, Kurnool–518002.

Masha T., Research Scholar, Department of Home Science, Gandhigram Rural Institute, Gandhigram–624302.

Maya D. Kem, Additional Director General, for Foreign Trade, Ministry of Commerce, Udyog Bhawan, New Delhi.

Mohanasundaram V., Reader, Department of Economics, PSG College of Arts and Science, Coimbatore – 14.

Mohd. Izhar Ahmad, Reader, Department of Economics, Aligarh Muslim University, Aligarh, India.

Mohd. Shamim, Lecturer, Department of Commerce, Aligarh Muslim University, Aligarh.

Nandhini Thiyagarajan, Lecturer, St. Joseph's College, Tiruchirapalli–2.

Narasimha Raghavan G., Research Scholar, Department of Economics, PSG College of Arts and Science, Coimbatore–14.

Nehru S., Senior Lecturer, Department of Economics, Gandhigram Rural Institute, Gandhigram–624302.

Nirmala Mary S., Research Scholar, Department of Economics, Gandhigram Rural Institute, Gandhigram–624302.

Paneer Selvam G., Lecturer in Economics, Adaikalamatha College, Vallam.

Perumal M., Selection Grade Lecturer in Economics, Urumu Dhanalakshmi College, Tiruchirapalli–19.

Raja Mohan Rao K., Reader, Department of Economics, Gandhigram Rural Institute, Gandhigram–624 302.

Ramakrishnan S., Selection Grade Lecturer in Economics, P.M.T. College, Melaneelithanallu.

Ranjitha Kumari B.D., Reader, Department of Plant Science, School of Life Science, Bharathidasan University, Tiruchirappalli-620024.

Reddappa Reddy V., Professor, Department of Rural Development Sri Krishnadevaraya University, Anatapur–515003.

Sabesh Manikandan M., Research Scholar, Department of Economics, Gandhigram Rural Institute, Gandhigram–624302.

Samwel Kakuko Lopoyetum, Senior Post Doctoral Research Fellow, Department of Cooperation, Gandhigram Rural Institute, Gandhigram–624302.

Selvaraj P., Voluntary Development Education Unit, Thoothukudi-628008.

Sivapragasam C., Reader, Department of Applied Research, Gandhigram Rural Institute, Gandhigram–624302.

Srinivasa Gowda M.V., Professor, & University Head, Department of Agricultural Economics, University of Agricultural Sciences, GKVK, Bangalore–560 065.

Suman Pandurang Yesane, Research Scholar, Department of Economics, Shivaji University, Kolhapur, Maharashtra.

Sundaramari M., Reader, Department of Agriculture & Animal Husbandry, Gandhigram Rural Institute, Gandhigram–624302.

Vaheed Z. Ubaidullah, Lecturer, School of Management SASTRA–Deemed University, Thanjavur.

Vaidehi S., Research Scholar, Department of Economics, Gandhigram Rural Institute, Gandhigram–624302.

Vaijayanthi P., Assistant Professor, School of Management SASTRA–Deemed University, Thanjavur.

Veera Sekaran R., State Liaison Officer, NSS, Govt. of Tamil Nadu, Chennai.

1

INTELLECTUAL PROPERTY RIGHTS–CONCEPT, CONTENT AND ENFORCEMENT

K. Raja Mohan Rao

"Intellectual property rights are the rights given to persons over the creations of their minds". They are the rights awarded by society to individuals or organisations principally over creative works: inventions, literary and artistic works, and symbols, names, images, and designs used in commerce. The creator is given an exclusive right to prevent others from making unauthorized use of his/her creation for a certain period of time.

Knowledge is much more than Intellectual Property; it is embodied in people, in institutions and in new technologies in ways that have long been seen as a major engine of economic growth. Ideas and knowledge are an increasingly important part of trade. Most of the value of new medicines and other high technology products lies in the amount of invention, innovation, research, design and testing involved. Music recordings, films, books, computer software and on-line services are bought and sold because of the information and creativity they contain, not because of the plastic, metal or paper used to make them. Many products that used to be traded as low-technology goods or commodities now contain a higher proportion of invention and design in their value—for example brand-named clothing or new varieties of plants.

Creators can be given the right to, like mentioned above, prevent others from using their inventions, designs or other creations, but they can also allow others to use those rights in return for payment. Protection of Intellectual Property rights is directed against unauthorized use. They take a number of forms, like for example, books, paintings and films come under *copyright;* inventions can be *patented;* brand-names and product logos can be registered as *trademarks;* and so on. Governments have given creators these rights giving them the opportunity to produce ideas that will benefit the society as a whole.

Intellectual Property Rights (IP) is, therefore divided into two categories:

(i) *Industrial Property (functional commercial innovations)* consisting of: inventions or patents, trademarks, industrial designs, geographic indications and protection against unfair competition.

(ii) *Copyrights (cultural creations):* literary and artistic works such as novels, poems and plays, films, musical works, artistic works such as drawings, paintings, phonographs and sculptures, and architectural designs. *Copyright related Rights* are those of performing artists in their performances, producers of phonograms in their recordings, and those of broadcasters in their television and radio programs.

I. INDUSTRIAL PROPERTY

Industrial Property is divided into four categories:

Structure of Industrial Property

1. *Patents for inventions*

Inventions are solutions to specific problems in the field of technology, related to a process or a product. They are protected by patents which are exclusive rights awarded to an inventor for a new invention. The inventor or the owner of the patent can prevent others from commercially making, selling, distributing, importing or using their invention, without licence or authorisation, for a fixed period of time (generally 20 years17).

These rights are granted by patent offices enabling the inventor property on his/her inventions and the possibility of exploiting them. The society requires inventors to disclose the invention, to put them into practice so that others can gain benefit from them and use them for further research.

The owner of a patent has the right to take action against unauthorised use of the patented invention in order to remunerate his effort, work and expenses spent for research and experimentation leading to the invention. This can be seen as the owner's most important rights.

- ***Protection***

A *patent is a territorial right* (there is no patent common to all states), it protects the invention only within the country for which the patent protection has been applied. Patent rights granted by the State are not automatically enforced, because it is up to the owner to take action against any infringements.

An Invention has to fulfil certain criteria in order to be protected. These are Novelty (invention has to be new), based on an "inventive step", and Industrial applicability (Utility). The WIPO includes two more requirements: Patentable Subject Matter and Disclosure (where the invention is clearly described by the inventor and published by the Patent Office).

2. ***Trademarks***

"A trademark is any sign that individualizes the goods of a given enterprise distinguishing it from the goods of its competitors."

There are several types of trademarks depending on: the sign that constitutes the mark (e.g. graphic marks, three-dimensional marks, etc.), on their popularity (common or well-known marks), on the holder (individual and collective marks), on the object they represent and finally, depending on the sense that perceives them.

Trademarks provide exclusive rights to use a variety of signs such as: colours, symbols, letters, shapes or names to identify the producer of a product, and protect its associated reputation. A Trademark does not protect ideas, unless it has been materialised and fulfils legal requirements for trademark protection. The key element of a trademark is its distinctiveness; the consumer distinguishes a product sold from one enterprise from other goods and services offered by other enterprises on the market. These two functions of individualism and distinguishment cannot really be separated.

- ***Protection***

A trademark can be protected either on a basis of registration in a Mark Office or by use. In countries where trademark protection is based on use, registration only confirms the trademark right that has been accomplished by use. Therefore, the first user has the right over the one who has fist registered the trademark. Through protection, the owner of the mark has the exclusive right over the mark, he can forbid others in using identical or similar marks, or authorise a third party for the use of the protected sign. The period of protection varies, in most countries lasting 10 years, but a trademark can be renewed indefinitely on payment of corresponding fees.[1]

Trademarks are only valid in the country where the person had applied for trademark registration. Depending on territory, the mark can be a:[2]

(i) *National mark:* valid in the country of request under national legislation,

(ii) *Community mark:* In the European level, there is a Community trademark valid for the whole EU territory, where a single application is submitted to the Office for Harmonization in the Internal Market (OHIM) and the holder has a trade mark valid for all EU Member States,

(iii) *International mark:* Group of national marks, with a common application procedure. Protection is granted by the World Intellectual Property Organization (WIPO), in accordance with the Madrid Agreement and Protocol.

Trademark protection is enforced by the courts, which in most systems have the authority to block trademark infringement. Trademarks promote initiative and enterprise worldwide by rewarding the owners of trademarks with recognition and financial profit. Its protection also keeps in the efforts of unfair competitors, such as counterfeiters, to use similar distinctive signs to market inferior or different products or services. "The system enables people with skill and enterprise to produce and market goods and services in the fairest possible conditions, thereby facilitating international trade".[3]

Legal Infrastructure includes both foreign treaty participation and local trademark laws. The main foreign trademark treaties signed were the Madrid Agreement, the Nice Agreement concerning the International Classification of Goods and Services for the Purposes of the Registration of Marks, the Paris Convention for the Protection of Industrial Property and the TRIPS agreement (Trade Related Aspects of Intellectual Property Rights). Transitional countries had a foreign treaty participation rate of 79,17%. The Local Legal Infrastructure was low.[4]

The time certain countries needed to get foreign trademarks approved differed from country to country. Transitional economies ranked slowest on foreign processing time, at 2,17 years. These countries expereinced the greatest percentage increase in foreign trademark application over the period-nearly 1780%.[5]

3. *Industrial Design*

An Industrial Design is an Ornamental aspect of a useful article: lines or colours or three dimensional elements. These are "Aesthetic creations determining the appearance of industrial products".[6] Industrial designs protect the aesthetic aspects like shape, texture, pattern, and colour of an object, rather than the technical features.

- ***Protection***

The design must fulfil certain criteria in order to be protected. These are: it has to be new (not made public before registration), original (author's work and not an imitation) or enjoy an individual character (consumer's impression when he sees the product). In some countries there is another criteria added, its useful function, meaning that the product has to have a function for which it has been created.

Community Designs, valid for the EU territory must fulfil the criteria of novelty and individual character in order to be protected under the Council Regulation on Community Design.[7] The TRIPS agreement requires that an original design be eligible for protection from unauthorized use by others for a minimum of 10 years.[8]

4. *Geographical Indications*

"A Geographical Indications (GIs) is a sign used on a good to identify the specific geographical origin of a product, and the associated qualities, reputation or other characteristics".[9] They usually consist of the name of the place of origin, for example, agricultural products sometimes have qualities that derive from their place of production and local environmental factors. Parties tending to use protected geographical indications for products not from the region or misleading the public as to the true origin of the product are prevented in doing so by the geographical indication.[10]

II. COPYRIGHTS AND RELATED RIGHTS

1. *Copyrights*

Copyrights are individual rights of an author to dispose his work, inventions of remuneration. Copyright grants exclusive rights to the creators of original literary, scientific and artistic works. They only prevent copying, not independent derivation. Copyright deals with the rights of intellectual creators in their creation. Works, like books, paintings, or drawings, exist only once they are embodied in a physical object. However, poems, or music are works even before they have been written down by a musical notation or words.[11]

- ***Protection***

Many different types of works are protected by copyrights like literary works (novels, poems, stories, etc.), musical works (songs, operas, etc.), artistic works (drawings, paintings, sculptures, etc.), maps and technical drawings, photographic works (Portraits, lands capes, etc.), motion pictures, computer programmes, data bases, etc.

Copyright protection is independent from the quality of the work and the author's purpose in doing such a work, as the final objective is not related to its protection. Copyright protection begins, without formalities (registration), with the creation of the work, and lasts (as a general rule), as stipulated under the TRIPS Agreement, for the life of the creator plus 50 years (70 years in the US and EU).

Protection prevents unauthorised reproduction, public performance, broadcasting, recording translation, or adaptation, and allows the collection of royalties for authorised use. Computer programs are protected by copyrights, as software source and code have been defined as a literary expression.[12]

In order of a copyright to be protected, a work needs to fulfil two conditions regarding its form of expression (materialisation of the form of expression like in a compact disc, computer program and so on) and originality (marked by the personality of its creator, meaning that the creator has played a decisive role in determining the form of the work).[13] Copyright protection comprises two main sets of rights: the economic and the moral rights. The economic rights are rights of the reproduction, broadcasting and so on, whereas moral rights include author's right to object to any distortion, or modification of his work that might have an effect on his honour or reputation.[14]

Related Rights include neighbouring rights of performers and broadcasters, moral rights of original artists, and copyrights for derivative products. It consists of the development of reproduction technology for printing to photography, radio, films, and television.[15]

- *Protection Against Unfair Competition:* The WIPO Model Provisions on Protection Against Unfair Competition defines the "failure to correct or supplement information concerning a product test published in a consumer magazine, thereby giving a wrong impression of the quality of the product offered on the market, or failure to give sufficient information concerning the correct operation of a product or concerning possible sideeffects of a product," as an act of unfair competition.[16] Article 10 was added to the Paris Convention trying to protect unfair competition.[17]
- *Trade Secrets:* Trade secrets consist of commercially valuable information about production methods, business plans, clientele, etc. They are protected as long as they remain secret by laws which prevent acquisition by commercially unfair means and unauthorised disclosure.
- *Database Protection:* The EU has adopted legislation to provide sui generis protection in respect of databases, preventing unauthorised use of data compilations, even if nonoriginal. Exclusive rights to extract or utilize all or a substantial part of the contents of the protected database are granted.[18]

AGREEMENTS PROTECTING INTELLECTUAL PROPERTY RIGHTS: AN OVERVIEW

The protection of intellectual property is governed by a number of international treaties and conventions, which are implemented by two main organisations, the World Intellectual Property Organisation (WIPO) which administers some 23 treaties and has

181 member states[19] and the World Trade Organisation (WTO).

International Treaties protecting Intellectual Property are: the Berne Convention for the Protection of Literary and Artistic Works; Brussels Convention Relating to the Distribuiton of Programme-Carrying Signals Transmitted by Satellite; Convention for the Protection of Producers of Phonograms Against unauthorized Duplication of their Phonograms; Madrid Agreement for the Repression of False or Deceptive Indications of Source on Goods; Nairobi Treaty on the Protection of the Olympic Symbol; Paris Convention for the Protection of Industrial Property; Patent Law Treaty (PLT); Rome Convention for the Protection of Performers, Producers of Phonograms and Braodcasting Organizations; Trademark Law Treaty (TLT); Treaty on the International Registration of Audiovisual Works (Film Registy Treaty); Washington Treaty on Intellectual Property in Respect of Integrated Circuits; WIPO Copyright Tretay (WCT); and WIPO Performances and Phonograms Treaty (WPPT).[20]

THE WORLD INTELLECTUAL PROPERTY ORGANISATION (WIPO)

The WIPO is one of the specialised agencies of the United Nations (UN), who is responsible for taking action in accordance with its basic instruments, treaties and agreements administered by it and it promotes creative intellectual activity and faciliates the transfer of technology related to the industrial property to the developing countries in order to accelarate economic, social and cultural development.[21] The WIPO is increasingly involved in helping, among others, developing and Central and Eastern European countries, to receive full benefits of the creations of their citizens, assisting them in the enforcement of laws, in the establishment of sound institutions, and administrative structures, and in the training of the appropriate personnel. WIPO's development program is closely interwoven with governmental and intergovernmental cooperation, including its agreement with the WTO's aimed to assist developing countries in the implementation of WTO's TRIPS Agreement.

The WIPO launched a project in 1999 which benefited to the sharing of valuable intellectual property information through the worldwide global IP information network WIPOnet, designed to establish a secure global network linking the IP offices of all WIPO's

Member states which have access to it and provides the exchange of information worldwide.[22]

THE AGREEMENT ON TRADE RELATED ASPECTS OF INTELLECTUAL PROPERTY RIGHTS (TRIPS)

The WTO's TRIPS Agreement, negotiated in the 1986- 94 Uruguay Round, which came into effect on 1 January 1995, introduced intellectual Property rules for the first time, creating new order and settling disputes more systematically. Before the Uruguay Round, no specific intellectual property agreements existed under the General Agreement of Tariffs and Trade (GATT) framework.[23] It was an attempt to narrow the gaps in the way of protection of these rights in different countries and bring them under international rules. The Agreement established minimum standards governing copyrighted literary, artistic works, rights related to copyright law, patents, trademarks, geographical indication, etc. and even touching related issues to unfair competition law.[24] The TRIPS Agreement covers five broad issues:

- The way basic principles of the trading system and other international intellectual property agreements should be applied;
- The way to give adequate protection to intellectual property rights-that all member states should have adequate standards of protection;
- The way countries should enforce those rights adequately in their own territories;
- How to settle disputes on intellectual property between members of the WTO; and
- Special transitional arrangements during the period when the new system is being introduced.[25]

The transitional periods depends on the level of development of the country concerned. Developed country Members were given 1 year (from 1 January 1995) to ensure that their laws and practices conform to all of the provisions of the TRIPS Agreement. For developing countries (under certain conditions), the general transitional period was five years, i.e. until 1 January 2000.[26] Least developed countries were given 11 years, until 2006–now extended to 2016 for pharmaceutical patents.

Any other Member which is in the process of transformation from a centrally-planned into a market, free-enterprise economy and which is undertaking structural reform of its intellectual property system and facing special problems in the preparation and implementation of intellectual property laws and regulations may also benefit from a period of delay of four years after the date of application.[27]

Protection of intellectual property can contribute to technical innovation and the transfer of technology. The TRIPS agreement includes a number of provisions on this, requiring developed countries governments to provide incentives for their companies to transfer technology to leastdeveloped countries. Both the producers and users should benefit improving the economic and social welfare.[28]

The TRIPS Agreement requires that the substantive obligations of the main conventions of WIPO, the Paris Convention and the Berne Convention in their most recent versions, must be complied with. With the exception of the provisions of the Berne Convention on moral rights, all the main substantive provisions of these conventions are incorporated by reference and thus become obligations under the TRIPS Agreement between WTO Member countries.[29]

The desire of transitional economies to join the WTO and at least agree to its terms may indicate that many more of these countries are expecting greater trade and investment relationships in the future.

PROTECTION OF GLOBAL BRANDS

Global Brands are becoming more attractive to buyers worldwide. International firms use these established brands to facilitate foreign market entry and exploit scale economies in the development of products, packaging and promotion. In order for global marks to be protected, international firms are concerned about the protection of trademarks in various national markets. In countries where trademark protection is weak, or it does not exist, the firm can face a loss because of pre-emption (legally registering a foreign brand name in the domestic market, to exploit brand equity in the domestic market or domestic use back to foreign owner); brand imitation (a product different but barely distinguishable from a famous foreign one) or counterfeiting (illegally copying the trademarks of others).[30]

The TRIPS Agreement requires member states of the WTO to grant special protection to wellknown foreign brands and it clarifies and enlarges both the definitions of well-known brands to the advantage of international firms. These brands do not have to be sold in national markets to be well known. The question arises how ambitious is the WTO vision of establishing global norms for trademark protection? How easy is it for countries to comply and comply quickly?[31]

Many countries are faced with the problems of a lack of enforcing laws and the continuation of counterfeiting are also mentioned. The establishment and enforcement of global norms for trademark protection has been a challenge for the WTO in the first few years. National governments have provided trademark protection in national markets. However this protection has varied. Developing countries are characterised as offering less protection than developed countries. In a survey of 120 trademark counsels, only two developing countries were rated among the top ten best countries for trademark registration, and only one among the top ten for trademark protection.[32] Transitional economies, or countries of the former eastern block have received examination as a distinct country group, because of their recent shared history as a communist command economies. There are clear differences along the dimensions of privatization not only between developed countries and developing countries but between these two groups and transitional economies, which shows why this particular category should be tested separately in future investigations.[33]

The incoming of economic and policy consultants from the West to the transitional economies during the early 1990s had some impact on the transitional economies, causing them to adopt policies similar to those of developed countries and provide trademark protection greater than that of less developed countries (LDCs).[34]

Therefore, there is a need for enforcing the IPRs because, strengthening IPRs enhances growth and development raising, The Enforcement of IPRs can generally take, according to the WIPO, four forms: Administrative Enforcement, Criminal Enforcement, Civil Enforcement, and Technological Enforcement.[35] Some countries do not have the institutional structures and financial resources to administer and enforce laws. The discrepancy is greater for countries that adopt strict measures which result in greater expectations regarding the administration of trademark protection. Transitional economies may administer laws better than LDCs.[36]

In this regard, Universities can play a vital role in propagation of IPRs by including IPR matters in the curriculum at all levels in the university systems of education and also by way of creating awareness among general public through public out reach programmes. Because, one of the major impediments to the effective participation of India in international negotiations and consultations on IPR matters is the absence of an articulate and well informed multi-disciplinary group of professionals dealing with IPR matters. The vision of the few copyright and patent law practitioners is limited to the respective national laws. Since IPRs encompass the whole of human achievement-all innovations, inventions and intellectual (scientific and artistic) creations–the country requires experts in various branches of IPRs with trans–disciplinary expertise spanning science, engineering, medicine, law, economics, and management. Protection of national interests also warrants that our engineers, scientists and other professional have a fair knowledge of IPR laws and practices.

NOTES AND REFERENCES

1. WIPO (2001), WIPO Intellectual Property Handbook: Policy, Law and Use, WIPO Publication No. 489 (E), in www under http://www.wipo.int/about-ip/en/iprm/index.
2. IPR-Helpdesk, Trade Marks Guide, in www under http://www.ipr-helpdesk.org, p. 9.
3. http://ww.wipo.org.
4. De Castro, Uhlenbruck (1997), pp.123-143, quoted in Gillespie, K., Krishna, K., Jarvis, S. (2001): Protecting Global Brands: Toward a Global Norm. In: Journal of International Marketing, Vol. 10, No. 2, pp. 99-111.
5. Gillespie, K., Krishna, K., Jarvis, S. (2001), Protecting Global Brands: Toward a Global Norm. In: Journal of International Marketing, Vol.10, No. 2, pp. 99-111.
6. WIPO (2001), WIPO Intellectual Property Handbook: Policy, Law and Use, WIPO Publication No.489 (E), in www under http://www.wipo.int/about-ip/en/iprm/index, p. 3.
7. IPR-Helpdesk, Designs Guide, in www under http://www.ipr-helpdesk.org, p. 3f.

8. Commission on Intellectual Property Rights (2002), Integrating Intellectual Property Rights and Development Policy, Report of the Commission on Intellectual Property Rights, in www under http://www.iprcommission.org, p. 14.
9. Commission on Intellectual Property Rights (2002), Integrating Intellectual Property Rights and Development Policy, Report of the Commission on Intellectual Property Rights, in www under http://www.iprcommission.org, p. 14.
10. Commission on Intellectual Property Rights (2002), Integrating Intellectual Property Rights and Development Policy, Report of the Commission on Intellectual Property Rights, in www under http://www.iprcommission.org, p. 14.
11. WIPO (2001), WIPO Intellectual Property Handbook: Policy, Law and Use, WIPO Publication No.489 (E), in www under http://www.wipo.int/about-ip/en/iprm/index, p. 41.
12. Commission on Intellectual Property Rights (2002), Integrating Intellectual Property Rights and Development Policy, Report of the Commission on Intellectual Property Rights, in www under http://www.iprcommission.org, p. 15.
13. IPR-Helpdesk, Guide on copyright, in www under http://www.ipr-helpdesk.org, p. 1f.
14. http://www.wipo.int.
15. Philips, J., p. 111 in WIPO (2001), p. 43.
16. http://www.wipo.org.
17. http://www.wipo.org.
18. http://www.iprcommission.org.
19. http://www.wipo.int.
20. http://www.wipo.int.
21. WIPO (2001), WIPO Intellectual Property Handbook: Policy, Law and Use, WIPO Publication No. 489 (E), in www under http://www.wipo.int/about-ip/en/iprm/index, p. 3-4.
22. WIPO (2001), WIPO Intellectual Property Handbook: Policy, Law and Use, WIPO Publication No. 489 (E), in www under http://www.wipo.int/about-ip/en/iprm/index, p. 4f.
23. Gillespie, K., Krishna, K., Jarvis, S. (2001), Protecting Global Brands: Toward a Global Norm. In: Journal of International Marketing, Vol.10, No. 2, pp. 99-111.
24. TRIPS Agreement, supra note 1, Arts. 9-39.
25. http://www.wto.org.

26. TRIPS Agreement, Article 65, Transitional Arrangements, Paragraphs 1 and 2; Articles 41- 51, Paragraphs 1- 4; Part 2, Section 1-6 in www under http://www.wto.org/ english/docs_e/legal_e/27-trips.doc. Paragraphs 1 and 2.

27. TRIPS Agreement, Article 65, Transitional Arrangements, Paragraphs 1 and 2; Articles 41- 51, Paragraphs 1- 4; Part 2, Section 1-6 in www under http://www.wto.org/english/docs_e/legal_e/27-trips.doc. Paragraph 3.

28. http://www.wto.org.

29. http://www.wto.org.

30. Gillespie, K., Krishna, K., Jarvis, S. (2001), Protecting Global Brands: Toward a Global Norm. In: Journal of International Marketing, Vol.10, No. 2, pp. 99-111.

31. Gillespie, K., Krishna, K., Jarvis, S. (2001), Protecting Global Brands: Toward a Global Norm. In: Journal of International Marketing, Vol.10, No. 2, pp. 99-111.

32. Nurton (1996), pp. 23-30, quoted in Gillespie, K./Krishna, K./Jarvis, S. (2001): Protecting Global Brands: Toward a Global Norm. In: Journal of International Marketing, Vol.10, No. 2, pp. 99-111.

33. De Castro, Uhlenbruck (1997), pp. 123-143, quoted in Gillespie, K./ Krishna, K./Jarvis, S. (2001): Protecting Global Brands: Toward a Global Norm. In: Journal of International Marketing, Vol.10, No. 2, pp. 99-111.

34. Gillespie, K., Krishna, K., Jarvis, S. (2001), Protecting Global Brands: Toward a Global Norm. In: Journal of International Marketing, Vol.10, No. 2, pp. 99-111.

35. Sharp and Barz (1997), p. 110, quoted in Smarzynska/Beata, K. (2002): World Bank, Policy Research Working Paper, the Composition of Foreign Direct Investment and Protection of Intellectual Property Rights, Evidence from Transition Economies, in www under http://www.worldbank.org.

36. Kaufmann (1995), pp. 26-31, quoted in Gillespie, K./Krishna, K./ Jarvis, S. (2001): Protecting Global Brands: Toward a Global Norm. In: Journal of International Marketing, Vol.10, No. 2, pp. 99-111.

2

ROLE OF UNIVERSITIES IN PROMOTION OF PATENTABLE RESEARCH UNDER INTELLECTUAL PROPERTY REGIME

R.P. Gangurde

INTRODUCTION

Intellectual property (**IP**) refers to certain kinds of exclusive rights to intellectual capital, some forms of which can expire after a set period of time, and other forms of which can last indefinitely.

The term *intellectual property* appears to have originated in Europe during the 19th century. French author A. Nion mentions *"propriété intellectuelle"* in his *Droits civils des auteurs, artistes et inventeurs,* published in 1846, and there may well have been earlier uses of the term.

Common types of Intellectual Property Rights Include

Copyrights, which give the holder some exclusive rights to control some reproduction of works of authorship, such as books and music, for a certain period of time.

Patents give the holder an exclusive right to use and license use of an invention for a certain period, typically 20 years from the filing date of a patent application.

Trademarks are distinctive names, phrases or marks used to identify products to consumers.

Trade secrets, where a company keeps information secret, perhaps by enforcing a contract under which those given access to information are not permitted to disclose it to others. These rights, conferred by law, can be given, sold, rented (called "licensing") and, in some countries, even mortgaged, in much the same way as physical property. However, the rights typically have limitations, sometimes including term limits and other exceptions (such as fair use for copyrighted works.)

LEGAL STATUS

Intellectual property rights are generally divided into two categories: those that grant exclusive rights only on copying/ reproduction of the item or act protected (e.g. copyright) and those that grant not only this but also other exclusive rights. The difference between these is that a copyright would prevent someone from copying the design of something, but could not stop them from making that design if they had no knowledge of the original held by the copyright holder. A patent, on the other hand, can be used to prevent that second person from making the same design even if they had never heard of or seen the original. Patent rights can thus be more powerful, and generally harder to obtain and more expensive to enforce.

There are also more specialized varieties of so-called *sui generis* intellectual property rights, such as circuit design rights (called mask work rights in USA law, protected under the Integrated Circuit Topography Act in Canadian law, and in European Community Law by Directive 87/54/EEC of 16 December 1986 on the legal protection of topographies of semiconductor products), plant breeder rights, plant variety rights, industrial design rights, supplementary protection certificates for pharmaceutical products and database rights (in European law).

Generally, the action regulated by intellectual property is unauthorized reproduction. However, as indicated above, some rights go beyond this to grant a full suite of exclusive rights on a particular idea or product. Generally, it is true to say that intellectual property rights grant the holder the ability to stop others doing something (i.e., a negative right), but not necessarily a right to do it themselves (i.e., a positive right). For example, the holder of a patent on a pharmaceutical product may be able to prevent others selling it, but (in most countries) cannot sell it themselves without a separate license from a regulatory authority.

Most intellectual property rights are nothing more than the right to sue an infringer, which has the effect that people will approach the right holder for permission to perform the acts covered by the right holder's exclusive rights. The granting of this permission is termed licensing, and IP licenses may be used to impose conditions on the licensee, generally the payment of a fee or an undertaking not to engage in particular forms of conduct. In many jurisdictions the law places limits on what restrictions the licensor (the person granting the license) can impose. In the European Union, for example, competition law has a strong influence on how licenses are granted by large companies.

A license is 'permission' to do something, in a contract form. Therefore a license is only required for activities which fall under the exclusive rights in question. The intellectual property laws of certain countries provides for certain activities which do not require any license, such as reproduction of small amounts of texts, sometimes termed fair use. Many countries' legal systems afford compulsory licenses for particular activities, especially in the area of patent law.

Many intellectual property rights are awarded by a government for a limited period of time. Such rights are justified as a reward for creating intellectual works. Economic theory typically suggests that a free market with no intellectual property rights will lead to too little production of intellectual works relative to an efficient outcome. Thus by increasing rewards for authors, inventors and other producers of intellectual capital, overall efficiency might be improved. On the other hand, intellectual property law could in some circumstances lead to increased transaction costs that outweigh these gains (see Coase's Penguin). Another consideration is that restricting the free reuse of information and ideas will also have costs, where the use of the best available technique for a given task or the creation of a new derived work is prevented.

University, as the very word suggests is a laboratory relating to the universe. The objective of the universities is to disseminate latest knowledge and create new knowledge through research. Pandit Nehru had outlined the objective of the university in 1947 as under:

> "A university stands for humanism, for tolerance, for reason, for the adventure of ideas and for the search of truth. It stands for the onward march of human race towards even higher objectives. If the

universities discharge their duties adequately then it is well with the nation and the people".

Universities have come to be seen as "engines of economic growth," supplying industry with basic research and new products and processes. Nowhere has this role been more apparent than in the biological sciences, where discoveries made by university scientists have spawned an entire new industry, the biotechnology industry, comprising over a thousand firms and billions of dollars in revenue in many countries especially in the U.S. On a more altruistic level, increased patenting and licensing has also provided new drugs for previously untreatable diseases, new approaches to managing and reversing pollution, and other socially valuable innovations.

Universities should have the right to seek patents for scientific discoveries made by their faculty and staff with support from government funds in order to facilitate the commercialization of potentially valuable discoveries and they should be allowed to have the right to license their patents to firms. Without clear intellectual property rights, firms have few incentives to invest in developing new products.

The Indian higher education system is one of the largest system in the world having more than 400 universities including Central Universities; State Universities having more than Deemed to be Universities; institutions established through State and Central Legislation and Institutions of National Importance established through Central Legislation. In addition, the country has a vast network of as many as 15,600 colleges. Strength of the teaching faculty in universities and colleges has been 4.27 lakhs in the year 2001. Out of 0.75 lakh teachers in the university departments, 20.22 per cent are Professors, 31.53 per cent are Readers/Associate Professors and 45.78 per cent are Senior Lecturers/Lecturers who are supposed to be involved in active research along with more than 1 lakh research scholars. The Government of India has been spending nearly 2.6 per cent of GDP on Education of which 8.00 per cent is being spent on Higher Education.

Therefore, if all these faculty members are encouraged to engage in appropriate outside professional relationships with private industry, such outside activities can provide the individual faculty member with experience and knowledge valuable to teaching and research and also help students gain valuable educational opportunities and experiences. Such activities also facilitate the transfer of technology to improve the well-being and productivity of society and offer research opportunities through which the faculty member can make a contribution to knowledge. Moreover, private industry continue to recognize universities for their engineering, basic science and medical colleges as rich sources of research brainpower. Many companies know that funding of research is prized highly by the University researcher. They may seek to pay minimal or no continuing royalty payments for continuing rights to practice developments from research they have partially funded. However, that could contravene state law and university policies. A continuing royalty stream for research developments will often be available, and that has the possibility of longer range and perhaps increasing benefits to the university, the researcher, and the researcher's department. In addition to income generation, these fuel the economy, create jobs and offer possible long-term income to the researcher and her or his institution. To pursue the full benefits of innovation, academic researchers should have a passing familiarity with certain aspects of patent laws.

Universities should establish collaboration with industry in the support of research, instruction, and public outreach to play the role of the "engines of economic growth," University-industry relations consist of a variety of activities, including:

- Direct funding of research costs through contracts and grants.
- Formal licensing to industry of University-owned patents and technology.
- Gifts and endowments (including endowed chairs) designated for colleges, schools, departments, or individuals.
- University-industry exchange programs and student internships.
- Specialized programs designed by the University for continuing education and training of professionals, primarily through University Extension.
- Participation of industry representatives on campus and University wide advisory groups.
- Cooperative research projects, some of which include government participation and the use of specialized facilities.

- Use of unique University facilities on a fee-for-service basis.
- Research and development facilities of industries housed on University property (industrial parks).
- Activities of Cooperative Extension.
- Faculty consulting.
- Research activities of the Agricultural Experiment Station and its affiliated field stations.

In recent years, across the world there has been heightened interest and activity in University-industry relationships. Federal patent and tax laws have changed to facilitate and encourage University-industry collaboration and technology transfer.

For those individuals and groups of faculty and the private sector who want to embark on cooperative efforts, the means for doing so should be readily made available. The Universities are expected to explore innovative organizational approaches to assure support of worthy research and education that provide significant contributions to the body of scholarship and knowledge, that are responsive to industry interests, and that advance the public's interest in these productive relationships.

3

ROLE OF UNIVERSITIES IN INTELLECTUAL PROPERTY, EDUCATION, RESEARCH AND PUBLIC OUTREACH

Maya D. Kem

It gives me immense pleasure to stand before you to inaugurate a National Seminar on the theme which is very much relevant in the context of Higher Education, today. I congratulate the Vice Chancellor of the Institute and the Organisers to have chosen such a theme and I wish that in the end of the Seminar we shall be able to formulate our views as to role of University in Intellectual Property, Education, Research and Public Outreach.

UNIVERSITY SYSTEM IN INDIA

The Indian higher education system, today, is one of the largest system in the World with nearly 350 universities of which 18 are Central Universities; 178 are State Universities; 85 Deemed to be Universities; 5 institutions established through State and Central Legislation and 11 institutions of National Importance established through Central Legislation. In addition, the country has a vast network of as many as 15,600 colleges of which 1,600 are the women's colleges. As per the recent record, the total number of students enrolled in the formal system of education in universities and colleges is 88.21 lakhs (11.66 lakhs in university departments and 76.55 lakhs in affiliated colleges). According to the recent report of All India Council for Technical Education (AICTE), there are 5,108 technical institutions (Engineering, Management, MCA,

Pharmacy, Architecture and Hotel Management) with 7,44,072 sanctioned intake.

84 per cent of the total enrolment is concentrated, in the faculty of Arts–46.13 per cent; Science–19.88 per cent; and Commerce–7.87 per cent while remaining 16 per cent has been attributed to the professional courses. The enrolment at the Degree level is about 89 per cent with 78.63 lakhs students, at the Postgraduate level 9.25 per cent with 8.16 lakhs students and the remaining students are enrolled in the university department for Research and Diploma/Certificate level. The enrolment of the women students has been calculated to be 35.14 lakhs at all levels constituting 39.84 per cent of the total enrolment. The women enrolment is the highest in Kerala to the tune of 60 per cent of the total enrolment in the state and the lowest in Bihar to the tune of 23 per cent of the total enrolment.

India is one country which produce the largest number of Doctoral degrees every year such a number in 2001 was to the extent of 11450 of which 4330 Ph.D. were in Faculty of Arts followed by the Faculty of Science with 3737 degrees, the remaining Doctoral degrees were in the rest of the subjects including the professional one.

Strength of the teaching faculty in universities and colleges has been 0.75 lakh and 3.52 lakh respectively totaling 4.27 lakhs in the year 2001. Out of 0.75 lakh teachers in the university department, 20.22 per cent are Professors, 31.53 per cent are Readers/Associate Professors and 45.78 per cent are Senior Lecturers/Lecturers.

The Government of India has been spending nearly 2.6 per cent of GDP on Education of which 8.00 per cent is being spent on Higher Education. In a given scenario of our country where population is already above one billion mark, nearly 6% youth of the country, in the relevant age group, have access to higher education. To extend the facility for the remaining youth who wish to get into the folds of higher education, the country has to spend a lot of financial resources to create infrastructure relating to higher education. The foremost concern of Government of India being the sanitation, health, drinking water, electricity, proper dwelling units for the masses, the finance available for the higher education always remain precarious and inadequate.

Therefore, it is now well established that desirable and needed expansion in higher education is not possible without the participation of private education providers. It is in this context that a proper policy document on private participation in higher education should be framed to provide guidelines for the formal entry of providers of education in the country so as to deter the gross commercialisation of education.

ROLE OF UNIVERSITIES

Every institution of Higher Education in the country must commit itself to provide all its students with in-depth knowledge and understanding in their chosen field of studies. This has to be done at a global acceptable level while keeping in view the ground realities of access and equity in focus. The universities across the country have to restructure their academic programmes by adopting the following ground rules:

- The present education structure is very rigid and riddled with the ills of annual examination system, evaluation in terms of marks etc. and has to be, therefore, more open and flexible adopting 'cafeteria approach'.
- The curricula for various subjects, being taught in the universities, has to be revised reflecting the need for national development with international benchmark.
- The university system in the country has to create possibility of enhancing the quality of teaching and learning experience through use of information path way.
- Laboratory teaching is to be innovated using multi-media teaching material and electronic communication network for sharing academic resources.
- Enhance research capabilities by upgrading scientific infrastructure in universities and Inter-university centres and give easy access to research funding.
- We have to identify and support few universities and colleges that have potential to do better both in undergraduate and postgraduate education.
- The need for social change and enhancing perception for human value is to be further recognised and revised the curricula accordingly.
- Since the job in Govt. sector are shrinking, the academic programme are to be revised to make them more job oriented

to cater the needs of human resources of service sectors e.g. Telecommunication, Hotel Management, Tourism etc.

- The world, all over, has since recognised the worth of Indian Higher education, attempts are to be made to export the Higher Education abroad and attract as many foreign students as possible to study in India. The UGC has recently commenced a scheme called "Promotion of Indian Higher Education Abroad (PIHEAD)". The universities and colleges should participate in the scheme and showcase their academic strength to the outside world so as to attract more foreign students to have quality education in India.

INTELLECTUAL PROPERTY RIGHTS (IPR)

Intellectual Property Rights are the rights given to persons over the creation of their minds. They usually give the creator an exclusive right over the use of his/her creation for a certain period of time.

Intellectual Property Rights are customarily divided into two main areas:

A. Copyright and rights related to copy right, and;

B. Industrial property;

A. Copy Right and Right Related to Copy Right

(Rights of authors)

The rights of authors of literary and artistic works (such as books and other writings, musical compositions, paintings, sculpture, computer programmes and films) are protected by copyright, for a minimum period of 50 years after the death of author.

(Rights of performers)

Rights of performances (actors, singers and musicians), producers of phonograms (sound recording) and broadcasting organizations are also protected.

B. Industrial Property

Industrial property can be divided into two main areas:

(i) One area can be characterized as the protection of distinctive signs in particular trade works (which distinguish the goods or services of one undertaking from those of other undertakings) and geographical indications (which identify a good as originating in a place where a given characteristic of the good is essentially attributable to its geographical origin).

The protection of such distractive signs aims to stimulates and ensure fair competition and to protect consumers by enabling them to make informed choices between various goods and services. The protection may last indefinitely provided the sign in question continues to be destructive.

(ii) Other types of industrial property and protected primarily to stimulate innovation, design and the creation of technology. In this category fall inventions (protected by patents), industrial designs and trade secrets.

The general agreement on trade of services is only set of multi-lateral covering international trade services negotiated in the Urguay Round, it was developed in response to the huge growth of the services economically over the past 30 years and the greater potential for trading services product about by the communication resolutions. Keeping this in view the intellectual property rights also known as trades was for the first time introduced in WTO. The agreement on trade related aspects introduced intellectual property rules into the multi-lateral system in the first time. Creation can be given to the rules to prevent others from using their invention, design or other creation and to use that right to negotiate payment in other using them.

THE GATS COVERS FOLLOWING BROAD ISSUES

(i) Basic Principles of Trade System

As in GATT and GATS the starting points of intellectual property agreement is basic principle. And as in the other agreement known discrimination features prominently i.e. national treatment (trade one own national and foreigner equally), most favoured nation treatment equally treatments for nationals of all trading partners of WTO, the national treatment is also keeping agreement outside the WTO. The trips agreement has an additional important principle i.e. intellectual property protection should contribute to technical innovation and transferred of technology both producers and user should benefit and Economic Social Welfare should be enhanced.

(ii) How to Protect Intellectual Property

The second part of the TRIPs agreement looks at a different kind intellectual property rights and how to protect them. The purpose to be ensured that educate standard of protection existents in all member countries. Here the supporting point is the obligation of the main international agreements of the World Intellectual Organisation that already existed before the WTO so created.

(iii) Implementation of Rights

There are different ways of enforcement those rights within the territories of the various countries depending upon the invention and the category it falls. Enforcement have not intellectual property laws is not enough they have to be enforced. The agreement says Government has ensured that intellectual property rights can be enforced under their laws and that the penalties for infrenchment are tough enough to data for their violation. Protection must be fair and equitable and not unnecessarily complicated or costly. They should not un-reasonally time limits or un-warranty deals. People involved should be able to ask a court to review an administrative decision or to appeal a lower court truly.

(iv) Transitional Arrangements

When the WTO agreements took a fact on Ist January, 1995 developed countries were given one year to ensure that there laws and practices confirmed with the trade agreement. The developing countries and transitional economics were given 5 years.

GATS IMPACT ON EDUCATION

GATS is the General Agreement on Trade in Services. It was created in April, 1994, where as the WTO came in to formal existence in January, 1995. It is the first multilateral agreement on trade in services as a whole. Essentially it aims to liberalize trade in the services. Two basic principles underlying the GATT (Goods) are preserved and adapted in the GATS (Services). These two principles are the "most favored national (MFN) and national treatment". It is now part of the fabric of the WTO in similar way to the GATT agreement on goods. GATS has not defined what is meant by services. It classifies services in to 12 sectors and education is one sector. This sector includes primary education, secondary education, higher education, adult education and other education services.

In terms of the Agreement, the WTO identified four forms of trade in services:

1. *Cross Border Supply:* This is the supply of services from the territory of one member country to the territory of another member country. In the case of education sector, distance education is included in this category. When the institution of a given country A provides distance courses to another country B, then country A is deemed to be exporting education services to Country B.
2. *Consumption Abroad:* This refers to situations whereby consumers of a service move into another member's territory to get the service. In the education sector, the most common example is undertaking a course abroad. When a student from a given country A takes a course in country B, the latter is deemed to be exporting education services to country A.
3. *Commercial Presence:* This is setting up of a branch of a foreign service in another member country. In the education sector, the activities carried out by foreign universities or other institutions fall under this category. Thus, when an institution from country A is operating on the soil of country B to perform education activities, then country A is exporting its services to country B.
4. *Individual Presence:* In WTO jagron this is called "presence of natural persons" It means services provided in a home country by foreign people who are national of another member country. In the education sector, this means courses offered by foreign teachers fall under this category. When a teacher from country A teaches in country B, his or her own country becomes an exporter of education services to country B.

It could be seen that the GATS has instituted a very broad and general framework. It has an agenda to progressively liberalize international trade in education, particularly in higher education. We will have to take cognizance of all this while deciding our strategy for facing GATS sanctions. Following, in the meanwhile, be done at home front:

- The foreign nations would be interested in higher education sector.
- They would like to use all the four modes to trade to get an advantage.

- They would target at economically affordable group in the society in order to maximize profits.
- The non-organised private education providers in India would be first one to take an advantage.
- There will unfavourable balance of payments as far as trade in education services are concerned.
- The public education providers would be marginalized in the race due to unequal play rules and ground.

4

IPRs: TOWARDS SCIENTIFIC APARTHEID

Devinder Sharma

The world's largest collection of plant germplasm, some 6,00,000 plant accessions, are in a safe custody under the control of the US Department of Agriculture. These genetic resources that lie stored at Fort Collins/Fort Knox in the United States are outside the purview of any international treaty. The countries from where these were collected have no control or say over these resources, nor do they get any benefit from providing these valuable resources.

Thirty years after the developing countries were made to believe that their economic interests were perfectly safe in collecting and conserving the massive plant germplasm that were getting lost, the world is at it again. And this time, it is the traditional knowledge that the international community is suddenly so concerned and worried about. This is in reality the green gold that lies unaccounted with the developing countries, including India. This knowledge is worth the entire gold that is stocked with the US treasury.

In India, the Department of Science and Technology, Council for Scientific and Industrial Research (CSIR), the Indian Council for Agricultural Research (ICAR) and numerous agricultural universities, institutes and civil society organizations are engaged in documenting traditional knowledge. Like the earlier efforts to misappropriate genetic resources in the name of mankind's heritage' and security', this time the same language is being used to document the traditional knowledge that tells the exploiters of genetic wealth as to what uses the plant species can be put to. World Intellectual Property Organisation (WIPO) is already putting together a mechanism to draw intellectual property rights over the traditional knowledge that comes from the developing countries.

It is said that traditional knowledge, which has been passed on form generations to generations by local and tribal communities in the developing worlds, is getting lost. These would soon be lost to posterity and the humanity would be paying a heavy price for not conserving and keeping the same alive for future generations. The answer, therefore, is to document the traditional knowledge. After all, it too is mankind's heritage.

It was in the mid–60s and early '70s that the same language and expression was used to seek monopoly control over the plant germplasm resources of the developing countries. The height of the green revolution, with the land grant system borrowed form the United States well in place, we were told that plants were a mankind's heritage but were being lost in the process of development. Letting the plant germplasm disappear would be at the world's own peril. So what needs to be done in to collect whatever is available and keep these safely in gene banks.

We did it. We made plan expeditions and picked up, classified and put the germplsasm resources in the gene banks. It was then that we were told that the society would gain if, for instance, all the rice–growing countries were to keep their rice collections at an international centre, which in turn would act as a custodian of the invaluable genetic wealth. We did it again in good faith. India provided a copy of its rice collections, for instance, for a common custody at the International Rice Research Institute, manila, in the Philippines. The wheat collections were kept at the International Research Centre for Maize and Wheat (CIMMYT) at Mexico City. The other collections went to the 14 other international agricultural centrs under the Consultative Group for International Agricultural Research (CGIAR).

We were then told that these collections are not safe at Manila or Mexico city. After all, there is a distinct probability that a terrorist group can blow the gene banks with the result that these resources would be lost forever. So what do you do? You keep a copy of these collections in safe custody. And where is this safe custody? At Fort Knox and Fort Collins in the United States. We did it again and of course in good faith.

The US has these plant genetic resources, has the finances for research, and has the mastery over genetic engineering. But what is coming in the way is as to what to do with these genetic resources. After all, you cannot work out the chemical composition and find out the pharamaceutical properties of each and every plant stored at Fort Collins. The best way is to revert back to the country which originally had these plant resources. To find out from the local communities as to how and what uses they were putting these plants to. And that would give the companies the chemical route to decipher the knowledge, draw industrial uses, seek patents and market the product back to those countries where it has been traditionally been used for centuries.

At a time when there exists so much of anger over biopiracy, sending a bio–prospecting team from a western university or a company would invite the wrath of the civil society in the developing

Box 1

MEXICO: People force Government to Stall Bioprospecting

Bioprospecting is a means to conserve and share endangered indigenous knowledge while making user that any resulting commercial benefits are share with indigenous people. Others contend that n the absence of effective community, national and international mechanisms, biprospecting equates to biopiracy. A US government initiative "Drug Discovery and Biodiversity among the Maya of Mexico" sought to identify, patent and commecialise Mayan knowledge and pharmalocially important biological materials through private biopharmaceutical enterprise and the university of Georgia. This project formed part of the International Cooperative Biodiversity Groups (ICBG) Program, which aims to address the Interdependent issues of drug discovery, biodiversity, conservation, and sustainable economic growth. It was a 5 year project that aimed to collect and evaluate thousands of plants and microorganisms used in traditional medicine by Mayan communities in order to promote drug discovery. The project proposed to patent and privatize resources and knowledge.

Many indigenous communities opposed the commercial exploitation of their genetic resources and traditional knowledge, even though the project was designed foster benefits sharing so that local communities could derive benefits from their biological resources. After two years of local opposition from indigenous peoplesi organizations in Chiapas, the bioprospecting project was definitively cancelled, by the Chiapas based partner ECOSUR due to the contentious political climate.

Source: http://www.law.unimelb.edu.au/ipria/research trad_know.html

world. The best way to legitimize biopiracy, therefore, its to encourage researchers, NGOs, and the public sector institutes to document the traditional knowledge. Give them a little research grant and you will have the civil society and cashstraved research institutes documenting the traditional knowledge virtually free for you.

Traditional Knowledge: Almost all donors are pumping in grants for documentation of the traditional knowledge. Except for the donors who continue to misguide the developing country researchers, no one wants to know what the documentations are for. No one wants to know why has the world become suddenly so conscious of the fast eroding traditional knowledge. No one wants to work out the economic price of the traditional knowledge that is being given on the an official platter. Moreover, who is using the documentation that is being done so speedily?

Once again, such documentations are safely going into the hands of the companies who need them desperately. But unlike the genetic resources, it will not take 30 years for these companies to draw IPR over traditional knowledge. International effort has already begun on how to draw a *sui generis* system over traditional knowledge. It is a matter of few years. The documented traditional knowledge will then be out of the control of the communities, which nurtured them. The tragedy is that unlike biopracy in the past neem, turmeric and the likes–the scientific community and the civil society is a willing partner this time.

Digital Library: India's proposal of setting up a 'Traditional Knowledge Digital Library (TKDL)', which has been selected for a pilot study in 170 countries. Is classic example of facilitating the process of biopiracy. Denials from the CSIR notwithstanding, the fact remains that the proposed digital library only helps to ensure that the biopirates don't have to work hard in collating information. They can get it on a VCD.

The digital library of traditional knowledge will have some 35,000 *lokas* or verses drawn from the available literature on one the Indian systems of medicine, *Ayurveda*. It will in addition have 1,40,000 pages of information, which will be easy to retrieve. The argument for the digital library is that these CD *roms* will be made available to each of the patent offices world wide with the hope and expectations that the patent applications will be matched with the details provided so as to ensure that a patent is not granted on something that was traditionally known.

At the face of it, the digital library seems to be a wonderful weapon against biopiracy. After all, public outcry and outrage against some of the better known cases of biopiracy or thefts of traditional knowledge–*neem,* turmeric, brinjal, ayahuasca and quinoa–could have been avoided if those who granted these patents knew that the medicinal or insecticidal properties of these plants were widely known among the traditional communities in the developing countries. In technical parlance, these patents were based on 'prior art'.

It is however not as simple as that. In a world where profit and greed has become the new economic *mantra,* private companies will go to any extent to manipulate what is already known to project it as an invention or a novelty. Any tinkering of the original medicinal remedy with a little cosmetic coverings can be easily *presented* as a novel product that was not previously known. It has happened in the past. For every successful revocation of a patent, whether it is *neem,* turmeric or ayahuasca, there are at least a thousand others that simply go unnoticed.

The TKDL Task Force itself was astounded to learn that of the 4,896 references on 90 medicinal plants in the United States Patent and Trademark Office (USPTO) database, 80 per cent of the references pertained to just seven medicinal plants of Indian origin. In other words, nearly 4,000 patents or patent applications are based on the medicinal properties of plants that were already known. The Task Force studied the patents and interestingly found that 360 of the 762 patents on medicinal plants that were granted by USPTO could be easily categorised as traditional.

Does it mean that once the digital library is in place, the USPTO will strike down these faulty patents? The answer is no. Does it mean that the USPTO will ensure that in future no such patents are granted? The answer again is no. After all, what is available in the Ayurveda Verses is not scientific decoded Language of the medicinal properties of the native plants. What is presented before the patent offices, on the other hand, is mired in technical details and legal complexities that is difficult to easily decipher. There are patent applications pending before the USPTO, for instance, which run into 1,000 pages. It has already been said that a complete examination of this patent application alone will not be complete before the year 2035!

The proposed digital library will therefore be only helping the companies to easily scout for the commercial uses of the medicinal and therapeutic properties from the database. A minor tinkering or value–addition will qualify it for the grant of a patent. And then, how will the infringement be checked, is something that has been very easily left to interpretation. Even in a country where patent and theft of intellectual property rights has become an emotive issue, it has been rather difficult to fight the piracy of traditionally known products like *basmati* rice. The Ministry of Commerce had, in fact, issued a circular saying that it has no money to take the *basmati* battle any further. If the government has no money and the political will to challenge and fight the patent on *basmati* rice, which is a culturally and politically sensitive issue, it is futile to expect any meaningful challenges to any more cases of biopiracy.

Box 2
Tragic Potion

Herbal Drug Stuck in IPR Jam, Tribal Group Biggest Loser

India's wonder drug Jeevani–developed by the Thiruvanthapuram–based Tropical Botanical garden Research Institute (TBGRI) using the traditional knowledge of Kerala's kani tribe–hit the headlines a few years ago. It was heraided as the world's first product that perfectly exemplified the access and benefit–sharing system involving indigenous people.

Media reports suggest that a US–based nutriScience Innovations, LLC, has surreptitiously patented the product and is doing brisk business on the line. At the same time, Jeevani's original licensee claims that there re no takers for the medicine. Yet it continues to manufacture the drug. And TBPGRI is at sixes and sevens over the position of the product with regard to intellectual property rights. Amid the tangled web, the kani tribals, who provided valuable inputs of the medicine's formation in the first place, have been sidelined.

Clearly, the gains from the venture aren't percolating down to the tribal groups. The Kanis received a one–time payment of Rs. 5 lakhs when the product was licensed. The tribe is also supposed to get a 1 per cent royalty on sales. In 2003, it earned a paltry Rs. 2,000 from this source. Experts are of the view that a chance to showcase a fruitful and equitable benefit sharing model has been lost. Furthermore, what's the guarantee that the other collaborative efforts won't go the Jeevani way?

Source: Varsheny, V. In down to Earth, New Delhi: March 31.2004.

To challenge and fight the patent infringements is simply prohibitive. In the case of *basmati* rice, the challenge came only from India while the scented rice is also grown in neighbouring Pakistan. Despite first making claims that it too will join the battle against *basmati* rice, Pakistan chickned out when the cost of the legal battle was worked out to something around US $ 3,00,000. Not only the developing countries, even the rich industrialized countries find it difficult to fight the legal patent battles in the US Courts. A British company BTG, for instance, had a filed a case for patent infringement over the use of hover crafts in use by the Pentagon. BTG won and the Pentagon was forced to fork out US $ six million in penalties. But the lesser known fact is that the company had spent a whopping US$ 2 million towards lawyers' fees.

In the absence of any global safeguards, the digital library will become a much wanted source of information on bio–prospecting for the private companies. If such digital libraries are constructed all over the world, the private companies will surely laugh their way to the banks. And if you are wondering as to why the WIPO and the UN is showing so much of interest in creating the database for traditional knowledge, the answer is obvious. Both these organizations are desperately pushing in for a system that legalizes the monopoly control over what was traditionally known.

Benefit Sharing: Documentation of traditional knowledge has therefore to be seen in the national interest before any move to make the community knowledge accessible globally. To say that such initiatives will come with benefit sharing is to duck the real and sensitive issues linked to its theft and misappropriation. Let us accept it, benefit sharing is for all practical purposes a dead concept. It hasn't benefited any country or a community. The famous case of InBio-merck deal in Costa Rica, which allowed the pharmaceutical company to do unrestricted bioprospecting in the jungles of the Central American nation, was in fact a classic example of exploitation. For a mere one million dollar, Costa Rica had made available five per cent of world's known biodiversity at the disposal of a multinational corporation *(See also Box 1).*

In India, the only example of benefit sharing that is being repeated time and again involves the Keni tribes in Kerala. It too is a failed project *(Box: 2).* The Convention on Biological Diversity (CBD) describes benefit sharing as a fair and equitable sharing of the benefits arising out of the utilization of genetic resources, including by appropriate access to genetic resources and by appropriate transfer of relevant technologies, taking into account all rights over the resources and to technologies, and by appropriate funding. Effective regulation of access to genetic resources and benefit–sharing is currently one of the principal focus of international negotiations relating to the CBD and the Plan of Implementation arising from the World Summit on Sustainable Development (WSSD) in 2002.

While voluntary guidelines and several options for equitable sharing of benefits and technology transfer are being tossed around, the fact remains that control and misappropriation of proprietary rights over genetic resources and traditional knowledge continue to be fortified. No wonder, native groups and some environment organization in Hawai, are calling for scrapping a contract struck two years ago between the UH Marine Bioproducts Engineering Center and a San diego biotech company called Diversa. The way research has been conducted and how proceeds from the work will be distributed have become concerns among native groups. This has strengthened the belief that research will produce profits for industry with no benefit to native communities, forcing some of the Indian tribes to pass laws banning the harvesting of living things on their property.

Bioprospecting however, comes in handy for university researcher to provide unlimited access to valuable genetic resources at a throwaway price. Take the case of Papua New Guinea, a hotspot of biological wealth and knowledge. Under the aegis of a International Cooperative Biodiversity Groups (ICBG)—a misleading title for a so–called partnership consortium—between the University of Papua New Guinea and the US National Institute of Health and the University of Utah, among others-the University of Papua New Guinea is taking a lead role in executing a US $ 4 million project aimed at the search for marine organisms and plant species that contain chemical properties for treatment of tuberculosis, malaria, cancer, HIV and other diseases.

Already, a random plant collection and inventory for anti-tuberculosis, anti-malaria, anti-HIV and anti- cancer drugs in the last three years has resulted in the collection of 250 plant samples from about 120 plant species for testing. Papua New Guinea is excited at the benevolence of the ICBG (US $ 4 million, much of it going to US researchers), which will help in capacity building by teaching the local researchers in preparing an inventory of plants, collection of ethno medicinal plant species, preparation of extracts and screening them. It will also enable the researchers to learn the process of economic valuation of natural products, developing intellectual property rights legislation and conduct outreach programmes to educate communities into further sharing their knowledge.

The US National Institute of Health and the University of Utah will in the bargain make a neat US $ 26 billion a year, if the drug discovery programme in Papua New Guinea proves successful. In any case, the US $ 4 million investment in Papua New Guinea is peanuts by any known international standards. This classic case of unbridled biological theft and exploitation comes at a time when meaningless international negotiations continue unabated. The Papua New Guinea benefit sharing example is in tune with the earlier and equally exploitative experience of Costa Rica that has been hailed by the pharmaceutical industry as well as researchers and policy makers as a success story.

Blocking Research: The writing is clearly on the wall. The United States Supreme Court's crucial ruling that upholds 'utility patents' over plant varieties has merely affirmed it. And in the bargain, the American farmers have for all practical purposes lost the right to save seed.

The US Supreme Court's judgment in December 2001 comes at a time when at the other end of the spectrum, India recognizes the right of the farmer to save seed under a newly formulated Plant Variety Protection and Farmers' Rights Act, 2001. For India, farmers' right to not only save seed but also to share and sell is politically correct considering that a majority of the estimated 110 million farming families comprises small and marginal landholders. For America, agriculture is an industrial activity and therefore the world must conform to the 'protective shield' laid down by the US government and its legal system for its seed and agri–business multinationals.

It is only a matter of time before the two diverse and diametrically opposite systems clash. The conflict that arises will surely have a profound impact on the farming communities in not only India but in the entire Third World where seed saving has been a practice ever since man began to farm. With the biotechnology industry throwing its weight behind any and every move that strengthens monopoly through a patent control over plant varieties and its genes and cell lines; it may not be long before the trade–related intellectual property rights (TRIPs) under the World Trade Organisation are reinterpreted.

Equally worrisome is the manner in which the US Supreme Court brushed aside two other laws—the Plant Patent Act and the Plant Variety Protection Act, which many thought were the only route for seeking patent protection for plants and plant varieties. The court rejected the argument that patents for plants reproduced from seeds were not authorized under section 101 of the federal patent law. By a convincing 6–2 margin, the US apex court finally concluded that the patent law authorizes patents for sexually reproduced plants. Such a patent protection would be available for 20 years.

It is not that the 'utility patents' were not in vogue earlier. Already hundreds of utility patents had been granted to seed multinationals like Monsanto and Pioneer Hi–Bred International Inc. Although the US justice Department had earlier warned that limiting the scope of the federal law to exclude sexually reproduced plants would reduce incentives for research and development in agricultural and horticultural areas, the fact remains that such 'utility patents' have been the greatest hurdle to crop improvement.

There is this classical case of a 'utility patent' over a hybrid maize variety. At the time when the International Centre for Maize and Wheat Improvement (CIMMYT) in Mexico made available the semi–dwarf improved varieties of wheat to the developing countries, literally sowing the seeds of green revolution, a single–cross hybrid variety of corn was denied to India. This variety, which was responsible for the growth of the corn sector in America, was covered under a 'utility patent', and therefore was never made available to India. With the result that despite India being the seat of the green revolution, maize production never really picked up.

The number of utility patents issued has grown up very rapidly in the US. By December 1994, 324 Utility Patents had been issued for new plants or plant parts and 38 were issued for animals. As with PVPC's, most utility Patents were awarded to the private sector (Fugile, Klotz, and Gill, 1995). Thus, IPR has encouraged the private sector to develop new agricultural technologies by enabling firms to capture greater share of the commercial value of their inventions.

But still what is equally more worrisome is the speed at which life sciences firms are drawing patents over genes, gene sequences and cell lines. For instance, Monsanto owns US patent (No: 5, 159,135) which covers all GM cotton but there are 228 other cotton gene sequences patented too. The Guardian (Nov. 15,2000) reports that there are 25 patents on pineapple, 25 on raspherries, 21 on grapes, six on kiwi fruit, 11 on oranges, nine on apples, eight on pawpaw, four on strawberries and cherries, two on grapefruit, one each on tamarind and peach. There are also 43 patents on silek genas, including several on the golden orb–weaving spider, which makes the strongest and finest thread.

The report goes on to say that although wheat is the greatest hope for mankind, gene companies have already drawn patent on 228 gene sequences. Genetically modified wheat is still far away from the market. Meanwhile, 152 patents have been applied for on rice. Those patents cover 584 genes or partial gene sequences. US Multinational Dow has applied for patents on 655 maize gene sequences, which is 30.3 per cent of the total number of applications. Du Pont has applied for another 587, Affymetrix (US) for 418, Monsanto for 102, AstraZeneca for 83. The top five maize companies have nearly 85 per cent of the total 2,181 applications between them. In the past four years, the patenting of life forms has continued unabated.

Much of the focus is on cereal crops with huge global commercial value like rice, maize, wheat, millet, sorghum, soya and cassava. Patent protection by agri–business companies now covers many of their genes and gene sequences, compounds and properties. And all this will have profound impact on the future agricultural research in the developing countries. Let us see how.

Patenting rice genes: As that brouhaha was unfolding several years ago, agribusiness giants kept on assuring the scientific community that crops like rice, wheat and other cereals are of no commercial interest to them. Their focus was on cash crops like strawberries, cut flowers, tomatoes and the likes, which could rake in big profits. This prompted universities, which developed such technologies in the first place, to license these to the private corporations. Knowing well that patenting alone will determine who wields power over farming and world food system, a tug of war began over who controls the rice plant genome–the raw sequences in the genetic code.

The tussle over the monopoly control of rice extends to its 12 chromosomes. These chromosomes contain 430 million base pairs of DNA, and are expected to have about 50,000 genes. Syngenta, in collaboration with Myriad Genetics Inc of USA, has beaten Monsanto in the game by sequencing more than 99.5 per cent of the rice genome. Syngenta has already made it clear that it will restrict access to the genomic map and expects proprietary control over any research carried out with the information.

Top executives of Syngenta have already told the *New York Times* that while the companies would not seek to patent the entire genome, they would try to patent individual valuable genes. They categorically stated that Syngenta and Myriad were well on their way to finding many of those. First Monsanto, which made international headlines in April 2000, for announcing to share its working draft (rougher, 60 per cent) of the genome map with international researchers sequencing the rice genome under a publicly funded International Rice Genome Sequencing Project (IRGSP), and then Syngenta making it clear of the efforts to seek patents on genes with visible commercial output, the race is on to draw proprietary control over something that existed in nature.

There are conflicting reports of the latest tally of patents over rice genes. Some researcher say that more than 900 genes have already been patented. Earlier, GRAIN had compiled a list of 609 patents on rice genes drawn till Sept. 2000, 56 per cent of which were owned by private companies and research institutes in the western countries. Top of the list was the American giant Du Pont with 95 patents, followed by Mitsui, Japan, with 45 patents. In the next three years, especially after the mapping of the rice genome by Syngenta, a majority of the patents would surely be in the lap of the handful of multinational agribusiness companies.

The control of the plant genes therefore is slowly being passed into the hands of private companies. Such a monopoly control is all about control and power over the food chain.

5

INTELLECTUAL PROPERTY RIGHTS AND INDIAN AGRICULTURE

M.V. Srinivasa Gowda

INTRODUCTION

The issue of intellectual property rights (IPRs) has attracted considerable academic and policy debate in India in the last decade. Intellectual property refers to "a creation of human mind that is of value to the society, while intellectual property right is the right granted by the State to a person or institution over this creation." The objective of IPR is to promote effective and adequate protection of the intellectual property, and at the same time to ensure that laws and procedures meant to enforce intellectual property rights do not themselves become barriers to legitimate production and trade.

The concept of property has changed over the years. When human beings were nomadic, the only objects that could clearly be recognized as property were movables and chattels. When agriculture became an important occupation, immovable property, particularly land, became a major form of property. With industrialization, technological progress and development of capital markets, non-physical objects including products human ingenuity also came to be recognized as property. The latest addition to this concept is that of intellectual property.

The demand for effective intellectual property protection has primarily been a demand articulated by the industrialized nations. The royalty incomes would go up for developed countries, their exports would face lesser competition from developed countries and gray imports into developed countries would be less likely. Expenditure on detecting and preventing unauthorized use of inventions would also decline. In a way the Uruguay Round has thrust upon the developing countries the norms of intellectual property protection and hence initially there was lot of opposition from the developing countries to the agreement on trade related intellectual property rights (TRIPs). The WTO agreement on TRIPs covers standards and norms on wide-ranging dimensions of IPRs including patents; plant and seed variety, micro-organism and related rights; copyrights; trade marks; geographical indications; industrial designs; layout designs of integrated circuits; trade secrets, etc.

INDIA'S COMPLIANCE WITH TRIPs AGREEMENT

The Uruguay Round GATT has a very forcefully worded Article 27 on patents; it says, "subject to the provisions of paragraph 2 and 3, patents shall be available for any inventions, whether products or process, in all fields of technology, provided they are new, involve an inventive step and are capable of industrial application". It further states that members shall provide for protection of plant varieties either by patents or by effective *sui generis* system or any combination thereof. It also stipulates that microorganisms, non-biological and microbiological processes must also be patented. That is why the WTO Agreement, *inter alia*, contains an agreement on intellectual property rights, namely, the Agreement on Trade Related Aspects of Intellectual Property Rights (TRIPs).

Currently India's major concerns in the area of IPR are: granting of product patents to pharmaceuticals and agro-chemicals, patenting of micro-organisms or life forms including patenting of products based on our bio-diversity and traditional knowledge in other parts of the world; and establishing an effective ***sui generis*** system for the protection of new plant varieties and plant breeders' rights, and for recognizing and rewarding the traditional contribution of rural communities to the conservation of bio-diversity.

Towards meeting these tasks, there has been a wave of new IPR legislations covering every field of activity/technology. Successive amendments of the Indian Patents Act 1970 since 1999 represent very elaborate legal framework along with amendments/ enactments of other laws such as the Indian Trade Marks (Amendment) Act 1999, the Copy Right (Amendment) Act 1999, the Designs Act 1999, the Geographical Indications of Goods (Regulation and Protection) Act 1999, Plant Varieties and Farmers' Rights Act 2001, the Biodiversity Act 2002, and the Competition Act 2002.

IPRs AND INDIAN AGRICULTURE

In order to protect the plant varieties and farmers' interest, the government has introduced the Plant Variety and Farmers' Rights Bill 1999 which, together with Geographical Indications of Goods (Regulation and Protection) Act 1999 and Biodiversity Act 2000, represents a set of progressive legislative measures to protect plant varieties developed by plant breeders and the traditional knowledge of farmers and other indigenous knowledge systems, from exploitation especially by the developed countries and MNCs. These legislations incorporate both the sui-*generis (self generating)* system of plant variety protection modeled on the UPOV Convention and the legal provision to protect farmers' and researcher's rights. The objectives of the Plant Varieties and Farmers' Rights Act in particular are: (i) to safeguard the interests of a plant breeder as an incentive to the development of improved plant varieties for agriculture, horticulture and forestry, (ii) to facilitate recovery of his costs and accumulation of the funds necessary for further investment, (iii) to prevent others from multiplying the breeder's seeds or other propagating material and selling the variety on a commercial scale, without providing recompense to the breeder, (iv) to ensure a continuous supply of new varieties by safeguarding the interests of plant breeders. Under this Act, plant breeders have exclusive commercial rights to any variety that is developed from germplasm. A breeder obtains exclusive rights to produce, sell, import and export the protected seed for fifteen years after the date of registration. In the case of trees and vines, the protection is upto 18 years.

A breeder can license his rights over the variety. These rights will extend to varieties that are already registered under the Seed Act, 1966, with retrospective effect from 1984. This clause is designed to prevent other countries/MNCs from acquiring rights over seeds that have been released in India. A plant breeder will also have to reward rural communities in recognition of their contribution. A national gene bank has also been proposed to protect the Indian germplasm. There are exceptions granted to researchers for free and complete access to the protected material. Farmers can also retain their traditional rights to save, use, exchange, share and sell propagated material or seeds from the harvest. But their right is restricted to non-conventional sales and branded seeds cannot be sold.

EFFECTS OF SEED/PLANT PATENTING ON TRADITIONAL FARMING COMMUNITIES

The WTO Accord on TRIPs, which implied patenting of seeds and genes, initially generated considerable controversy and apprehensions. The farmers were given to understand that they would have to buy their seeds every year from multinational seed companies, that they could not change seeds with the fellow farmers and, so on. While the WTO authorities opine that these apprehensions are unfounded, it is also true that the new IPR regime has put the developing countries at a disadvantageous position since the advanced countries have a distinct advantage and decisive lead over the developing countries in matters of scientific inventions and technological breakthroughs in many fields, including agriculture.

There is considerable debate over patenting of plant varieties and microorganisms. Much of this debate borders on speculation since there is certain degree of information vacuum on this aspect. There can be several explanations to the criticisms advanced against patenting plant varieties and microorganisms. The foremost concern is about patent protection being granted to life forms, the philosophy being that only inanimate matter should be eligible for patent protection and patenting of animate matter is regarded as quite unethical. It is argued that in a technology driven world, the question of distinction between animate and inanimate objects is not pertinent. What is pertinent issue is whether the object in question is a discovery or an invention.

The second concern is about the dominance of the MNCs in the seed trade. It is feared that the resultant monopolies would lead to an increase in seed prices and restrict the free flow of germplasm. In addition, new varieties would not be readily available and indigenous capability of adapting seeds to local conditions would be limited. This is due to the fact that royalties would have to be paid for protected varieties and further innovation in these varieties would not be possible without the permission of the right holder. However, this sort of apprehension probably underestimates the Indian strengths in seed research and seed production. On the other hand, the varying agro-climatic zones, the rich biodiversity and existence of expertise in developing new varieties of crops should offer India a comparative advantage.

The third criticism relates to fertilizers, similar to that relating to seeds. Patenting of microorganisms like Rhizobium and Blue green algae as well as organic manures such as vermiculture can be done if the new forms are accepted. These are new bio-fertilizers, which can boost agricultural yields considerably, but it is apprehended that with patent protection these too would become the monopoly of multinational firms. However, as in the case of seeds, the apprehensions in this regard also seem to be rather farfetched in view of the comprehensive legislative measures introduced to protect farmers' and plant breeders' rights.

The implications of TRIPs for biodiversity have often had strong ideological overtones, because of perceived threat to biodiversity as a result of the possibility of gene pool piracy. Although, patents can only be granted for inventions and not for discoveries, the dividing line between the two gets blurred in the area of biotechnology. The argument here is not clearly articulated. The fact is, developing countries have inadequate system of registration. Wild germplasm, plant and animal varieties are, therefore, likely to be stolen and patented as inventions elsewhere. Several examples can be quoted to substantiate this argument. For example, 'Sarpagandha' plant has many medicinal values. A multinational pharmaceutical firm isolated the active alkaloid ingredient known as 'reserpine' and came up with drugs for controlling blood pressure. These were patented. One can also cite the example of the MNC, W.R. Grace, obtaining a patent on a neem seed derivative in the form of 'Margosan-O' in the USA.

Similarly, turmeric and basmati rice are other examples, the patents for which continue to be contested by India in the WTO's Dispute Settlement Body. In fact, ever since it signed the TRIPS Agreement, India has been steadfastly fighting one legal battle after another in respect of natural life forms. The ranges from basmati rice, neem and turmeric Hessian, a coarse product of jute, naturally grown in, and exported from, the Bengal region for centuries. A Britain based company Geo-Hess had patented under the European Patent No. 0728048 the use of Hessian cloth/sheet to cover waste/dumping grounds. A royalty of 65 per cent on the cost of Hessian was charged by Geo-Hess the use of Hessian covers for waste in Europe on grounds of claimed invention.

The Kolkata based Jute Manufacturers Development Council with help from the Indian Jute Industries Research Association made in the European Patent Office a well documented and substantiated opposition to Geo-Hess's patent claim and eventually succeeded in getting the patent revoked on grounds of lack of inventive merits. This legal success has avoided what would have been a substantial loss to the Indian industry. Taking advantage of the environment friendly and biodegradable nature of this jute product, which had gained increasing acceptability for waste/garbage disposal in Europe, the patent holder had already earned billions of Euros as royalty payment.

BIOLOGICAL DIVERSITY ACT

After the Rio summit in 1992 and the agreement reached under the International Biodiversity Convention, efforts have been made to regulate the illegal flow of genetic material across nations. The convention on biological diversity signed by 65 countries came into force in December 1993 and India ratified it on February 1994. The convention accords sovereign rights to nations over their genetic material and biological resources. It is estimated that India is endowed with 6.5 per cent of the world's stock of plant and animal species. It is also estimated that there are 45,000 species of wild plants and 77,000 species of wild animals in India. Documenting this germplasm is a huge task but it is necessary. The Biodiversity Act provides for protection of the Indian germplasm. However there is need for harmonizing the provisions of Plant Varieties Act and Biodiversity Act. This is essential for protection of bio-diversity and to regulate trade in germplasm as well as to recognize traditional knowledge of biomaterials for which local communities need to be compensated. An international consensus should be evolved in this issue.

India had signed the International Convention on Biological Diversity in 1992 and ratified it in 1993. The objectives of the convention are conservation of biological diversity, sustainable use of its components and fair and equitable sharing of benefits arising out of utilization of genetic resources. India is one of the countries having rich biodiversity. There was no specific legislation for regulating the access to natural (genetic) resources of the country, for enabling export of such resources, and for facilitating sharing of the result of their use or for transfer of technologies using them in India.

Keeping these view and also in order to follow upon the obligation under the Convention on Biological Diversity, India has brought into force a very comprehensive Biodiversity Act in 2002 followed by Biological Diversity Rules 2004. The main objectives of the Act are: (i) To regulate access to biological resources of the country with the purpose of securing equitable share in benefits arising out of the use of biological resources and associated knowledge relating to biological resources; (ii) To conserve and facilitate sustainable use biological diversity; (iii) To respect and protect knowledge of local communities relating to biodiversity; (iv) To secure sharing of benefits with local people as conservers of biological resources and holders of knowledge and information relating to the use of biological resources; (v) To conserve and develop the areas of importance from standpoint of biological diversity heritage sites; (vi) To protect and rehabilitate the threatened species and (vii) To involve the institutions of self-Government in the broad scheme of implementation of the Act through the constitution of the committees.

The Indian Patent Act 1970 provided for process patent for food, medicines, drugs and chemicals only. No patents of life forms, plants varities and products were allowed. The biodiversity Act provides for patenting the biological process, biological technology and biological product. The Act's provisions for regulating Biological Diversity are as follows.

(i) All foreign individuals, associations and organizations would be required to seek prior approval of the National Biodiversity Authority to access any biological resources or the results of research taking place in India for any use.

(ii) The Authority's prior approval would be required before seeking any form of intellectual property right on an invention based on biological resources. The authority will have the power to impose conditions to ensure a share in the benefits accruing from the acquisition of intellectual property rights.

(iii) Indian citizens, body corporate, association or organization registered in India are required to give prior intimation to the State Biodiversity Boards about obtaining biological resources for commercial utilization. However, local people and communities of the area including *vaids* and *hakims* who have been practicing indigenous medicine are exempted from giving prior intimation to the State Biodiversity Boards.

The National Biodiversity Authority: The National Biodiversity Authority shall be established by the central Government to regulate transfer and use of biodiversity resources at the national level. The head office of the Authority shall be located at Chennai. The Authority shall consist of a chairperson, eight ex-officio members and five non-official members. The chairman shall be an eminent person in the field of conservation and sustainable use of biological diversity and in matters relating to equitable sharing of benefits. The ex-officio members include representatives of the ministries dealing with environment and forests, agricultural research and education, ocean development, agriculture and co-operation, Indian and homoeopathy systems of medicine and tribal affairs. The non-official members include specialists and scientists in the field of biological diversity, representatives of industry, conservers and holders of knowledge about biological resources.

The functions of the National Biodiversity Authority are:

(i) To grant permissions to persons who intend to obtain a biological resource occurring in India or knowledge associated thereto for purposes of research or for commercial utilization or for bio survey and bio-utilization or for transfer of results of any research relating to such biological resources;

(ii) To grant approval to persons making applications for patent connected with biological research in foreign countries;

(iii) To impose such terms and conditions as it may deem fit for payment of royalty, determine and secure equitable sharing of benefits arising out of the use of accessed biological resources, their by-products, innovations and practices associated with their use and application and out of the use of knowledge relating thereto;

(iv) To frame guidelines for access and equitable sharing of benefits;

(v) To advise the state Governments in the selections of areas to be notified as heritage sites.

(vi) To take necessary measures to oppose grant of intellectual property rights in any country outside India on any biological material obtained from India or associated knowledge, which is derived from India.

(vii)To make appraisal of and either approve subject to terms and conditions or reject the application giving reasons of the application for obtaining biological resources or the knowledge associated thereto for purposes of research or for commercial utilization or for bio-survey and bio-utilization; for transferring results of research outside India; for getting prior permission for seeking intellectual property rights.

Equitable Sharing of Benefits: It is just and reasonable that persons and/or communities who preserved and conserved matter and material shall have a share in the monetary gain obtained from exploiting the biological material. Benefits sharers may be individuals or communities of some specified localities where rare and useful species or germplasm is found which on its use is found to help exceptional improvements and yield superior results in biotechnology. The National Biodiversity Authority and the State Biodiversity Board shall determine the proportion of the gain to be shared to the conserver person/communities. Benefit sharing shall be determined in any of the following methods; (a) Grant of joint ownership of IPRs to the National Biodiversity Authority; (b) Transfer of Technology; (c) Location of production, research and development units in such areas where it facilitates better living standards to the beneficiaries or where beneficiaries are identified; (d) Association of Indian scientists, beneficiaries and the local people with research and development in biological resources and bio-survey and bio-utilization; (e) Setting up venture capital fund for aiding the cause of beneficiaries; (f) Payment of monetary compensation and other non-monetary benefits to the beneficiaries.

The State Biodiversity Board: The State Biodiversity Board is to be set up by the state concerned. The Board shall consist of a chairman, five ex officio members representing various departments of the state Governments and five non-official members. The state board shall advise the State Government on the matters relating to conservation and sustainable use of biological diversity, in the selection of areas to be notified as heritage sites and in equitable sharing of benefits. It shall regulate activities relating to obtaining biological resources for commercial utilization by Indian citizens, body corporate, organizations or associations. It shall monitor such activities and see that they are not contrary to the objectives of conservation or sustainable use of biodiversity and equitable sharing of benefits.

Duties of Central and State Governments: The Central Government shall develop national strategies, plans, and programs for the conservation and sustainable use of biological diversity including measures for identification and monitoring areas rich in biological resources, promotion of conservation of ecosystems and natural habitats and maintenance or recovery of viable populations of species in their natural surroundings and in the case of demonstrated or cultivated species in the surroundings where they have developed their distinctive properties (*in situ* conservation), conservation of components of biological diversity outside their natural habitats (*ex situ* conservation). The Central Government shall integrate conservation and sustainable use of biological diversity into relevant sectoral or cross-sectoral plans, programs and policies.

The Central Government shall take measures for assessment of environmental impact of projects and with public participation and to regulate, manage or control the risks associated with the use and release of modified living organisms resulting from biotechnology. The Government shall endeavor as per the recommendations of the National Biodiversity Authority to respect and protect knowledge of local people relating to biodiversity. The Central Government may notify certain species as threatened species and prohibit or regulate collection thereof for any purpose and take appropriate steps to rehabilitate and preserve those species. The Central Government in consultation with the National Biodiversity Authority may designate institutions as repositories for different categories of biological resources. The Central Government may in consultation with the National Biodiversity Authority declare that the provisions of this Act shall not apply to any items including biological resources normally traded as commodities. The State Governments may in consultation with the local bodies, notify areas of biodiversity importance as biodiversity heritage sites; frame rules for management and conservation of heritage sites in consultation with the central Government; formulate schemes for compensating or rehabilitating people economically affected by such notification.

Biodiversity Management Committee: Every local body shall constitute a Biodiversity Management Committee for conservation, sustainable use and documentation of biodiversity; The National Biodiversity Authority and State Biodiversity Boards shall consult the Biodiversity Management Committees while taking any decision relating to the use of biological resources and associated knowledge occurring within their jurisdictions. The Biodiversity Management Committee may impose collection fees for collecting biological resources from their territories.

Offences and Penalties: Offences under this Act shall be cognizable and non-bailable. No court shall take cognizance of any offence under this Act or Rules and Regulations made there under except the complaint made by the National Biodiversity Authority or State Biodiversity Board. No Suit, prosecution or other legal proceeding shall be brought against the Central Government or the State Government or any officer concern or any member officer or employee of the National Biodiversity Authority or the State Biodiversity Board for anything which is done or intended to be do in good faith under this Act or rules or regulations. The provisions of this Act shall have effect notwithstanding anything inconsistent therewith contained in any other law under force.

The following shall be punishable with imprisonment for a term which may extend to five years or fine which may extend to ten lakh rupees or both; (a) Non-Indian participation shall if he undertakes biodiversity related activities without prior permission, (b) Any person whether a citizen or not, transfers the results of any research relating to any biological resources for monetary consideration to any non-Indian, (c) Any person who makes an application for any Intellectual Property Right on any invention based on any research or information on a biological resource obtained from India without previous approval of the National Biodiversity Authority.

The Following shall be punishable with imprisonment for a term, which may extend to three years or with fine which may extend to five lakh rupees or both; (i) Any Indian citizen excluding *vaids* and *hakims* who are practicing indigenous medicine, who obtain any biological resource for commercial utilization or bio-survey without giving prior intimation to the State Biodiversity Board, (ii) Any citizen, body corporate, organization, association in India intending to undertake any activity of obtaining biological resources for commercial utilization without giving prior intimation to the State Biodiversity Board. If a person contravenes any direction given or order made by the Central Government or the State Government or the National Biodiversity Authority or the State Biodiversity Board, he shall be punished with a fine which may extend to one lakh rupees and in case of second or subsequent offence, with fine which may extend to two lakh rupees every day during which the default continues.

Offences by the Companies: Where the company is accused, every person who at the time of offence was in charge of responsibility as well as the company shall be deemed guilty and shall be punished unless such person proves the commission of offence or contravention is in bonafide. In the case of a person in charge of the conduct of business of the company, he is deemed to be guilty unless he proves the committal of offence is in bonafide. In the case of a person who is a director, manager, secretary or other officer of the company, it shall be proved that the offence has been committed with his consent or his connivance or attributed to his neglect to bring home his guilt.

REACTIONS TO BIODIVERSITY RULES 2004

In April 2004, the Ministry of Environment and Forests, Government of India, notified the Biological Diversity Rules 2004, under the Biodiversity Act 2002. These Rules have come in for severe criticisms and protests from various quarters. Several NGO's, citizens groups, Panchayats and Gramsabhas have been protesting against the Biodiversity Rules. The proposed rules undermine both communities dependent on biodiversity and conservation itself. They also dilute the Biodiversity Act in letter and in spirit, weakening the already inadequate provisions of the Act relating to rural community rights and powers.

After the draft rules were notified by MoEF, about 220 Gramsabhas and Panhayats across India have signed declarations rejecting these rules and have said that they will not implement these rules. The demand is that the rules notified by MoEF be withdrawn, and a process initiated to draft new Rules that would ensure protection of biodiversity and peoples' rights. In particular, the framing of a new set of Rules should involve widespread consultation with village communities, NGOs, and independent experts.

Some of the critical problems emanating from the Rules are:

Faulty Process: After the draft Rules were put up for public comment in 2003, several citizens and groups sent in detailed comments to MoEF, but each of these was completely ignored in the finalisation of the Rules. Indeed, the draft Rules finally notified on 15th April are almost identical to the draft put up for public comment, including repeating scientific mistakes! This is a mockery of "public participation".

Faulty Content: There are several problems with the Rules which would only facilitate privatisation of biological resources and knowledge, allow biopiracy, weaken the communities' rights over natural resources and allow vested interests to exploit India's biodiversity.

One of the critical issues is around the powers on constitution of Biodiversity Management Committees (BMCs) to be established by every local body. The Act supposedly empowers the BMCs to take decisions on conservation and control. However the Rules severely dilute this and state that the main role and function of the BMC is to merely maintain Peoples Biodiversity Register (PBR). The PBR is only part of a larger plan of the government to document and record the diversity of species of flora, fauna, crops, livestock and knowledge of the same. As on date, there is no legal protection available for the knowledge recorded in the PBR. This is problematic when it comes to the question of access to this document and the knowledge it contains.

Even though communities create and maintain a database of their resources of knowledge, there is no requirement that their consent would be sought when it comes to accessing the information in the PBRs. Although Rule 17 says local bodies will be consulted before approval for access to bio resources is given, the definition of "consult" is not clear and in many cases it might remain a mere formality and not a prior informed consent. Though the Act has clearly spelt out criteria for rejecting applications for the grant of access to resources and knowledge, it has not listed community consent as one of them. Also Rule 7 is clearly biased, as it gives BMC only an advisory role in the of grant approvals.

Therefore in many ways the Rules do not facilitate community decision-making and control on their resources and knowledge and hence are not step toward community sovereignty. Before the

Parliament gives the final nod to the Rules, it is essential to modify them by incorporating the following.

1. Full rights and powers to panchayat raj institutions to manage their natural and agricultural surrounds;
2. Full legal protection to traditional knowledge including whatever is documented in Community Biodiversity Registers;
3. Transparent and stringent procedures that govern access to biological resources and knowledge by foreign and industrial entities;
4. Clear provisions for conservation of threatened ecosystems, species, and genetic varieties, with the full involvement of relevant communities.

6

INTELLECTUAL PROPERTY RIGHTS AND AGRICULTURAL TECHNOLOGY DEVELOPMENTS

A.A. Dange

INTRODUCTION

Advancements in agricultural technology in recent years have been accompanied by a stronger intellectual property rights (IPR) regime under the WTO TRIPs Agreements. The new IPR regime is used for protection of technology and are highly exclusionist in their nature. This development poses a challenge for developing countries as advances in agriculture technology are largely in the private sector in present days. IPRs do provide commercial incentives for research and innovative activities. These financial rewards will accrue from market sales of patented products developed and fold. Social rewards also do arise by licensing the product at lower rates to non-commercial users. The commercial value of IPR protected products essentially depends on the breadth (scope) of protection. Moreover IPR laws are national in nature and are applicable in those countries where they are available.

In the field of agriculture more so research due to IPRs both scientific knowledge and its commercial application are increasingly becoming proprietary. Proprietary rights are claimed by both private firms mainly multinationals and public institutions. Such rights include trade secrets, patent rights, plant varietal protection (PVP) and contractual rights arising from the use of material transfer agreements. These developments have a bearing on the agriculture sector in developing countries as agricultural productivity increase depends crucially on improved technology. Today agricultural biotechnology opens up new vistas for productivity improvement and can have a beneficial impact on global food and livelihood security. It can reduce the incidence of poverty, and starvation in developing countries and increase food security. Agricultural biotechnology advancements are protected by a strong IPR regime and hence the impact of IPRs on Agriculture becomes crucial for analysis especially for countries like India which has a rich bio-diversity and where majority of the farmers are small and marginal. The present paper attempts to study the IPR system as applicable to agriculture and its consequences especially for small and marginal farmers.

Plant Breeders' Rights (PBR) or Plant Varietal Protections (PVP) systems are synonymous terms to describe specialized (sui generis) IPR systems for cultivated plants. PBRs were first systematized under the International Union for the Protection of New Varieties of Plants (UPOV). UPOV is an intergovernmental organization which was established under the 1961 UPOV Convention signed by its member governments. The purpose of the UPOV Convention is to ensure that the member states acknowledge the achievements of breeders of new plant varieties, by making available to them an exclusive property right, on the basis of a set of uniform and defined principles. The UPOV Convention entered into force in 1968 and was revised in 1972, 1978 and 1991. The 1991 Act of UPOV Convention entered into force on April 24, 1998. Membership of UPOV among other steps requires that signatories adopt national legislation along the lines of the 1978 (e.g. China) or 1991 (e. g. USA) UPOV Conventions. As of March 23, 1999,39 governments had become member states of UPOV. As of January 22, 1991 eleven out of 38 member states had developed legislation in lien with the UPOV 1991 Convention while the remainder had legislation in line with the UPOV 1978 Convention.

In place of the novelty, nonobviousness, and utility requirements of patent law, PBR uses the requirements of novelty, distinctness, sufficient uniformity, and stability (DUS). Uniformity and stability are measures of reproducibility true-to-form, respectively among specimens within a planting and inter-generationally. The principal test then is distinctness to determine novelty, i. e. that the variety be "clearly distinguishable from all" known varieties. PBRs differ from patents in a number of key respects and it is generally not useful in discussions of IPRs to confuse or conflate these two different IPR systems.

It is worth noting also that both trademarks and trade secrets are widely used intellectual property rights in the agricultural biotechnology sector. For instance, trademarks can be associated with a particular companies name (e.g. Pioneer Hi-Bred), or individual products like the FlvrSvr tomato. Note that the FlvrSavr tomato genotype may also be patented so the two forms of IPR can be complementary. Within agriculture, the parent inbred lines used to generate F-1 hybrids may be considered a form of trade secrets. So long as the crosses and/or the inbred lines are protected, the product is difficult to copy. However, the self reproducible nature of most living organisms precludes a major role for trade secrets as IPR protection systems for agricultural products. In other technological areas, trade secrets may substitute for or complement patents. When a product or process is difficult to copy, the trade secrets can be a substitute for patents.

The vast majority of patents in plant biotechnology research are taken out by private or public sector institutions in OECD countries (e.g. USA, Japan, EU countries, Australia). The same trend is evident for plant varietal protection or plant breeders rights certificates. It would seem that domestic innovation in plant biotechnology research in the majority of non OECD countries has to date yielded few IPR protected technologies or products.

TECHNOLOGY USE FEES AND CONTRACTS

Intellectual property rights (IPRs) are not the only legal means that can be used to ensure that proprietary technologies are not mis-appropriated. There is an emerging trend for some companies to also use bilateral legal contracts with growers to ensure that their products are grown in a particular manner and to ensure that value is captured from such downstream end-users. Agricultural biotechnology which focuses on output traits will result to some extent in a shift from agricultural production of commodities towards more specialised production for lucrative niche markets.

Agribusiness projections suggest that by 2028 farmers will be responsible for 10% of the added value in end-products, whereas food processing and distribution will be responsible for over 80%.

This contrasts with relative value added contributions of 32% and 50% in 1950 for farmers and food processing/distribution respectively. It is thought that an increasingly large percentage of varieties containing such specialised output traits will be produced under strict contractual guidelines. It is further suggested that such contracts are likely to be managed by input suppliers who, in partnership with the farmer, will produce within contract parameters for specific niche markets. A number of companies are using such types of legal contracts with farmers who act as contract growers. In some cases farmers buying such proprietary seed have to sign contracts guaranteeing no reuse of seed in the following year. Such contracts can also require that the growers use particular brands of inputs (e. g. herbicides) on the proprietary seed varieties.

Another development has been that of technology fees. To recapture private investments in plant biotechnology research some companies now make a legal distinction between the value of the original seed or variety per se and the value of the new technology embodied in the improved seed. Such companies now charge a 'technology premium' to farmers when they purchase improved seed. For example, the 1996 technology premium for Bt based insect protection in cotton was reported to approx $75 per hectare and $25 per ha for maize. More recently, the technology premium list prices ranged from $32 per acre for Bt cotton, to $5 per unit for herbicide resistant soyabeans. In some cases, such technology fees have been waivered to facilitate market entry and it is expected that such fees would decline as more competitors bring substitute technologies to the market.

In some instances, the developers of novel biotechnologically generated foods may opt to internalize the entire production and distribution process to the exclusion of other producers and suppliers. Calgene, owner of the Flavr Savr tomato, for example, was reported to be producing exclusively under contract or using their own facilities. Where labour costs are lower in developing countries it is possible that contract growing of proprietary varieties containing output traits (e.g. especially for export crops) will begin to emerge.

TECHNOLOGY PROTECTION SYSTEMS

There has been some controversy generated over the development of 'technology protection systems' (TPS) which aim to ensure that saved seed containing proprietary technologies or genes is not re-planted without adequate payment for the novel embodied technologies. Such systems are likely to work for all self-pollinated and out crossing seed propagated crops. And may have distinct biosafety benefits. At present no such systems have been developed for clonally propagated crops. Such systems may promote private investment in crop research for crops where the extent of re-planting of saved seed is a disincentive for recouping investments. One such technology dubbed the "Terminator" which was originally developed by the USADA and Delta & Pine, and is now owned by Monsanto, has been the focus of much attention. However, other companies are developing similar technology protection systems using a different suite of transgenes. A number of countries (e.g. India) are reported to have banned the use of such TPS systems and the CGIAR has stated that such systems will not be used in its research programmes.

None of the technology protection systems under development have yet been commercialised (i.e. reached farmers fields) and are unlikely to be commercialised in the near future (e. g. 5-7 years). If developed further, the next generation of systems are likely to involve the failure of the proprietary genes to express their useful traits when the variety is re-planted, rather than the failure of the entire varietal genotype to replicate itself. The 'switching on' of such proprietary traits which rest upon the varietal platform may be contingent upon the application of proprietary chemicals which induce the proprietary transgenes to express the useful trait. Hence, farmers could choose whether on not to buy the proprietary chemicals which switch on the improved traits. The impact of such gene use restriction technologies (GURTs) is currently the subject of an independent international expert review process conducted by the CBD Secretariat as an agenda item for consideration at the next SBSTTA meeting.

RESEARCH EXEMPTIONS UNDER PATENT AND PVP SYSTEMS

A key consideration for researchers, and hence for the public concerned about the efficiency of agricultural research, is access to IPR protected materials and technologies for research or non-commercial purposes. An IPR research exemption refers to the permissible use of protected materials for certain research and product development/improvement purposes e.g. non-commercial use. Research exemptions under IPR systems are critical to future scientific innovation and competitiveness. However, there are signs that research exemptions under both patent and PVP systems are becoming less standard and more restrictive in the favour of the IPR holders.

Most patent legislation provides an exemption for scientific research or non-commercial uses of the patented technology. However the practical nature of such research exemptions can differ significantly between different patent systems. For instance, the nature of the research exemption under the US and Canadian patent systems is more restrictive than the research exemption provided under the European and Japanese patent systems. In some cases the research exemption is explicitly stated in national patent laws while in others it is not. Furthermore, there can be significant legal differences between experimenting on a patented invention - that is, using it to study its underlying technology and invent around the patent, which is what the exemption covers-and experimenting with a patented invention to study something else, which is not covered by the exemption. Many researchers in the USA and Canada work on the assumption that patent holders are unlikely to file a lawsuit against an academic researcher whose use of their invention is commercially insignificant.

The research exemption under most PVP systems (e.g. UPOV) is typically called the breeders exemption. The breeders exemption refers to the right to use protected materials as the basis for developing a new distinct variety or other research use. Research or experimentation exemptions under patents are not as well defined. However, to prevent copying of research the breeders exemption under PVP laws such as promoted by UPOV 1991 is now contingent upon the questions of essential derivation and dependency. The 1991 Act of the UPOV Convention requires that varieties eligible for PVP shall not be essentially derived from other protected varieties or require the repeated use of the protected variety (e.g. inbred lines for F1 hybrid production). Essentially derived varieties may be obtained for example by selection of natural or induced mutants, by selection of somaclonal variants, by backcrossing or by genetic engineering.

The definition, either by molecular or phenotypic means, of thresholds which would define what extent of essential derivation and/or dependency would constitute an infringement is currently under discussion in UPOV, ASSINSEL and FIS. It is likely that molecular profiling of varieties will be increasingly used to identify varieties which are essentially derived from commercially valuable elite germplasm. Some seed companies (e.g. Pioneer HiBred) are now hiring germplasm security officers trained in molecular diagnostics who will specialise in identification and prosecution of essential derivation situations where proprietary germplasm is being misappropriated. Unlike the case of state promoted DNA forensics for identification of humans in criminal situations, it is likely that the DNA forensics will be performed by the companies themselves rather than by independent agencies. It is also likely that criteria for judging what constitutes an "essentially derived" variety will have to be defined on a crop-by-crop basis.

In the area of IPR protection for plants, utility patents are considered to be the IPR of choice in situations where the technology holder would like the strongest protection and the most minimal research exemption. However, the legal interface between plant breeders rights and patents is currently unclear in many countries. Because plant molecular biotechnology is conducted in a modular fashion, a single variety (or transgene) can be subject to multitude of different patents, each on different genetic components or processes, and each possibly owned by different owners in different countries. In addition, such varieties can also be subject to PVP and the legal provisions therein. ASSINSEL has stated that patented plant genetic components, traits or characteristics and commercialized varieties including their patented genetic components, traits or characteristics should be unrestrictedly accessible and/or usable for developing new plant varieties. However, to commercialize a variety incorporating a patented genetic component or expressing a patented trait or characteristic, ASSINSEL recognizes that the authorization should be requested from the patent holder.

Patent lawyers are typically paid to submit claims for IPR protection which are as strong and broad as possible. There has been much international debate on the issue of agricultural biotechnology patents which are increasingly broad in scope. In particular, when broad patents, or patents on basic research/ enabling technologies occur there can be a tendency for the patent holders to engage in cross-licensing or patent pooling. Such practices can act as significant barriers to market entry for competitors and can act as disincentives for follow on innovation.

Some of the larger companies with powerful patent portfolios on agricultural biotechnologies are now involved in cross-licensing or bartering of one patented technology for another. By comparison isolated public sector research institutions or smaller companies with relatively weak patent portfolios and legal expertise are not in a strong bargaining position to gain access to many useful proprietary technologies under standard research exemption clauses. Threats of litigation or 'sham litigation' to slow down competitive entry into markets will also be disproportionately felt by weaker institutions or organizations.

In the area of agricultural research, there is a greater need for more detailing of valid criteria for research exemptions under national patent law to ensure that researchers can gain access to proprietary technologies for research and non-commercial purposes. In the context of food security in developing countries there may be some scope for obtaining research exemptions on use of proprietary technologies for non-commercial purposes e.g. orphan and neglected crops, non-export crops, subsistence farmers.

A more transparent elaboration of the research exemption criteria for non-IPR holders coupled to a greater specification of the utility and enablement doctrines for patent holders could increase incentives for follow-on and incremental research and help to deter anticompetitive cross-licensing schemes. In particular, stronger research exemptions or compulsory licensing might be sought in situations whereby the patent owner "fails to practice" the patent in certain unprofitable "public good" type situations e. g. for improvement of non-commercial subsistence crops or for less lucrative markets. Generic material transfer agreements (MTAs) concerning genetic resources or technologies could also be developed which would broaden access to germplasm or technologies for certain purposes (e.g. non commercial use, non-export crops etc.).

The relative lack of participation of public sector scientific NGOs as observers in international for a concerning food security, environment, agriculture and genetic resources may mean that important issues regarding research exemptions and access to technologies remain off policy agendas. There is a pressing need at the national or international level for greater involvement of membership based organizations representing public sector scientists in the elaboration of criteria and approaches for maintaining IPR research exemptions in a manner which best promotes research competition and equitable technology transfer.

FARMERS PRIVILEGE TO SAVE AND RE-SOW PROPRIETARY PLANTING MATERIALS UNDER PATENT AND PVP SYSTEMS

The farmers' privilege is the right to hold PVP protected germplasm as a seed source for subsequence seasons (farmer-saved seed). Where the privilege exists, farmers can use the harvested product of a protected variety for propagating purposes on their own holdings, where the harvested product was obtained by previous planting on their own holdings. Under Article 15 of the UPOV 1991 Convention, the farmers' privilege is optional, within reasonable limits, for governments to include in their national PVP legislation.

The farmers' privilege to re-sow saved seed would generally be an infringement with most patented materials. Under most current patent systems, there is no farmers privilege to allow the saving and re-propagation of patent protected seed. This contrasts with the farmers privilege' under the UPOV plant breeders rights system where countries have the option to allow such a farmers privilege for PVP protected seed.

The International Seed Trade Federation (FIS) has stated that there is a need for a clear limitation or definition of those practices, which are carried out in some countries under the name of "farmers' privilege". FIS considers that it should not happen that a situation of unfair competition should arise between the participants in the seed market because of the use of farm-saved seed with subsequent commercial use of the product obtained whether it comes from the production of seed or from the production for consumption purposes. FIS has also stated that despite the benefits of the UPOV system for protection of plant varieties, it will be useful for companies to take advantage of patent protection also for plant varieties, in case of maintenance of the abusive application of the possibility for the farmer to use his own seed without paying royalties, which is considered by FIS to not be justified. This would happen because the patent system, with its stronger degree of monopolization, legally excludes such a possibility.

Nonetheless for both social equity and food security reasons there are justifications for providing a 'farmers' privilege' for smallholder and resource poor farmers, especially in developing countries. This would essentially require a disaggregated, farmers privilege' in both PVP and patent legislation whereby poorer farmers who do not represent an immediate or lucrative market would enjoy the 'farmer privilege' to save seed, while their richer counterparts would be required to pay royalties on saved proprietary seed. Interestingly, both the EU's Directive on Protection of Biotechnological Inventions (Article 11) and the Andean Pact countries have opted to enshrine the farmers' privilege for a segment of their farmers, namely subsistence or smallholder farmers, whose livelihoods can be dependant on farm saved seed and planting materials.

REFERENCES

httt/www.upov.org.

http/www.upov.org.

see http/www.agbioforum.missouri.edu.

Kindinger PE (1998), "Biotechnology and the Ag. Chem. Industry, Ag Bioforum", No. 1, pp. 74-75.

Hayenga M. (1998), "Structural Change in the Biotech Seed and Chemical Industrial Complex See http./www.agbioforum. Missouri.edu.

See http/www.rafi.org/.

See http./www.nap.edu/reading groom/books/property.

See http./www.world seed.org/assise/pos^2.htm.

Ibid.

http./www.upov.org.

See http:/www.world seed.org/assinsel/pos-fis.htm.

7

IPR FOR FOOD SAFETY TECHNOLOGY AND MANAGEMENT

V.G. Dhanakumar

INTRODUCTION

The Agreement on Sanitary and Phytosanitary Measures (SPS) and the Agreement on Technical Barriers to Trade (TBT) define the international rights and obligations of member countries with respect to the development or application of measures that affect trade. Especially, SPS acknowledges a country's right to protect itself from risks to human, animal and plant life and health, and it confirms the need to constrain countries from using such measures as excuses to create unnecessary barriers to trade. In short, the purpose of the agreement is to enable the legitimate protection of life and health while not giving rise to illegitimate protectionism. In this way, only measures truly aimed at protecting life and health are allowed, and measures that are either not related to life and health issues at all or that are excessively strict are ruled out.

India has lost sufficient trade because of failure to meet food safety standards. Different countries in the past had rejected Indian products. To quote some examples, European Community banned fish imports from Gujarat, Chilli exported from India was detained by Spain due to aflatoxin contamination. Indian spices were detained by Italy and Germany for pesticide residues and microbial standard for shrimp cost India nearly 58 metric tones. More than trade, human health is under threat due to physical, chemical and biological contaminants. For example, Polycyclic Aromatic

Hyderocarbons (PAH's) contamination with copra & fish in the process of smoking cased carcinogenic and mutagenic effects on human. Aflatoxin contamination in chilli and groundnut caused hepatic necrosis and hepatomes. Salmonella and E. coli 0157:H7 contamination in fruit juices caused deadful illness.

Therefore, TBT Agreement is intended to ensure that WTO Members do not use technical regulations and standards as disguised measures to protect domestic industries from foreign competition. In international trade law, health and environmental standards and regulations, labeling, symbols, packaging and markings can be considered as technical barriers to trade. In the agrifood sector, the TBT Agreement applies to all rules other than those specifically covered by the SPS Agreement. The TBT Agreement does not permit requirements for the labeling of some products whereby "like products" remain unlabeled (Article 2.1). For example, GM crop commodities that have been assessed and found to be "substantially equivalent" to their conventional counterparts would be considered "like products" and thus would not require specific labeling. Critics of the WTO stance argue that "substantially equivalent" is an unacceptable outcome of the risk assessment of GM products and assert that these products are not "like products" for purposes of labeling, and in fact, can be subjected to labeling would not be viewed as a legitimate objective within the context of the TBT Agreement.

In the present debate about health and safety, the "precautionary approach" is often opposed to a "sound-science approach". Varying perceptions about public health risks, different levels of acceptance of them, divergent priorities, and dissimilar economic interests have driven countries to take quite opposite positions in this field and have created acute tensions among them. International trade magnifies the problem.

PATENTS FOR FOOD SAFETY TECHNOLOGY

Knowledge is not merely power, but also wealth. If, a knowledge becomes wealth, he who acquires it, seeks to monopolize it. "know how" consists of knowledge and experience acquired for the practical application of a technique. The notion of property (patents) is employed by those who deal in technical know-how. Until it is patented, it can be treated only as "know-how", Patents enjoy statutory protection.

Example, "Knowledge on" frozen shrimps helps in the identification of salmonella and vibrio infection. "Know–how" of how to control this infection is termed as technological "Know–how" which is irradiation at the rate of 3 to 7 kGy.

One reason for greater interest in patents, especially in the organization for Economic Cooperation and Development (OECD) countries, is the rapid development of biotechnology and its application in agriculture. A patent prevents someone from making commercial use of what is claimed in the patent without the authorization of the patent holder. To be patentable, an invention must be:

- Nonobvious for someone skilled in the art, that is, not simply be an extension of something that already exist – it must require some inventive step;
- Novel or not previously known; and industrially applicable in some way.

Patents can be given for products and processes and are limited to a fixed period of at least 20 years under TRIPS–after which the invention moves into the public domain and can be used by anyone. Patents are territorial and apply only in the countries in which they are granted. Each country decides its own patent rules and how to interpret the meaning of different terms, but WTO Members must meet the minimum standards in TRIPS. Using a toxin–encoding gene the breeder are developing new seed or variety to minimize the use of agri–chemical and pesticide in the plant. The above technique meets the requirements of chemical toxin of SPS agreement, but fails to meet total role of "food safety technology (or) know-how" such as prevention as prevention of chemical, biological, physical and genomic residue aspects of SPSs.

In return for the temporary monopoly granted by the patents, the inventor must make a full disclosure of the nature of his or her invention that is understandable to anyone else skilled in the necessary arts or sciences. In this way, inventions do not "die with the inventor". Moreover, others can try to invent something better, but sufficiently different so as not to infringe the claim of the original patent. Clear evidence that the patent system in food safety has stimulated the development of new products and technologies, which otherwise would not have been developed, is available only for a few sectors (such as pharmaceuticals). In other sectors of the economy, patents are sometimes considered to have mainly anticompetitive effects: they serve to secure and strengthen the position of market leaders and limit the entry of new competitors. In the extreme, they may actually slow the pace of innovation if a dominant firm possesses a powerful group of patents that limits the ability of other firms to improve existing products and technologies.

RESEARCH AND DEVELOPMENT PRIORITIES

The importance of patents is increasing, partly because of changes in the funding of R&D for agriculture. Until relatively recently, agricultural R&D was largely publicly funded. Research results were given to farmers through extension services. The financial returns for publicity financed R&D into improved farming productivity are high for both developing and developed countries. The U.S economy, for example, benefited from its long-term investment of US$134 million worth of support to international wheat and rice research aimed at developing countries by up to US$14.7 billion, according to research by the IPGRI.

In theory, stronger IPRs should encourage more research and development (R&D) in countries where thy exist, but there is "limited empirical evidence", even in industrial countries, that IPRs protection leads to increased investment in R&D. This is partly because of the difficulty of separating cause and effect–IPRs may stimulate more investment, but countries and firms that invest more in R&D may demand more protection.

The Code Alimentarius Commission, a U.N. body, complies agreed measures into the Codex Alimentarius, the Codex Food Code (CFC).

> Article 27, section 5 of TRIPS agreement on agriculture states that an invention in all fields of technology is patentable if it is new, innovative and capable of industrial application.

In India, a vicious circle of R&D and corporate sectors are exclusively working around patents of products and processes, protection of seeds and disputes. The key features of IPR implications for agricultural technology, especially in terms of "food safety" technology development, access and profitization are limited.

FEATURES OF IPR IN AGRICULTURE & AGRI-BUSINESS

The implementation of the new SPS Agreement has raised significant problems for developing countries. Some result the lack of capacity to develop the institutional arrangements that permit them to meet their SPS-related WTO commitments. Even if the capacity exists, these commitments are costly to implement: standards, along with testing and certification, represent between 2 and 10 per cent of overall product costs, which impose a burden on agriculture in the developing countries.

> Article 10.1 of the SPS Agreement says that "in the preparation and application of Sanitary and Phytosanitary measures, Members shall take account of the special needs of developing country Members and in particular of the least-developed country Members".

A recent paper found that a 1998 European Commission regulation that raised the standards for the minimum level for certain types of aflatoxin (a toxic substance found in foodstuffs and animal feed), to levels higher than those required by the Codex Alimentarius (the food standards code) is estimated to cost close to US$700 million in lost revenue to African groundnut exporters, many of them LDCs (1).

India has immense potential for the export agri-livestock and its products; the presence of livestock disease of economic importance (e.g., FMD) shall be eradicated /controlled with appropriate patentable technology. The office International des Epizootic (OIE), which is considered as the top most international agency with regard to animal activities. It recommends creation of "Disease Free Controlled Zones" in selected areas of the country, to meet the WTO-SPS agreement that act as a non-tariff barrier.

(a) For example, prioritizing Foot and Mouth Disease (FMD) prevention With suitable technology (FMDV) is sensitive to environmental and patentable importance.

(b) Another high priority in crop husbandry is contamination of microorganisms (e.g., Ochratoxin, aflatoxin, etc), which is highly carcinogenic has truncated export.

(c) Generation and patterning of technology to prevent chemical residue in food sector is warranted. The SPS standard should be formulated on par or equivalence with codex by R&D system in India.

(d) In the past, materials and machines are produced to enhance productivity and quality rather than food safety dimension. It is recommended that technology to patent food-engineering design must focus on food safety aspects.

It is difficult to argue against developed-country actions that aim to protect consumer health and safety. But when such actions result in significant costs to developing-country exports, it would seem fair that the developed countries to legally committed to take steps that will help the developing country to meet the problem that the developed-country regulation has created. Under the agreement, WTO members are encouraged to adopt international standards (where they exists), but may define even higher standards provided these are based on a sound scientific risk assessment and do not discriminate against imports. Recognizing that a complete risk assessment may not possible in the short term because of scientific uncertainty or the lack of sufficient evidence,

> Article 5.7 of the SPS Agreement allows member countries to adopt temporary restrictive measures.

In such cases, members are expected to seek the additional information required to complete a full risk assessment within a reasonable period. Maintaining restrictive measures indeterminately in the absence of scientific evidence of risk solely for "precautionary" reasons is not allowed. The TBT Agreement is intended to ensure that WTO members do not use technical regulations and standards as disguised measures to protect domestic industries from foreign competition.

OPERATIONAL DIMENSIONS OF IPRs TECHNOLOGY

The features of future agriculture and agri-business solemnly depend upon identification of critical control points (CCP) and patenting of critical limits (CL) related to HACCP.

A Critical Control Point (CCP) is defined as "any point step or procedure at which control can be applied and a food safety hazard can be prevented, eliminated (or) reduced to an acceptable level of SPS". The identification of critical control points is based upon the assessment of severity and likely occurrence of hazards and upon what can be done to eliminate, prevent or reduce the hazards at a process step. The selection of CCPs are made on the basis of:

(a) Identified hazards (knowledge) and likely occurrence in relation to that constitutes unacceptable contamination
(b) Operations (know-how) to which the product is subjected to during processing and preparation, and
(e) Intended use of the product.

It should be noted that a separate critical control point does not have to be designated for each hazard. However, actions must be taken to ensure elimination, prevention or reduction of all identified hazards. Examples of CCPs may include heating, chilling, formulation control and its limits. The steps to identify critical control points are:

- Use decision tree approach to identify CCP.
- With the help of experts verification of the control of all the identified hazards.
- Develop parameters attached to CCPs.

There must be a column in hazard identification form where CCPs are identified. CCPs should be identified numerically with a category qualifier "B", "P" or "C" for biological, physical and chemical respectively. For example, if the first CCP identified will control a biological hazard, it will be recorded as CCP-1B. If the second CCP identified will control a chemical hazard, it will be recorded as CCP-2C. If a biological and a chemical hazards are controlled at the same processing step, and this is the fifth CCP, then the CCP number used will be CCP-5BC. This identification protocol was developed to sequentially identify CCPs independent from process step numbering and readily inform the user of the HACCP model which type(s) of hazard needs to be controlled at a particular process step.

Critical limits are defined as criteria that separate acceptability from unacceptability. A critical limit represents those boundaries (technology) that are used to judge whether an operation is producing safe products. Critical limits may be set for factors such as temperature, time (minimum time exposure), physical product dimensions, water activity, moisture level, etc. These parameters, if maintained within boundaries will confirm the safety of the product.

Article 4 of SPS agreement encourages to give positive consideration to accepting as equivalent the SPS measures of other WTO members.

Table 1

Sl. No.	Area of Operation	CCP (Know-how)	CL (Technology for IPR)	Remarks
1.	**Chemical Hazard** Minimize Deposition of Polycyclic Aromatic Hydro-carbons(PAHs) µg/kg in Coconut	• Controlled combustion and use of right fuel in smoke kilns • To prevent PAHs occurrence in copra use either frond (divided foliage leaf) or shell as a source of fuel and charcoal	• Optimize combustion temperature below 140°C to minimize PAHs in copra • Regulatory limits of 25 µg/kg for total PAHs and 5 µg/kg for heavy PAHs for export copra	• The higher level of PAHs may serve as trade barrier • Consumption of PAHs contaminated products emerged as carcinogenic and mutagenic effects on human (2).
2.	**Biological Hazard** Drying of Chillies	• Optimum moisture level • Redrying to avoid rewetting	• < 11% moisture content (It is recommended to use microwave technology in drying & sterilizing of chilli) • Drying period 10-21 days	• 11% moisture level leads to mould growth and intern produce aflatoxin (3). • Specifications for aflatoxin B_1 is 2ppb while for $B_1+B_2+G_1$ and G_2 together the limit is 4 ppb (4)
3.	**Physical Hazard** Spices grinding process (Iron filing in the spice powder)	• Removal of iron filing with metal detector	> 10 ppm	• > 10 ppm for iron filings is considered to be hazardous for human consumption (5) • Use of metal detectors GENIUS GLS tunnel detectors for application in conveyor belt systems and GENIUS RZ tunnel detectors for monitoring sectional and pressure conveyor pipes(6)

The recognition of the equivalence of SPS measures through appropriate CL to Indian products with appropriate patent would represents a key instrument to enhance WTO led market access to our products. The examples of CCP and CL with reference to SPS is given in table 1.

CONCLUSION

The prospects of identifying patent related R&D, education and outreach in the up-coming hinge on how Indian agriculture and agri-business can take maximum advantage of the existing clauses of the TRIPs and to what extent it is successful in amending some of the clauses are the thrust areas. Using modern biotechnology, plant breeders are able to introduce specific genetic material taken from any species of plant, animal, or microorganism, or created synthetically within the laboratory, into many different species of plants or animals, to create transgenic-organisms. The "first generation" of genetically modified (GM) products has generally included crop plants with new input traits, such as pest resistance or herbicidal tolerance. These have included insect-resistant varieties of maize, potato and cotton, containing a toxin-encoding gene from strains of the bacterium Bacillus thuringiensis; plants with tolerance to broad–spectrum herbicides, such as glyposates (Round-up tolerant canola, maize, and soybean), and glufosinate ammonium-tolerant canola, maize, rice and soybean; and plants, such as melon, papaya, potato, and squash, with resistance to disease caused by specific plant viruses. In addition, there are a very few products with modified quality traits, such as high-oletic acid canola and soybean, and delayed-softening melon and tomato.

In international trade law health, environment, standards, regulations, etc can be considered as TBT. Therefore, SPS thus serve as a strict interpretation of the precautionary approach for generation of "wholesome technology" to protect human, animal & plant health and life. This paper calls for commodity and agri-business strategies for the promotion of India's Agri Export and evokes policy discussions and implications on IPR with special reference to food safety technology (or) wholesome technology for patent. The conceptual framework to understand inter-relationship between agreements and its relevance in agri-business sector with special reference to IPR is illustrated in Figure 1.

Figure 1: Conceptual Framework to Understand interrelationship of WTO-SPS-AOA-TBT-TRIPs Agreements & Its Relevance in Agri-Business Sector

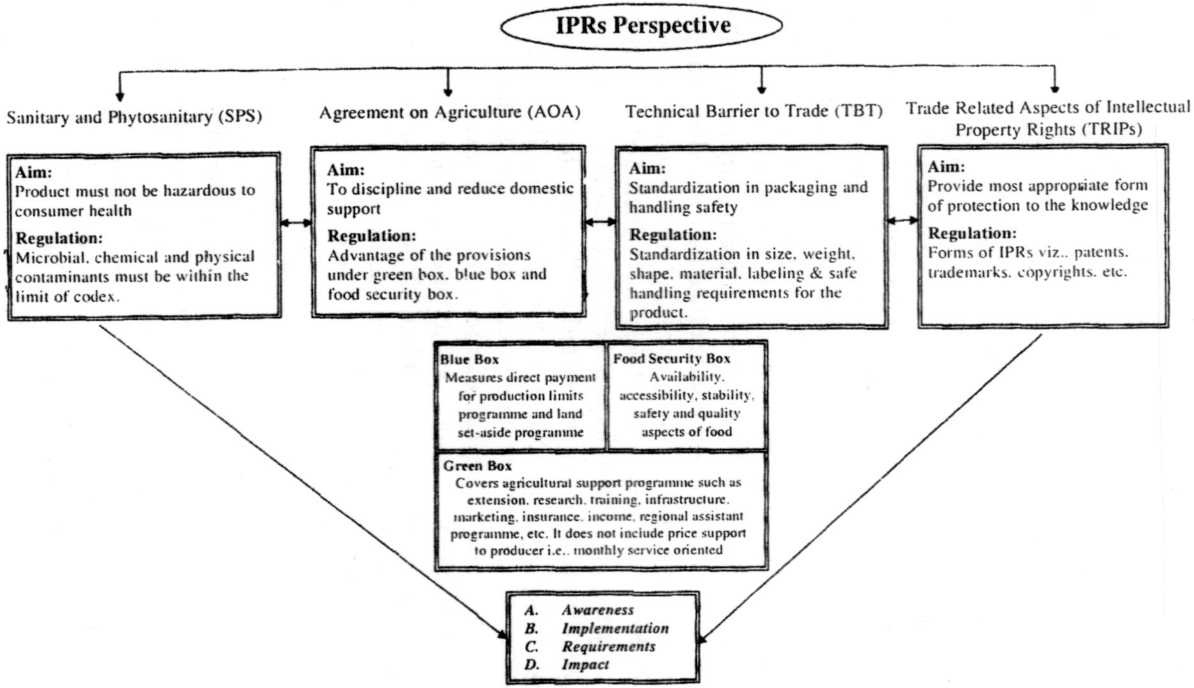

IMPLICATIONS

It is expected that over the coming years there will be newer of "patentable food safety technology" for market. These next-generation products will include plants enhanced resistance to diseases caused by fungal and viral pathogen; agricuticles; improved tolerance to abiotic stresses such as heavy metal contamination; improved nutritional quality or medicinal value; vehicles for delivery of oral vaccines and therapeutics; factories for the production of pharmaceutical proteins; safety technology for food chain from genomics to government and farms to super market to consumers. The **SPS** agreement sets out the basic research, education and outreach for food safety and animal and plant health standards. Although it allows individual countries to set their own standards, it demands that regulations be based on science, and that be applied only to the extent necessary to protect human, animal, or plant life and health.

WTO also instruct countries to enter into consultations with the aim of achieving bilateral and multilateral agreements on recognition of the equivalence of specified sanitary and phytosanitary measures between academic and industry partnership domain to enhance market access. It also instructs countries to develop and document "CL" for each patentable technology with the aim to achieving agreements of SPS and TBT.

REFERENCES

Otsuki, T.,J.S. Wilson, and M. Sewadeh (2000), What Price Precaution? Europen Harmonization of Aflatoxin Regulations and African Food Exports. Processed. World Bank, Washington, D.C.

Samarajeeva, W. (1998), Current Staus on Health Hazards from Pplycycile Aromatic Hydocarbons in Foods: Their Control, Globalisation and Perspective of Export Trade. Proceedings of Technical Sessions, CFTRI, Mysore.

Donna R. Tainter and Anthony T. Grenis (2001), Spices and Seasonings– A Food Technology Handbook. WILEY–VCH, A John Wiley & Sons, Inc., Publication, New York.

Anonymous (1998), World Spice Congress Proceeding, Spices Board and All Indian Spices Exporters Forum, Cochin, p. 43.

Kalyanaraman, K.(2002), Quality Specifications for Spices and Spice Products in Europe, Tata Spices Centre, Cochin.

Markarand Mandke (2002), 'No' to Metal in Food. Agro India, September –October 2002, p. 32.

Aditya Matto and Robert M. Stern (2003), India and the WTO. A Co-Publication of the World Bank and Oxford University Press. Washington.

Dhankumar, V.G. (2004), Safety Management for Fruits & Vegetables. Journal of Agri-business ans Food Industry. Vol. No. 1, Issue 6, pp. 19-23.

Dhankumar, V.G. (2003), Biological Risk Management (Biodiversity) in Coffee: An HACCP Perspectives. Indian Coffee (part I & II). Vol. LZVII, April 2003, pp. 14-17 and Vol. LZVII, No. 7, July 2003, pp.18-21.

Dhanakumar, V.G. (2002), Total Quality Management in Tea through Quality, Safety and Risk Management: An HACCP Perspectives. International Journal of Tea Science Vol. 1, No. 2 & 3 2001-2002, pp.12-27.

Tiwari, S.C. (2003), Paradigm Jump in Indian Agriculture: Natural or Coercive?. Current Science. Vol. 85, No. 5, 10th September, 2003, pp. 578-581.

WTO (World Trade Organisation). (1994), The WTO Agreement on Technical Barriers to Trade (TBT Agreement). Office of the Secretary General, Geneve.

WTO (World Trade Organisation). (2002a), Information on the Utilization of Special and Differential Treatment Provisions. February 7, WT/COMTD/W/77/Rev. 1/Add. 4. Office of the Secretary General, Geneva.

8

INTELLECTUAL PROPERTY RIGHTS FOR BIOTECHNOLOGY–A PERSPECTIVE

B.D. Ranjitha Kumari

INTRODUCTION

One of the most important issues which have been raised due to the emergence of modern biotechnology is the legal characterization and treatment of trade related biotechnological process and products popularly described as Intellectual Property Rights (IPR). IPR includes 'patents, copy rights, trade secrets and trade marks'. The right to protect this property prohibits others from making, selling, copying or using the proprietary subject matter. Due to these intellectual properties, many legal and public policies, which are impediments to biotechnological research, are also being challenged and are undergoing changes. IPR's may adversely affect (1) Food security, (2) Use of evolved agricultural practices, (3) Biological diversity and ecological balance, (4) The livelihood of the poor in developing countries.

In a broader sense, biotechnology has been with us ever since farmers first began "artificially" selecting and breeding plants and animals, and bakers and brewers harnessed a microorganism-yeast -in their craft[1]. Only in the last two decades, however, has it been possible to operate directly on the heart of biological matter, transcending the reproductive barrier between species, and creating entirely new life forms that either would be impossible to bring about through breeding or would take many generations, and much trial and error, to develop[2].

THE U.S. LEGAL REGIMEN

Under current law it is possible to obtain a US patent on any sort of "artificial" life-from cells and plant parts to microorganisms, plants and animals. Indeed, the developer of a new plant variety may obtain either a patent or a specialized plant patent, or a patent-like, "plant variety certificate". This scheme comports with the TRIPS Agreement, which allows, but does not require, member states to "exclude from patentability.... Plants and animals other than microorganisms", as long as they "provide for the protection of plant varieties either by patents or by an effective *sui generis* system or by any combination thereof"[3].

The Supreme Court landmark decision in *diamond* V. Chakrabarthy[4] finally changed all that in 1980. Chakrabarthy involved an application claiming a genetically engineered microorganism with a unique ability to completely breakdown crude oil into compounds edible to aquatic life. Such an organism was thought to be quite useful in cleaning up of oil spills. Chakrabarthy thus cleared the way for patenting biological matter under the Patent Act. In its wake, the PTO (Patent and Trademark Office) extended its rule first to plants in *Ex parte hibberd,* a 1985 case involving claims to new variety of maize genetically engineered for elevated tryptophan levels, and then to animals 2 years later[5].

THE REQUIREMENTS OF NOVELTY, UTILITY, AND DISCLOSURE UNDER THE PATENT ACT

An applicant for utility patent protection must, above all, prove that the subject mater claimed is worthy of the name "inventive" or "discovery". In a word, that means that the thing or process claimed must be "new". Newness, however, has come to have two distinct aspects–novelty" and "nonobviousness" ("inventive step" in European parlance). These concepts, which are defined in the second and third sections of the Patent Act, respectively, are also reflected in the TRIPS Agreement.

Generally speaking, acclaimed invention is said to lack novelty if the exact same thing or process already exists in the public domain (although if the inventor himself put it there, he has a year to file a patent application). This is determined by comparing the language of the claims by which the applicant has described his or her invention with the "prior art" in the field which includes everything from earlier patents to papers published in scientific or technical journals[6]. If the claim language more or less perfectly describes a single piece of prior art, the claimed invention is said to have been "anticipated" and thus lack novelty under the second section of the Patent Act.

The term novelty is somewhat misleading, however, because a claimed invention also must be new in the sense that it does not represent an "obvious" combination of elements from several prior inventions. The test is whether all of the significant elements of the invention can be found in the prior art and, if so, whether the hypothetical "person of ordinary skill in the art" would have some reason, suggestion, or motivation" to combine them.

The "nonobviousness" requirement is probably the most common stumbling block for Patent applicants, and it poses unique challenges to applicants claiming biotechnology [7]. Indeed, because the development of new plant varieties through conventional-breeding techniques does not really involve an inventive step, as a practical mater, protection for such creation may be available only under the PVPA, which eliminate the nonobviousness concept and require only novelty for this reason.

The last of the three basic requirements of patentability–in addition to subject matter eligibility and novelty or nonobviousness–is that the claimed invention must be "useful". Similarly to the eligible subject matter requirement, most inventors have little difficulty in satisfying the utility requirement. It is not particularly strict, mainly because applicants can be expected not to claim useless things. It is not particularly strict, mainly because of invention has some apparent, lawful use-however slight-in the "useful arts" (as opposed to the liberal arts, fine arts, or pure sciences).

Again, however, biotechnology has been somewhat of an exception to the rule. Applications that assert no use beyond laboratory research, for example, may be rejected, on the ground that the invention falls within the ambit of pure science (or lacks "substantial" utility[8], whereas those who assert a utility in curing a putatively "incurable" disease such as cancer or AIDS) may be deemed inherently incredible absent proof to the contrary. Recent judicial decisions finally have adopted a more relaxed stance, however.

THE NATURE AND SCOPE OF RIGHTS CONFERRED BY A PATENT

A patent gives its owner a "right to exclude" others from the intellectual property staked out by the claims. Specifically, a patent entitles its owner to sue in federal court to stop anyone who, without permission, "make[s], use[s], or sell[s]" a thing or process that "infringes" the patent monopoly or be compensated monetarily.

A doing or process can infringe a patent in two ways: either "literally" or under the "doctrine of equivalents". Literal infringement means that a thing or process is more or less perfectly described by the words of the patent claims, properly interpreted[9]. The doctrine of equivalents, by contrast, is rooted in the ancient legal principle, traceable through the civil law tradition back to Aristotle, that a thing may be within the ambit of a legal text if it is within its spirit, even if it is not within its letter (and vice versa). The test for infringement by equivalence is whether the accused thing or process performs substantially the same function in substantially the same way to achieve to achieve substantially the same result as the thing or process described by the claims[10]. Pointing to an insignificant difference between the claimed invention and the accused thing or process will not do. To avoid, infringement, then, one must steer clear of not only the literal terms of the claims, but also the fuzzy zone of equivalents that lies at the periphery of the claims.

CLAIMING AGRICULTURAL BIOTECHNOLOGY UNDER THE PATENT ACT

This heading discusses surveys of few recently published decisions involving efforts to patent agricultural biotechnology under the most challenging and protective of the three statutes–the Patent Act.

The first is a 1992 decision involving an application claiming "a method of combating plant insect pests" by "applying to the plant environment or plant seed plant-colonizing bacteria" containing DNA that encodes for a protein toxic to insects, but harmless to humans[11]. This and inventions like it promise to reduce reliance on chemical insecticides and the attendant risks to health and the environment.

A year later, in 1993, the board had occasion to address an application claiming a "recombinant DNA molecule" with a

"DNA" sequence encoding a polypeptide displaying the biological activity of swine growth hormone" and a method for producing this polypeptide[12]. Identifying the gene for swine growth hormone allowed the manufacture of a synthetic hormone that could be used to make larger pigs–a use that had been "limited since extracting swine growth hormone from pituitary glands of swine adequate to provide the needed commercial quantities."

CONCLUSION

The differences between the three modes of protection outlined in this brief survey are significant and must be carefully considered by plant variety developers. For although one may protect a new variety under either the Patent Act or one of the plant-specific statutes (depending on whether the variety is sexually reproductive or not), that is not to say that one may protect the same variety under both a utility patent and a plant-specific title of protection. There is a judge-made rule against "double patenting"-that is, obtaining two patents on the same invention or an additional patent or an obvious variation first. Under this rule, one cannot obtain both a utility patent and a plant patent on the same variety. The courts have yet to decide whether this rule applies equally to plant certificates. It is also not entirely clear how they would, because difference in the scope of protection patents and variety certificates is sufficiently to be considered as distinguishing from double-patenting[13].

NOTES AND REFERENCES

1. Elizabeth Joy Hecht (1992), Beyond animal legal defense fund v. Quigg: The controversy over transgenic animal patents continues. 41 Am. U.L. Rev. 1023, 1026-27.
2. Reid G. Adler (1986), Can patents co-exist with breeder's rights? Developments in US and International Biotechnology Law. Int. Rev. Ind. Propr. Copyright L. p. 195, 207 and 80.
3. TRAIP Agreement, Supra note11, art. 27 (3) (b)
4. 447 US 303 (1980), *aff'g* 596F. 2d 952 (C.C.P.A. 1979).
5. *Ex Parte* Allen, 2 USPQ2d (BNA) 1425 (Bd. Pat. App. & Interf. 1987) (allowing claim to a genetically–engineered in the prescribed polyploidy oyster), *aff'd* without published op., 846 F. 2d 77 (Fed. Cir. 1988). The first patent actually granted on a multicellular animal was the famed "Harvard Mouse" Patent, US Patent No. 4, 736, 866

(1988), which claimed any nonhuman mammal, such as mouse, genetically engineered in the prescribed manner to increase its susceptibility to cancer.

6. Donald S. Chisum (1981). Prior Invention and Patentability 63 J. Pat. and Trademark Off. Soc. J. p. 397.
7. Brian C. Cannon (1994). Toward a clear standard of obviousness for Biotechnology patents, 79 Cornell L. Rev. 735.
8. Maebius (1992). Novel DNA sequences and the utility Requirement: the Human Genome Initiative. J. Pat. Trad. Off. Soc. p. 651.
9. Builders Concrete, Inc. v. Bremerton Concrete Prods (1985) 757 F. 2d 255, 257.
10. Graver Tank and MFG. Co. v. Linde Air Products Co., (1950), 399 US 605.
11. *Ex parte Obukowicz*, 27 USPQ2d (BNA) (1992). 1063 (Bd. Pat. App. And Interf.).
12. *In re* Deuel, 34 USPQ 2d (BNA) (1992). 1063 (Bd. Pat. App. And Interf.).
13. Straus (1984). Patent protection for new varieties of plants produced by genetic engineering–should "Double protection" be prohibited? 15, Int. Rev. Ind. Prop. Copyright L. p. 426.

9

CONTEXT, CONTENT AND METHODS OF INTELLECTUAL PROPERTY EDUCATION

V. Reddappa Reddy

THE CONTEXT

Academics and development must always go together hand in hand. Any gap between the two does not augur well, and may lead to lopsided growth of either of them or both. This does not mean all academic subjects matter in the same way. But the subject of Intellectual Property Education (IPE) is one such that matters. If one of these two, i.e. either IPE or development slowing down the other, it is more likely a case of IPE slowing down the actual development than the other way round. It is with this view, the subject of IPE needs a closer look vis-à-vis the actual development.

Intellectual Property Rights (IPRs) and IPE are the two sides of the same coin. Let IPRs be dealt first. If one has to understand the importance of IPRs, the concept and content of globalisation and the need for social, economic, political and cultural relations across political borders must be properly understood, since opening or closure of the economy for imports and exports of consumables, capital goods and technology and use of employment opportunities abroad are all closely linked to IPRs. Because respecting and paying for the IPRs is an accepted policy arrived through international agreements. None, naturally, can violate such policies and still remain part of the globalised economies. Which in the final analysis implies a country can either be a part of the world comity or a castaway from it; based on recognizing and respecting or not recognising and not respecting the IPRs. However, there are many other aspects that govern the participation or otherwise in the world comity, which are beyond the scope of this paper.

Academic subjects current to the development stage always received utmost care and support in the West. Academic institutions and universities specializing or imparting trainings and expertise on industrial development, financial management, insurance, science and technology and IPE have all received state and/or public support. Linkages with industrial houses and support from philanthropists and state's anxiety to exploit the research and academic expertise for public good always kept the academics in tandem with the stage of development. But in case of India, though many other currently relevant subjects received state and private support the IPE did not find place in the corridors of academics and administration.

The subject of IPRs and IPE gained its currency long ago in the West. This is more because, the resource rich western countries achieved development much earlier, and IPRs and IPE had role in it. With partial globalisation (globalisation within the West) the West experienced a radical change in their lifestyles and livelihood opportunities due to industrial revolution. As a result, the people in the West experienced the benefits of partial globalisation in the overall development process. Naturally, the industry related IPRs had both internal as well as cross country relevance in the West. With this the IPRs along with IPE gained their relevance and grew to contribute to the development of those countries. The IPRs did not gain currency in India especially owing to nominal partnership in international trade as compared to its GNP, exports being largely revolved around subsistence goods with little need and scope for IPRs protection and due to late entry into international agreements on globalisation. Still more, a large political body is opposed to the globalisation, especially when they are in opposition. As a consequence the IPE remained far beyond the scope of academic curricula in India.

Interestingly, even within these limitations the subjects like international trade, international markets and international banking did find a place in the academic curricula since long. However, the IPRs and IPE, having cross country relations and encompassing several fields did not grow as academic subjects.

Can India bypass the IPRs? Due to historical and current policies and administrative reasons, the IPRs remain a little/non-understood subject in India. Incidence of poverty, hunger, disease, homelessness, untouchabililty, absence of livelihood opportunities that guarantee minimum levels of living, degradation of natural resources, etc. continue to cause distressful situation in India. Further, India has no chance of bypassing the left over stages of development and directly concentrate on globalisation and international trade and specialization in IPRs in the background of subsistence oriented indigenous resources and outputs. The positive contribution of globalisation and IPRs to India's development still remains doubtful. But at the same time, it may be impossible to avoid globalisation and still be part of world comity. More important, India has no resources or capacity to survive as a castaway from the world comity by refusing to be part of world IPR regime, at least in the present juncture.

From the political angle, there are two sides here. Firstly, the political body fighting for anti-globalization from Indian side is too small to influence the decision making or unwilling to influence. Communists stand testimony to this. Secondly, though a large political body appears fighting for this cause when they were in opposition, they simply toe the same line of supporting globalization when they comeback to power. The case of Bharatiya Janata Party and Congress stand testimony to this.

With SRI (System of Rice Intensification) rice picking up and giving better yields as compared to HYV seeds, the traditional seeds will have better market in the near future.

Can India too benefit from IPRs? Yes, to some extent. There are innumerable patentable goods and services in India. Traditional Ayurveda medicine and Yoga are born here and still we have them in the blood and sinews of India. The country is a source for many indigenous varieties of seeds, plants and practices. Already some of these are registered by others as their own inventions. Some such things include registration of turmeric and basmathi rice, both very natives of India. All these need to be corrected with the intervention of state and well meaning institutions and individuals.

THE CONTENT OF IPE

The IPE includes large number of areas, and all areas cannot be pushed into academic curricula at once. But, most important cannot wait, and must be incorporated into the curricula of IPE without loss of time. The important areas and the need for their inclusion in the curricula are discussed below.

Globalisation: The globalisation may be explained as a situation of integrating all the world economies into one, which remain politically and geographically as different entities. The first efforts towards globalisation were made by the delegates of 23 countries to provide a common set of guidelines on import and export trade practices with no restrictions on trade across borders through first round of General Agreement on Tariffs and Trade (GATT) meet held in 1947 at Havana. Six more meetings were held at different locations covering many subjects. The eighth round of negotiations based on Arther Dunkel's text was initiated in September 1986 at Puntadel este, Uruguay. This round involved 137 countries and covered areas like agriculture, services, banking, insurance and telecommuni-cations and an agreement reached by April 1994. The link between globalisation and IPRs can be explained in the following way. Successful RAD of a product and its patenting in one area within the borders of a political entity need not yield dividends if similar work is done elsewhere, because globalisation helps marketing of products of RAD and patents across borders without restrictions. This simply means patent has no borders. Irrespective of the country and location a relevant patent may impact the lives of people of all corners of the world. Hence, naturally, the globalisation and its impact on patenting and patent rights must become part of common man's knowledge.

General Agreement on Trade and Tariff: The main objective of 1994 GATT treaty was said to reform the distorted trade, allowing 'level playing' for all the countries in international competitiveness. In the context of GATT treaty all countries that agreed for the globalisation has to oblige on five important provisions. The important provisions are: (1) the market access of every economy to all legal economies across borders; (2) not to provide domestic support to producers exceeding the targets fixed by international community; (3) reduction of export subsidies by member countries to provide a level playing field for all the economies; (4) protection of Trade Related Intellectual Property Rights; (5) following internationally approved sanitary and phytosanitary standards. The fourth provision makes the IPRs an obligation on all countries. The IPE, a natural ally of IPRs becomes crucial knowledge input.

Intellectual Property Rights: Globalisation under GATT principles seeks to encourage research by way of providing rights over the inventive research. The property rights are conferred on the researcher responsible for any inventive research. The researchers are allowed to patent their findings. This patenting makes the individual or institute as owner of that invention, idea and goods and services, and they will have intellectual property rights on them. Anybody subsequently using these inventions, ideas or goods and services for further use are to pay for the use. The price for the use depends on the demand from the patent holder. The GATT guidelines allow the patent registration and the patent holder will have the economic earning power on these patents. The legality of these intellectual property rights is spread over the entire world.

India, as a member of World Trade Organisation and as a signatory to its 1994 agreements has to introduce patent protection for pharmaceutical and agro-chemical products by January 1, 2005.

Patents: A patent may be obtained for 'any new, useful and unobvious invention'. The invention could be a new invention or identification of an untold idea or identification of goods and services that were not identified so far. Such things can be patented in the name of an individual or an institute.

There are two types of patents normally allowed. The first type is known as 'object patents'. Under this category, the patent holder will have the right to make, use and sell the patented object. For example, plant varieties and the seeds of the plants. The second type is 'process patents' that are granted to micro-organisms and non-biological and microbiological processes. Under this category, the patent holder will have right on not only on the 'object' but also on 'process' by which the object is obtained.

Patentable Subjects: All subjects are not patentable. Some patents make no sense: duplication, already on the pipeline, unviable both in the short and long run, outdated, already patented, useless and failed. For example, a wheel is patented by giving a name as 'circular transportation facilitation device' in Australia. This is hardly original. There are few others which are original but utterly without any apparent rational utility. Still others are simply intriguing and obscure. Other side of this is the state may not allow certain subjects for patenting, especially on issues like defence and internal security. People must have knowledge on all these aspects, and must patent products that are new, useful and unobvious invention that is also marketable and economically viable.

Process of Patent Registration: To register a patent, there must be a patentable good or service that is new, useful and unobvious invention. The agency or the individual or individuals seeking the registration must have no competitors at least immediately for patenting the same good or service. For all practical purposes, state takes up the obligation of registration of patents. On line registration after paying registration fee has been the internationally accepted registration method. The community must be made aware of the process of patent registration, agencies for patent registration and advantages of patent registration.

Research and Development Costs and Benefits: A patentable product emerges after considerable investment on research and development (RAD). Private investments in RAD are generally made with profit motive. Many a time private funds are also tapped for RAD from donors in the name of a 'noble cause'. Donors too might have benefited by way of tax concessions. Making cost-benefit analysis without taking these donors money and tax concessions into consideration accounts to double/multiple benefits to the patent holders and loss to the immediate patent user; ultimately the consumer. The rate of royalty on a patent is the ultimate weapon in the hands of patent holder. Most of the west is allowing four per cent royalty. India may have to reduce this rate to protect the poor, especially in the case of medicines and agricultural inputs. The final consumer must be made aware of this cost-benefit ratio so as to prevent the exploitation by the patent holder.

Monopoly Period: The cost-benefit analysis of a patent from the start of efforts to identify a problem to completion of patent registration and to advertisement costs for marketing the patent makes clear of rate of return and time required for recouping the principle and profit. To recoup the RAD costs and make profit from the patent a time frame becomes necessary, which can simply be called monopoly period. Another dimension is that all investments on RAD need not result in an economically viable patent unfailingly. Risk and uncertainty are part of such investments. What should be the rate of return on such investments facing risk and uncertainty? It is also here the monopoly period comes into picture. State can fix this monopoly period based on the amount spent, risk and uncertainty involved and recouping period. Monopoly period is, normally fixed at 20 years. Beyond this monopoly period the patent holder looses all his legal and monitory rights on the patent and all the literature and research output becomes the property of the state. But the monopoly holder, as all others are eligible, may retain the right for further RAD in the area. This helps the production of patented goods and services without paying the monopoly price beyond the allowed period.

Patents and Social Concerns: Issues of health and agriculture are the prime areas that need immediate answers from the promoters of patent rights, patents and patent holders. Thrusting prohibitive patent costs on medicines and medical equipment makes the cost of medical-care beyond the poor man's reach. Another important point here is that relatively low-cost and locally manufactured generic drugs that are currently available may need to be withdrawn from the market when the patents are given to high-cost non-obvious invented medicines, affecting the poor. Likewise, patenting of agricultural equipment and inputs makes farming, mainly subsistence in nature in India, un-remunerative and farming community exploited. This calls for restricting the use of monopoly powers by the patent holders. The community at large must be made aware of the relation between patents and social concerns, especially of poverty, agriculture and medicine, to prevent the exploitation.

Social Cost-Benefit Analysis: Economic cost-benefit analysis from RAD point of view makes little sense if social cost-benefit analysis from the angle of larger society is ignored. All the patents need not lead to benefit to the society. In some cases the social cost may be high as compared to the social benefits. For example, a patent on generic medicines makes the medical care costly and makes the poor to spend a large share of their income on diseases that may not, in general, require a visit to the doctor. When large share of income is spent on such generic medicines the households become more vulnerable and may lead to their empty stomachs. Similarly, a patent in brick-making by a multi-national company makes the life of traditional brick-makers worse and the poor may end up as homeless.

Responsibility of Patent Holders: Patents are not gifts for the patent holders to make money without responsibilities. Patent holder is responsible for any adverse effect either on the state or on individual due to the holding of the patent and use and misuse of patent rights. In a system where the duties and responsibilities are generally earmarked to the state and only rights to the individuals, use and misuse of patent rights by patent holders cannot be ruled out. Unless the community is made aware of responsibilities of the patent holders and the community develops the capacity to politically and socially pressure them, the responsibilities of patent holders are likely to be buried in the existing political system.

State and Patents: The state has to protect the rights of not only patent holders but also society at large. Legal arbitrations between firms within a country and outside the country are not the same. Role of state in international arbitrations is essential, especially if poorer countries are to maintain equal rights and responsibilities as people and firms of rich countries can afford economic costs of international arbitration and not from poor countries.

METHODS OF IMPARTING IPE

Intellectual property rights became part of everybody's life even before people realised this point. The actual rights and responsibilities of intellectual property right holders became more than an important defence secret, keeping the common man in complete darkness. Along with intellectual property rights, intellectual property education too became important to ignore.

The IPE has two important dimensions. First and most important one is targeting the community to bring awareness on all sections to empower them to resist any misuse of patent rights. And, the second one is to educate the community to help patent their inventions, at least which are already available but not patented. There are two targets for IPE; first is the students and the second is the community. The IPE can be introduced at high school, pre-university and university levels. Like national income and Indian planning, the IPE can be introduced at the above three levels. The teachers may be given orientation on the relevant aspects. The subject brooks no delay.

In the case of larger community, workshops, seminars, group discussions and electronic and print media can be utilized for imparting the IPE.

10

PROGRAMMES FOR INTELLECTUAL PROPERTY EDUCATION THROUGH UNIVERSITIES AND RESEARCH INSTITUTES

S.V. Hariharan

INTRODUCTION

The concept of IPR is not given at present its due importance and recognition in the university and collegiate education India. The public in general, and the business community in particular, in India, do not have adequate awareness about this concept. The economic implications of IPR on trade, technology, investment and other fields, in short–run and long–run, should be familiarized among the exporters, importers, industrialists, investors, business people, engineers, scientists, academicians and students. The lack of awareness about this concept and its consequences has already caused severe losses to the economy in various fields.

In this context, Universities, and research Institutes can play a significant role in familiarizing the various issues related to IPRs through their curriculum and also through a number of programmes. This paper enumerates the various programmes and activities through which Universities and Research Institutes can create a thorough awareness among the students, academicians, business people and other groups of people and also can promote research in IPR related issues.

INTRODUCTION OF A SUBJECT IN VARIOUS COURSES

The concept of IPR, meaning of patents, trade marks, copyrights, lay out designs, breeder's rights, trade secrets, industrial designs and other relevant concepts, the detailed Agreement on Trade Related Intellectual Property Rights, their historical perspective, the advantages, disadvantages, various consequences and other relevant aspects should be offered either as a full paper or as part of the relevant papers for the courses on Economics, Applied Economics, Commerce, Management, Business Administration, Foreign Trade, Export Marketing, International Law, International Relations and International Studies.

At present, in some of these courses, International Economics is offered as one or two papers. IPR and related issues may be included in this paper with more weightage.

At M.Phil level, this may be offered as an optional or special Area Study. The various aspects of IPR provide adequate scope to undertake research works for Project works and of dissertations works.

MAKING THE LITERATURE AVAILABLE

The foremost constraint for the students is the non–availability of literature or inadequate literature. Perhaps, the university libraries and college libraries may have some literature in this area. However, they are not adequate. Most of the libraries do not have sufficient literature in this area. Recently books are priced very highly and hence it may not be possible for the students to own these books within their budget limit. Therefore, one of the basic requirements to popularize the concept of IPR among the students is to make all the relevant literature available within the reach of students. As such, in all the relevant departments of the universities and colleges, all the relevant literature should be made available in multiple copies.

The another major problem for the students in this regard is that a siezeable proportion of students study through their regional language. Hence these literatures should be made available in the regional languages also. This will help the students to have a better understanding about the concept and the related issues.

REFERENCE CENTRES AND DATA BANKS

Due to the financial constraints on one side and the rising prices of books and increasing establishment costs on another side, it has now become extremely difficult for the general libraries to get all the relevant books in all the subjects. Hence, they are now selective in their approach. Therefore, General Libraries do not give adequate concentration to its area.

Under these circumstances, it becomes absolutely necessary to build Reference Centres and Data Banks in this area at least one center in each region. This Will enable the researchers to get the relevant materials for their project works, dissertations and other research works at one place.

ORGANISATION OF SEMINARS

Periodical seminars must be organized for the students from relevant disciplines to create a thorough awareness and understanding about this area. These seminars will also be useful to impart the recent developments in this field to the students.

WORKSHOPS TO THE RESEARCHERS AND COLLEGE TEACHERS

To encourage researchers and college teachers to undertake research works in this area and also to help to identify the potential areas of research, workshops and short–term courses may also be organized specifically on these thems. In these workshops, the rrecent research works undertaken in this field may be discussed and reviewed. Further, the methodological issues may also be discussed. This will certainly motivate the researchers to undertake more research works in this area.

FORMATION OF EXPERT TEAM

At present, the researchers specializing in this area are very very limited and they are scattered in different parts of the country. They may work as a team, meet periodically and identify the potential areas of research. This will be helpful to provide guidelines to the researchers regarding the research works to be undertaken and also to co–ordinate the research works and programmes depending on the requirements.

SCHOLARS–EXPERTS MEET

To guide the research scholars working in this area in identifying the research problem, in finalizing the research hypotheses, in developing the Research Methodology and also in deciding the appropriate rools of analysis of data, the scholars experts meet may be arranged periodically. Already, the MIDS is and organizing this type of meeting under the guidance of ICSSR for the researchers in Economics in general. However, under this programme, the research scholars working this area and the experts in this field may alone meet. This programme will definitely help to speed up the process of research work in the field of IPR undertaken by the research scholars.

SERIES OF SEMINARS TO THE DIFFERENT SECTIONS OF THE PEOPLE

Seminars may also be arranged to various sections of the people like, investors, industrialists, entrepreneurs, domestic traders, managerial staff of production units and marketing agencies to impart the various developments taking place in this field.

AWARENESS PROGRAMMES TO EXPORTERS AND IMPORTERS

These programmes may be organized to the exporters and importers and also to beginners of exporters to create a complete awareness about the various aspects of IPRs and related aspects. Special progarmmes may be arranged for different industries, for example, textiles products, leather products, food products and various agricultural commodities.

GOVERNMENT OFFICIALS–TRADERS MEET

To exchange the view and experiences and also to identify the problems faced by the exporters and importers, periodical meet of officials of Export Promotion Councils, Trade Development Authorities, State Trading Corporations and Other related departments may be arranged to review the current situation and to adopt suitable measures to extend necessary assistance to the traders.

CONCLUSIONS

The programmes suggested above are some guidelines only and more comprehensive progarmmes may be designed depending on the requirements. The traders may show a good response for the programmes designed for them since these programmes may help them to take necessary efforts to promote and expand their trade.

However, for the academic community, these programmes may serve only as necessary conditions. The sufficient conditions will be the involvement of devoted teachers, sincere and hard working students and the researchers who do research for the sake of research. The efforts to impart the knowledge about the Intellectual Property will be successful only if these conditions are satisfied.

11

UNIVERSITY EDUCATION: A CRITICAL REVIEW

J.A. Arul Chellakumar &
Nandhini Thiagarajan

The contents of higher education are usually derived from agehold disciplines, the emerging disciplines and the world at large. One of the education's major tasks is to keep abreast new knowledge and of new knowledge areas so that a decision can be taken regarding what of new should replace the old at any given point of time.

The contemporary world has a substantial influence on the educational contents and therefore its pattern for it is not possible to ignore the outside world. Therefore this paper aims to analysis as to whether the educational pattern and the curriculum designs of the Indian Universities are aiming at linking socio economic cultural backgrounds of the society of the world, without losing its identity.

HIGHER EDUCATION AND SOCIAL CHANGE

The relationship of education to social change has been greatly emphasized and examined in considerable depth in the last four decades. Quiet obviously the analysis depends upon our understanding of concepts of education and social change and of their inter relationship.

Generally social change is considered to be a process towards 'Modernization'. Here the term modernization should not be misconstrued as a synonym for westernization. Given its socio-cultural basis, a country can have its own brand of modernization. But, in consensus, the sociologists have arrived at a fairly general concept of modernization as an essential characteristic of social change... modern society seems to encourage rationally, as the calculus of choice, shapes individual behavior and conditions its rewards; people come to see the social future as manipulable rather than ordained and their personal prospects interms of achievement rather than heritage. As regards the modern personality, it is further believed that he is distinguished by a high capacity for identification with new aspects of his environment and he comes equipped with the mechanism needed to incorporate new demands upon himself that are outside his habitual experience... list of modern attitudes includes such personality characteristics as disposition to accept new ideas and try new methods, readiness to express opinions, time sense that makes men more interested in the present and the future than in the past, better sense of punctuality, greater concern for planning organization, and efficiency, tendency to see the World as calculable, faith in science and technology, and finally, belief in distributive justice (Hans nagpanl, 1980).

The segment of modern society in India has beer, nurtured and shaped by an educational system, by and large, inspired by the western style. Not only the course pattern and curricular methodology have been western, but also the medium of Institution/learning continues to be English. As a result, there is an inevitable social gap between the English-educated urban and the uneducated rural. There is literally a communication gap between the so-called modern society and the traditional rural society. The people under traditional segment feel, and rightly so, 'abienated' from the educated modern segment. This sense of alienation leads to a evidencing social disparity with no perceptible tendency towards integration.

AS OBSERVED BY A SOCIOLOGIST

The Impact of British colonialization on India in general and influence of western education on Indian society in particular have been phenomenal. India has been the only non-western country which has undergone almost 200 years of westernization. The various new trends found in India society today and many formative, far-reaching social changes in the tradition-oriented society are described by certain political scientists by the term 'amalgamate', a pattern, consist of one part western, one part traditionl (Girish Chandra Roy, 1983).

So, we have copied western education in its course-content and structure; but it seldom seeks to bear upon our indigenous culture and values. This education supplies just a body of knowledge, with little impact on attitudes and values of the educated.

SANSKRITISATION

With little effect of education on the social attitudes of the educated, the caste hierarchy and other social divisions continue to hamper the social change, despite education. In the given caste structure, the social change in India happens to be a process called 'Sanskritisation'.

Such an urge for upward movement in the caste-ladder may not itself necessarily result in any sort of modernization. On the contrary, there is a greater possibility of reverse-modernization (Sanskritisation consist in the faithful observance of the rituals of higher caste by the low cast) and hence an obsessed-traditionalism. Education incidentally helps and hastens this process. Caste and other social sub-divisions get further sharpened by education. In otherwords, education perhaps happens to be an instrument for developing grater caste loyalty.

We cannot resist our templation to quote once again Gunnar Myrdal: In south Asia, the stronger loyalty to less inclusive groups-family, caste, ethnic, religious or linguistic community and class-invites the special type of corruption we call "nepotism" and tends in general to encourage moral laxity (Gunnar Myrdal, 1969, Vol. II, p. 950).

PURPOSE OF HIGER EDUCATION

The relationship between Education and social change can be discussed under the following aspects:

- Education as a condition for social change
- Education as a instrument for social change and
- Changes in education resulting from social change

Education of the individuals, may change their attitudes and values and create in them a desire for change and development. Education helps in increasing the knowledge and spread of scientific ideas.

Education can impart knowledge, training and skills and also inculcate new ideas and new attitudes. Backwardness and poverty of various communities are largely due to illiteracy and ignorance. Several religious missions have also used education as a tool to bring about a social change. It has to be accepted that they have proved to be effective. Many thinkers and leaders in various fields have been educated from such institutions and our country has definitely got benefited from the facilities created by the various religious missions for purpose of education.

CONCLUSION

Education is expected to promote, the values of democracy, egalitarianism and social justice, good personnel, social moral as spiritual values, and the value of tolerance for others views, and the value of tolerance for others views, languages and religions. Education must necessarily emphasize excellence, productivity and the capacity to tackle problems encountered in life. It should prepare the younger generation to achieve a quality of life that is desirable, feasible and sustainable and to lead a useful, purposeful life. Therefore the university education imparted to the student community can be of the 3 of the followings:

- Value based Education - Benefiting the society
- Skill based education - Benefiting the individual and company or Organization he is working for
- Knowledge based education - This is so very basic that the skill based Value based education concurrently to emerge.

12

INTELLECTUAL PROPERTY RIGHTS AND ECONOMIC DEVELOPMENT

K. Raja Mohan Rao & C. Sivapragasam

INTRODUCTION

Intellectual property is the commercial application of imaginative thought to solving a technical or artistic challenge. It is not the product itself, but the special idea behind it, the way the idea is expressed, and the distinctive way it is named and described.[1]

The expression "property" is used to describe this value, because the term applies only to inventions, works and names for which a person or group of persons claims ownership. Ownership is important because the potential economic gain provides a powerful incentive to innovate. It is also important to note that Intellectual property results from innovation based on existing knowledge. It is the result of creative improvements on what has worked well in the past, or of creative new expressions of old ideas and concepts.[2] With information and communication technologies, knowledge has become the principle source of competitive advantage for both companies and countries.[3]

Technology and creative arts pervade modern society, but not many actually realize that their daily lives are surrounded by Intellectual creations, from which legal rights of all sorts, including their own, arise. Building public awareness of the role of Intellectual property is a key to fostering a broad understanding of, and respect for it, and the system that promotes and protects it. "To truly convince the public, including civil society activist groups, it is essential to engage them in such a way that they all see themselves as stakeholders in a healthy and robust Intellectual property system".[4]

Intellectual property is divided into two main areas: Copyrights (rights of authors, and artistic works) Copyrights related rights (e.g. performer in their performances), and industrial properties (trademarks, geographical indications, patents, industrial design, etc.). The protection of intellectual property is governed by many international treaties and conventions, which are implemented by two main organisations, the World Intellectual Property Organisation with its Berne Convention, Paris Convention, etc., and the World Trade Organisation with its TRIPS Agreement. Countries have additionally their national Laws protecting these rights.

Economic development can be promoted or hindered by an effective system of Intellectual Property Rights (IPRs). It can play a positive role in encouraging business development, rationalization of inefficient industry stimulate technology acquisition and creation. The development may be harmed by raising cost of imitation and permitting monopolistic behaviour by owners of IPRs. Empirical evidence supports that product innovation is sensitive to IPRs in developing countries, while FDI and technology transfer go up when patent rights are strengthened. There is an overall positive impact on growth which depends on the competitive nature of the economy.[5]

Stronger IPRS can either *enhance* or *limit* economic growth. Stronger and more certain IPRS could well increase economic growth and as mentioned, foster technological change, improving development prospects, if they are structured that way that promotes effective and dynamic competition.[6]

There are two objectives of any system of Intellectual Property Protection. The first purpose of Intellectual Property rights is to promote investments in knowledge creation and business innovation by establishing exclusive rights to use and sell newly developed technologies, goods and services. Without these rights, firms would less be willing to incur the costs of investing in research and commercialization activities. The second purpose is to promote widespread dissemination of new knowledge encouraging right holders to place their inventions and ideas on to the market. Information is like a public good, where developers find it difficult to exclude others from using it. It is socially efficient to provide wide access to new technologies and products, once they are developed at marginal production costs. Such costs could be quite low, causing copying of that certain product.[7]

Having too strong protective systems of IPRs could limit social gains from inventions by reducing incentives to distribute its fruits. However, on the other hand, a weak system could reduce innovation by failing to provide adequate return on investment. There has to be a policy balance found appropriate to the market conditions and conducive to growth.

Intellectual property rights which are protected have also to be enforced. These are punishing infringements and disciplining enterprises that try to extend their rights beyond the level by acting in an anti-competitive manner. These objectives however, require the development of extensive legal and scientific enterprise.[8]

National regimes of Intellectual Property protection strongly depend on the level of economic development. Therefore, IPRs and its development operate in both directions. Governments that strengthen their IPRs systems become wealthier and attain a basis of technological sophistication.[9] Not only legislated IPRs become stronger as economies develop, but enforcement and compliance also rise with income levels. Weak enforcement in developing countries reflects both an unwillingness to pay the high cost of administering an effective IPRs system and an inability to manage the complex legal and technical issues such a system entails.

BENEFITING FROM INTELLECTUAL PROPERTY RIGHTS

There are several ways how IPRs can stimulate economic development and growth. As mentioned above, IPRs can play a significant role in encouraging innovation, product development, and technical change. Developing countries have IPRs systems favouring dissemination through low-cost imitation of foreign products and technologies. This shows that domestic innovation and invention is insufficiently developed to provide protection. However, inadequate IPRs could stifle technical change even at low levels of economic development, because much invention and product innovation are mostly aimed at local markets and they could benefit from domestic protection of patents, utility models, and trade secrets.

Developing countries have to adopt new management and organizational systems and techniques for quality control, which can markedly raise productivity. Such investments are costly, but have high social returns because they are crucial for raising productivity toward global norms. Countries keeping the weak standards could remain dependent on dynamically inefficient firms that rely on counterfeiting and imitation.

Through developing their IPRs regimes, unilaterally or through the TRIPS Agreement, developing countries hope to attract greater inflows of technology. The transfer of technology across Borders can be achieved through three channels: *international trade* in goods, *foreign direct investment (FDI)* within multinational enterprises, and *contractual licensing* of technologies and trademarks to unaffiliated firms, subsidiaries, and joint ventures. Transfer of technology in each channel depends on local protection of IPRs.

- *International Trade:* Importing of goods and services leads to a transfer of technology. Importing capital goods and technical inputs could directly reduce production costs and increase productivity. Stronger patent rights in developed economies would reduce trade because of a market-power effect and diversion of trade to developing countries. Trade volume impacts are significant for developing countries that undertake extensive patent revisions. Many of the largest predicted impacts are in nations with strong imitation capacities like Argentina and Brazil, whereas India would experience relatively weak, though positive, trade impacts.
- *Foreign Direct Investment:* The second main channel of technology transfer is FDI. IPRs have varying importance in different sectors. Firms that invest in low-technology goods and services should depend less on the strength of the IPRs and more on the input costs and market opportunities. Investors with products or technologies which are costly to imitate, would pay little attention to local IPRs. However, firms with easily copied products and technologies, such as pharmaceuticals and software, would be quite concerned about the local IPR system to deter imitation.[10]
- However, licensing to unrelated firms has been seen as riskier with weak IPRs. This can be seen in other industries as well, and the findings show that licensing was viewed as insecure compared to FDI in high-technology sectors when there is a weak IPRs protection. Firms therefore, likely undertake FDI

than licensing when they own complex technology, produce highly differentiated products and face high licensing costs. These firms tend to internalize through direct investments in a majority-owned subsidiary, and as IPRs are upgraded, licensing cost fall and it becomes easier to discipline licensees against the misuse of a trademark or a technology.

Stronger IPRs have a significant and positive impact on the transfer of technology to developing countries through each of these channels (Imports, FDI and market-based technology transfer). This has especially an impact in middle-income developing countries with significant imitative capabilities. In least developed economies the impact would be positive but small. The reason for this is that the countries with weak IPRs could be isolated from the modern technologies and would have to develop their own technical knowledge from their own resources, which would be difficult and costly. These countries would also gain little spill over benefits of new technologies in their economies and the technologies available in those nations would be outdated. Finally, countries with weak IPRs would experience limited incentives for domestic innovation and relatively few inward technology transfers.[11]

From these findings, one can conclude, that the strength of IPRs and the ability to enforce contracts have important effects on decisions by multinational firms on where to invest and whether to transfer advanced technologies.[12]

CONCLUSION

Since, an effective system of Intellectual property Rights can play a positive role in accelerating in achieving Economic Growth by encouraging business development and by stimulating Technology acquisition and creation, the Governments should take it seriously in the protection and enforcement of IPRs simultaneously by propagation of their (IPRs) Importance among the general public.

NOTES AND REFERENCES

1. http://www.wto.org
2. WIPO (2001), WIPO Intellectual Property Handbook: Policy, Law and Use, WIPO Publication No. 489 (E), in www under http://www.wipo.int/about-ip/en/iprm/index.
3. Commission on Intellectual Property Rights (2002), Integrating Intellectual Property Rights and Development Policy, Report of the

Commission on Intellectual Property Rights, in www under http://www.iprcommission.org, p. 14.

4. WIPO (2001), WIPO Intellectual Property Handbook: Policy, Law and Use, WIPO Publication No.489 (E), in www under http://www.wipo.int/about-ip/en/iprm/index.
5. Maskus, K.E. (2000), Intellectual Property Rights and Economic Development. In: Case Western Reserve Journal of International Law, Special Supplement 2000, Vol. 32, p. 471.
6. Evenson, R.E., Westphal, L.E. (n.a.), Technological Change and Technology Transfer, in 3A Handbook of Development Economics 2209.
7. Maskus, K.E. (2000), Intellectual Property Rights and Economic Development. In: Case Western Reserve Journal of International Law, Special Supplement 2000, Vol. 32, p. 471.
8. Maskus, K.E. (2000), Intellectual Property Rights and Economic Development. In: Case Western Reserve Journal of International Law, Special Supplement 2000, Vol. 32, p. 471.
9. Maskus, K.E. (2000), Intellectual Property Rights and Economic Development. In: Case Western Reserve Journal of International Law, Special Supplement 2000, Vol. 32, p. 471.
10. Ibid. p. 471.
11. Ibid. p. 471.
12. Mansfield, E. (1994), Intellectual Property Protection, Foreign Direct Investment, and Technology Transfer: Germany, Japan and the United States, World Bank Discussion Paper No. 19, at 1.

13

MARKET STRUCTURE, VALUATION AND COST OF ENFORCEMENT OF INTELLECTUAL PROPERTY RIGHTS (IPRs) ARGUMENTS FOR FURTHER INVESTIGATION

V. Mohanasundaram & G. Narasimha Raghavan

"The process of maximizing the value of patents, trademarks, copyrights, know-how–the most tangible of intangibles. We call it the bottoms up approach to knowledge management"

—Gordon Petrash[1]

INTRODUCTION

Incompatibility of the mindset of the people is the single most influential reason for the non-acceptance of 'knowledge'–the creation of the mind[2]–as a property. More to the point, this knowledge needs to be managed, to achieve social goals (like national copyrighting of the works of a National Poet–Subramania Bharathiar) or economic objectives (like profiting from patents). The primary objective of this paper is the facilitation of comprehension and an appreciation of the researchable issues in IPRs–market structure, valuation and cost of enforcement–with the derivative purpose being the recognition of such issues as legitimately binding the holistic understanding of the IPR framework in the contemporary era of WTO/TRIPS[3]. The discussion in the paper is generic. The paper is delineated into three sections: section one relates to a discussion on the elements of market structure; section two encounters the nuances of valuation of IPRs; and the third section explicates the aspects of cost of enforcement of IPRs. Eventually, the outweighing intention of the paper is the persuasion of appreciating the juxtaposing of law and economics in any deliberation involving IPRs.

SECTION - I

Indicating a demonstrable pattern in every economic fete, the market structure referred to here relay the characteristics of the firm, like market share and number of competitors. Prominent studies by Schumpeter (1942), Symeonidis (1996) and Sutton (1991)[4] build on these aspects of the market structure. This, then, remains to be organic for evaluating the impact of IPRs apropos rivalry of goods, aspect of rights attenuation and repercussion of competition policy.

Rival vs. Non-rival Goods: The incidence of rivalry of a good prevents simultaneous use of the good, while a non-rival good doesn't so. Beginning the discussion with the premise that the good to be endowed with an intellectual property is a non-rival good (rival good does not entail, normally, multiple concurrent usages), awarding an intellectual property to it is but making it non-excludable and consequently a private good[5]. The argument for research in this direction is twofold: The cost of producing a non-rival good (on detection) is zero, and hence affixing an IPR to it, constitutes a market inefficiency, since the price of the good is over and above its marginal cost; will the adjudication of a non-rival good as an intellectual property desist the society from eliciting socially desirable products, in the face of nil returns?

Rights Attenuation: The central theme of discussion in this sub-section is the justifiable principle for social, state or collective ownership of IPRs. The basis for assigning intellectual property is to pass on the costs and benefits to the individual who has created it. However, there are situations where a community holds the specific privileges[6] to a body of knowledge (like traditional knowledge of *Ayurveda*). In this case, dynamic inefficiency cannot be ruled out, in the event of mutual possession of IPRs. Sooner or later, such knowledge become public, for its propagation cannot be inhibited. This raises two important areas for inquiry: Will public expenditure on IPRs result in rights attenuation (weakening of rights, in the event of a fragile relationship existing between the cost and the benefit)? and will the idea of creating a market for IPRs with strong legislations ensure immunity for commonly held IPRs?

Competition Policy: Undeniably, an IPR confers a monopoly right on the holder of the idea or good. This results, *inter alia*, in pricing the 'right', to be understood in the presence of competition policies[7]. Competition Policies aim at removing monopoly practices in the market. This creates an inevitable strain between competition policy and IPRs. The issue, though, is not all that all concerned with such friction. In the event of the market tolerating the production and distribution of a close substitute, will the competition policy itself turn inadequate? And, how is a mechanism to be fitted in, when "excessive compounding"[8] (getting a large number of related patents in order to stifle competition) of patents arise, notwithstanding the attendance of a competition policy?

SECTION - II

The disinclination for valuing IPRs is not just out of lack of measurement apparatuses, but also out of the identification of such rights[9]. In general, IPRs come under the tag of intangibles. The International Accounting Standards Committee (IASC)[10], an independent private sector body, has also been working to develop internationally acceptable accounting standards. The IASC publishes its standards in a series of pronouncements called International Accounting Standards (IAS). In 1998, IASC published IAS 38, a revised standard on intangible assets. It applies to expenditures on advertising, training, start-up and R&D activities. The customary methodologies followed in valuing IPRs are:

(a) *Cost Approach:* The expenses for acquiring IP from external sources or for generating IP assets internally are indicated. This method measures future benefits by quantifying the amount of money that would be required to replace the future service capability of the property.

(b) *Income Approach:* The income approach focuses on a consideration of the income generating capability of the property. The underlying theory is that the value of property can be measured by the present worth of the net economic benefit on the assumption that IP is capable of producing the income. It is generally agreed that this approach often proves to be the most reliable for the valuation of IP[11].

(c) *Market Approach:* The market approach is the most direct and the most easily understood appraisal technique. It measures the present value of future benefits by obtaining a consensus of what others in the marketplace have judged it to be. There are two requirements: the existence of an active and public market and an exchange of comparable properties[12].

The catch here is not the inscrutability of the components of the methodologies; rather the crux of the issue is the uniformity in valuation of IP assets, coupled with the deficiency in undertaking an intellectual portfolio audit (where all kinds of economically exploitable IP assets are legitimized, even if the IP asset is not related to the main business area).

SECTION - III

Non-physical assets like IPRs, besides being difficult to value, are effortlessly replicated in many instances. Now, this calls for stricter monitoring and supervision, in addition to penalizing. Nonetheless, in many circumstances the costs to the owner for monitoring and preventing unauthorized use are insuperable, thwarting the efforts of individuals to realize rewards for their creative activity[13]. Replication engenders counterfeiting, while higher level of enforcement might lead to development of the acclaimed grey market (where legitimate IPR products are sold, but without the requisite licence). Even though definitional problem lies in understanding the costs of enforcement of IPRs (like counterfeiting for commercial purposes only)[14], this subdivision spotlights on the market assistance question (the market indicating the infringement of IPR and following up with enforcement) and its related costs, and the costs of ensuring a political preference for IPR enforcement (an example would be ensuring IPR awareness by making the citizens stakeholders in it).

CONCLUSION

As researchable areas, the arguments put forth, define to a limited extent, activities that do not always remain with the purview of a particular discipline. The two entry-points for exploring the above-mentioned issues are: cost/price and legal/statutory legislation. Assuaging the effects of discipline-centric approach, the present paper would like academic and otherwise intellectual endeavours to be on familiar terms with both law and economics as an indissoluble pair, while investigating IPR-related issues.

NOTES

1. Gordon Petrash is the Competency Leader at Pricewaterhouse Coopers. Quoted in Waterfalls Institute for Technology Transfer (2000), *Valuation of IPRs in Technology Transfer,* New Delhi. This is a report prepared for the Department of Scientific and Technology Research, Government of India.
2. Refer Isaac and Park (2004) for a detailed discussion on IPRs as creations of the human mind. Justification for IPRs is discussed in the contexts of philosophy and metaphysics. This article will appear as Chapter 18 in the forthcoming The Elgar Companion to Economics of Property Rights edited by Enrico Colombatto.
3. The significance of TRIPS as an international agreement is highlighted in the article "Patently problematic", published in *Economist* dated Sep. 12 2002. A detailed schema for phasing in the TRIPS Agreement Obligations for developing, developed and least developed countries are given in Arai (1999).
4. Studies cited in Dixon and Greenhalgh (2002). Detailed discussions on Joseph Schumpeter's 1912 work *The theory of economic development: an inquiry into profits, capital, credit, interest, and the business cycle* (New York: Oxford University Press) and his 1942 book *Capitalism, socialism, and democracy* (London: Routledge) are carried out, especially on the Schumpeterian issues of market structure and innovation.
5. The article "Property Rights and Intellectual Monopoly" available at *http://www.dklevine.com/general/intellectual/coffee.htm* provides an insight into rivalrous and non-rivalrous goods, in the wake of IPR regime. Also see the commentary "A Case against Intellectual Property" accessible at *http://www.economicprincipals.com/issues/02.07.21.html.* Simple and undemanding explanation of rival and non-rival goods through examples can be got from Barder (2003).
6. For a further clarification see Phillips (1995). Besides deliberating on the issues of weakening of rights and collective ownership of property rights, reference is also made to the Pigouvian notion of free distribution of products that have zero or negligible marginal cost.
7. Pricing under monopoly conditions arising out of the IPR regime are dealt with in detail in Gans, Williams and Briggs (2000).
8. "Excessive compounding", a term used by Gangi, ensures that the market becomes difficult for potential entrants to get their hands on

industry expertise. Alternatively, Shapiro dubs this phenomenon as "patent thicket".

9. Among the other reasons identified for slower acceptance of valuation of IPRs are the lack of approximation of competition in an economy (especially in a developing nation like India) and presence of asymmetric information regarding the worth of IPRs. Greenhalgh and Rogers (2004) spell out an econometric model for market valuation of IPRs.
10. Additional information can be viewed at *www.iasplus.com*
11. Details on the other two methodologies are dealt with in Idris (Undated) in a WIPO Report, Chapter Three.
12. With respect to developing nations, the two requirements exist with an uncertainty disposition. Lack of political will and laxity in the implementation of IPR legislations haunt developing nations. This is underscored in an article by Giannakas (2003).
13. Other factors that affect cost of enforcement of IPRs like litigation charges and innovation inducements are outlined in Lanjouw and Lerner (1997).
14 The Intellectual Property Rights Enforcement Recommendation of the Global Business Dialogue on Electronic Commerce (2002) gives a detailed investigation of the definitional problems of piracy and counterfeiting.

REFERENCES

A. Books, Articles and Reports

________, "Patently Problematic", *Economist*, Dec.12, 2004. Available at *www.economist.com.*

________, "Property Rights and Intellectual Monopoly". Available at *http://www.dklevine.com/general/intellectual/coffee.htm.*

________, "The Case against Intellectual Property". Available at http://www.economicprincipals.com/issues/02.07.21.html

Arai, Hisamitsu (1999), "Intellectual Property Policies for the Twenty-First Century: The Japanese Experience in Wealth Creation". Available at *www.wipo.int.*

Barder, Owen (2003), "Intellectual Property And Market Failure: The Economic Ideas, For Non-Economists". Available at URL *http://www.owen.org/musings/ip/.*

Bekkers, Rudi, Geert Duysters and Bart Verspagen (2000), "Intellectual Property Rights, Strategic Technology Agreement and Market Structure: The Case of GSM". Available at *www.tue.nl*

Bjornstad, David J, Steven Stewart, Christine Dummer and John Cogburn (2000), "Economic Implications of Intellectual Property Rights and the Human Genome Research Program", prepared as a background paper for Licensing Executives Society Franklin Pierce Law Center. Available at *http://www.ornl.gov/~webworks/cpr/misc/107712_.pdf*.

Dixon, Padraig and Christine Greenhalgh (2002), "The Economics of Intellectual Property: A Review to Identify Themes for Future Research". Available at *www.oiprc.org*.

Gans, Joshua, Philip Williams and David Briggs (2000), "Clarifying the relationship between intellectual property rights and competition". Report prepared on behalf of the National Copyright Industry Alliance for submission to the Review of Intellectual Property & Competition. Available at *http://www.ipcr.gov.au/SUBMIS/docs/78.pdf*.

Gerken, Peter J. (2002), "Gray Matters: Protecting and Increasing the Value of Intellectual Property". Available at *http://www.mmc.com/views2/spring03Gerken.php*.

Giannakas, Konstantinos (2003), "Infringement of Intellectual Property Rights: Developing Countries, Agricultural Biotechnology, and the Trips Agreement". Available at *http://www.ifpri.org/pubs/rag/br1001/biotechbr5.pdf*.

Global Business Dialogue on Electronic Commerce (2002), The Intellectual Property Rights Enforcement Recommendation. Available at ***www.gbde.com***.

Greenhalgh, Christine and Mark Rogers (2004), "The Value of Innovation: The Interaction of Competition, R&D and IP". Available at *www.oiprc.org*.

Idris, Kamil (Undated), *Intellectual Property: A Power Tool for Economic Growth*. Report prepared by WIPO. Available at *http://www.wipo.int/about-wipo/en/dgo/wipo_pub_888*.

Isaac, Alan G and Walter G Park (2004), "On Intellectual Property Rights: Patents vs. Free and Open Development". Available at *http://www.american.edu/cas/econ/faculty/isaac/wp/isaac_park.20030818.pdf*.

Lanjouw, Jean O and Josh Lerner (1997), "The Enforcement of Intellectual Property Rights", NBER Working Paper 6296. Available at *http://www.nber.org/papers/w6296*.

Phillips, Paul (1995), "IPRs and Regional Development" in Nair, K.R.G. and Ashok Kumar (Eds.), *Intellectual Property Rights*, Allied Publishers, New Delhi.

Schweihs, Robert P. (2002), "Valuing Intellectual Property". Available at *http://www.willamette.com/pubs/presentations/SchweihsIP.pdf*.

Soon, Jason (1999), "An Economic Perspective of Intellectual Property: The Case of Copyright", *Policy*. Available at URL *http://www.cis.org.au/policy/autumn99/aut99-7.pdf.*

Waterfalls Institute for Technology Transfer (2000), *Valuation of IPRs in Technology Transfer*, New Delhi. Report prepared for the Department of Scientific and Technology Research, Government of India.

WIPO (2004), WIPO Intellectual Property Handbook: Policy, Law and Use. Available at *http://www.wipo.org/about-ip/en/iprm/pdf/ch4.pdf.*

WIPO (Undated), WIPO Guide to IP Worldwide–Country Profiles Part One (India). Available at *www.wipo.int.*

Wyhe, Phyllis Van (Undated), "Placing a Value on Intellectual Property". Available at *http://www.insurancece.com/resources/articles/.*

Yang, Guifang and Keith E. Maskus (2003), "Intellectual Property Rights, Licensing, and Innovation", World Bank Policy Research Working Paper 2973. Available at *http://econ.worldbank.org/files/24162_wps2973.pdf.*

B. Websites:

http://dipp.nic.in/ipr.htm

http://europa.eu.int/

http://grants1.nih.gov/

http://www.iasplus.com/

http://www.interpol.com/

http://www.ipria.org/

http://www.nipo.org.in/

http://www.wto.org/

14

INTELLECTUAL PROPERTY RIGHTS AND THE COMMONS: A CASE OF INDIGENOUS KNOWLEDGE IN INDIA

M. Sabesh Manikandan, K. Raja Mohan Rao
R. Veera Sekaran & A. Annadurai

INTRODUCTION

India is a continent endowed with a rich diversity of biological resources. Since time immemorial, India's people have depended upon free and open access to that diversity for food, fuel, medicine, shelter and economic security by exchanging and trading of such resources among themselves. For the vast majority of the sub-continent's people, this diversity of biological resources serves as a buffer against poverty, drought, environmental change and war.

In India, local communities have accumulated a broad traditional knowledge base to conserve and sustainably use biological resources. They deploy different and unique technological systems to conserve and use plants and their genetic components. These systems include home gardens, seed banks, and sacred groves. Unlike many other parts of the world, where knowledge about biodiversity and the technology on the use of diverse species is held by geographically distinct indigenous groupings, such knowledge in India is found virtually most in rural households and some urban households.

Moreover, it is also expressed in the enormously diverse cultures of the more than 2000 ethnic groups that inhabit the continent, and in the central role played by plants and animals in Indian indigenous systems of medicine and agriculture. The following traditional technologies or traditional knowledge systems as they pertain to biodiversity-farming practices (e.g. inter-cropping, mulching); soil and water conservation (e.g. stone lines); wild food products (e.g. gathered fruits); fermentation techniques (e.g. brewing, food processing); storage (e.g. grain stores, local additives) and medicinal products (e.g. plant or animal derivatives) etc. It is also generally accepted that biodiversity survives through the conservation and sustainable use strategies employed by indigenous and local communities.

It is generally accepted that Traditional/Indigenous and local communities are distinguishable from each other and have different political needs and aspirations. The main rights demanded from indigenous people with regard to genetic resources and associated knowledge; include those relating to self-determination or control, territory and the recognition or renegotiation of existing treaties with States. Local communities do not seek these rights rather; they require secure land and resource tenure, equitable access to natural resources, participation in decision-making affecting the exercise of their rights in respect of biological resources, control over their resources etc. However, indigenous and local communities share common characteristics; e.g. genetic resources and associated knowledge are not privately owned, but are typically shared within communities.

Indigenous and local communities also have common concerns with regard to genetic resources and associated knowledge. For example, they seek:

(a) the right to control the physical access of outsiders to the land and sea areas that they inhabit or use and where genetic resources are located; and

(b) the right to control access to and subsequent use of genetic resources and associated knowledge.

In connection with this Indigenous knowledge system and the sustainability in local based resource management is guaranteed where there is participation, the local people should be consulted on how they would want to organize themselves between the two types. It however seems appropriate to use the traditional setup since it is more related in its constitution to resource distribution.

However the people who will lead the company should be chosen on the basis of ability rather than heritage.

THE COMMONS–MEANING

The word "commons" in relation to property primarily refers to assets, resources, or things owned by nobody but available for use by all without restriction with it's peculiar characteristics of both non-excludable and non-rivalry. The "Communal" property or resource, however, differs from "commons" property or resource. According to Posey and Dutfield "Communal property is the prevailing system used in most Indigenous societies *to control access* to basic resources like food and fuel, but rights are multiple in that individuals, elders, women, clans, lineages, etc., each have ownership rights within a given resource area and over specified resources within them. Such rights may vary in their extent from one group to another, but they are inalienable (others cannot take away or undermine them)".[1]

In international law, "commons" or "common property" is synonymous with areas or resources beyond state jurisdictions or territorial boundaries. The high seas, the superjacent airspace, the living resources[2] thereof, and the moon, belong to this category of resources.[3] They are collectively referred to as the global commons. They are also regulated by international treaties.[4]

In non-international law parlance, such as sociology and anthropology, common property resources have a different meaning from what we have described above. Simply put, commons are areas or resources "co-owned and actively stewarded by a specific community."[5] Under these disciplines, "common property" is nearer in meaning to "communal property resources" than "open access resources." For sociologists and anthropologists, common property owners enjoy the benefits of a determinate management that is compensated for overseeing the common property. With such management, there is no likelihood of overuse occurring.

Hardin credited with the phrase, "tragedy of the commons"[6] it was Pardo who popularized the concept of the "common heritage of mankind" at the debate on the exploitation and uses of the resources of the seabed.[7] The international community agreed with Pardo that certain resources outside the territorial jurisdiction of states, such as the ocean seabed should be utilized in such a way as to benefit both the technologically advanced countries and those not too advanced. In other words, access to and exploitation of such resources should not be on the basis of the survival of the fittest, which is the hallmark of capitalism[8] and trade liberalism.[9] Rather, the concept endorsed "all states to share in the rewards, even if unable to participate in the actual process of extraction."[10] Moreover, the concept of "common heritage" differs both in meaning and character from "open access property," "common property resources," and "communal ownership" or "communal resources." For instance, "communal resources" or "communal ownership" is noted for having an identifiable leader or management that oversees their uses. This is not an attribute of "open access property," "common property resources," or resources within the common heritage paradigm. Notwithstanding this difference, the principle of benefit sharing is a characteristic that permeates communal ownership resources, shared natural resources, and common heritage resources.[11]

In practice, it is difficult to make the distinction between these two concepts, namely "common property" and "common heritage of mankind" notwithstanding that managing common property resources is harder than managing common heritage resources. For common property resources, there is no restriction on uses and therefore capacity to exploit is vital.[12] In contrast, the concept of common heritage acknowledges the weaknesses of some of the "common" owners and therefore endorses the principle of benefit sharing. Under this arrangement, it is irrelevant that any particular state lacks the capability to exploit the resources described as common heritage. Furthermore, for this category of property there is an inbuilt responsibility to exploit the resources in a sustainable manner because common heritage resources are available for both the living and those yet unborn. In contrast, common property resources are available for the living, albeit the most capable because of this thin line distinction between these resources that Birnie and Boyle warned: "The common property doctrine is not to be confused with the more recent 'common heritage' concept, a specialized regime applied to certain mineral resources, nor with 'shared natural resources', where, ... rights are shared by a limited number of states."[13]

Consequently, Hardin's commons would be interpreted differently in legal and non-legal disciplines. For instance, common property in international law signifies availability of a free resource susceptible to overexploitation. There is no doubt that this is a resource to which Hardin's *Tragedy of the Commons* applies.[14] It is such resources' character of "open access" that may have triggered Hardin's concern. In sociology and anthropology, however, Hardin's tragedy of the commons would only apply to "open access" resources and not to "common property resources" because unlike the commons resources, the common property resources have identifiable owners and determinate management.

However, in view of the foregoing, classifying the indigenous knowledge on their uses as part of the commons would be inappropriate. With adequate legal protection, both have the characteristics of excludability and rivalry, the hallmark of items capable of ownership, including patent protection.

DEFINITION OF TERMS

Intellectual Property Rights

Property is a claim to a benefit or income stream whilst property rights constitute claims to a benefit stream protected through institutionalised regimes from interference by other potential users (Kameri-Mbote, 2000). Property rights define the relationship, rights, responsibilities, between a holder of the property and the property itself. They also define the relationship between non-holders of the property and the property. IPRs are designed to confer ownership and specify rules of access over inventions, processes, and ideas (George and van Staden 2000; Swinson J. 2000). They are private legal rights that apply to the intangible human contribution that goes into the production of a particular technology (IUCN, 1994).

The distinction is made between tangible and intangible property as well as the rights pertaining to such property. Tangible property refers to real property that is made up of physical goods or commodities (for example such as house, building or land). Intellectual property on the other hand deals with informational services that are intangible and amorphous, not readily susceptible to either possession or delineation (Kameri-Mbote, 2000). It is argued that real property is relatively scarce and therefore expensive to protect and capture, whilst on the other hand the value of intellectual property is associated with creation of shortage of information by limiting the capacity of non-owners to capture it. A major distinguishing factor between property rights as they relate to tangible and intangible property, is the aspect of time. Rights of an intangible property, such as intellectual property, have got a time period over which they hold. After the lapse of the time allotted the rights of the holder of Intellectual Property will no longer hold, meaning that anybody wishing to use the property can do so without fear of incrimination.

Information generated through intellect has the general characteristic that it is highly liable to use by others without paying for it. It is very difficult to limit or exclude others from this type of good. Under current intellectual property regimes, information of this nature is more of a public good. Production of an intellectual good, such as information, takes a lot of resources in the form of time, effort and even money. Since such resources have an opportunity cost associated with them, the person producing an intellectual good would need compensation for his/her investment. If the good is not protected to deny access to those who did not incur any costs in its production, others may use the good to produce other economic goods from which they will enjoy benefits. Intellectual property rights are therefore designed to facilitate and protect investments into generation of information so that those who would want to use their goods can reward investors for their creativity. IPRs enable companies and individuals to legally protect themselves against counterfeiting of their products, technologies and services. (IUCN, 1999).

A Community-Definition

The definition and identification of a community is a difficult exercise. Can one just go in the countryside and point at a community? Much depends on what one calls a community. There is great diversity within and among communities. There is therefore no standard community that can be taken as a stereotype to represent all other communities. The relationship between a particular community with its environment or biological resources differs from what one finds in the next.

It refer to 'local communities' and to this extent, a local community means "a human population in a distinct geographical area, with interests or rights over biological resources, knowledge, innovations, practices and technologies governed partially or wholly by its own customs, traditions or laws." An indigenous population refers to "a homogenous society identified by self-ascription and ascription by others, who have continuously lived as a community sharing common bonds of language, customs, traditions and other distinctive cultural traits, and who through political, social and cultural factors, became differentiated from the majority of the population."

Mayet (mimeo) indicates that there is no one definition of a local community. It can be defined in terms of shared social and economic relationships, the transmission of knowledge, values and customs. Some communities are said to define themselves in territorial terms or in terms of a particular natural resource or set of natural resources or in terms of shared activity.

Types of Intellectual Property Rights

IPRs generally fall into the following categories; copyrights, trademarks, trade secrets, industrial designs, geographical indications and patents (Kameri-Mbote, 2000). Products and technologies that are protected by property rights are major exports of most developed countries as well as are the rights themselves in the form of licenses to use patented processes, techniques and designs, copyrights and trade marks.

Copyrights: Copyrights protect the creative expression of ideas in tangible form. They are extended to scientific publications, computer software and databases. These generally require no formalities to obtain. In most countries as soon as one writes they are protected by copyright (Swinson J. 2000).

Trademarks: Trademarks protect symbols, words and marks that are designed to distinguish goods and services of one person or company against those of the other in the market (Kameri-Mbote, 2000; Swinson J. 2000).

Trade Secrets: Trade secrets are used to protect subject matter, which is either unpatentable due to failure to fit into the requirements for patenting, or because the holder of such information does not want to publicly reveal the subject matter fearing that a competitor may commercially use the information to the holder's disadvantage.

Examples of information that can be protected through trade secrets are scientific information or a traditional healers' knowledge. Trade secrets differ from patents in that trade secrets do not prevent others from developing and using the same information in a different way.

Plant Breeders Rights: Plant Breeders Rights (PBRs) are rights granted to plant breeders to exclude others from commercialising material of the plant varieties they have developed (Mpofu, mimeo). For a plant variety to be eligible for protection through PBRs, it must be clearly distinguished from other protected varieties, uniform and stable. PBRs are designed to attract the private sector into engaging in plant breeding activities. They are also designed to allow other plant breeders to use the protected plant for their own breeding activities and research as long as they refrain from selling the protected plant itself.

Patents: Patents confer exclusive rights on an inventor which, for fixed period, prevent others from producing, using, or engaging in commercial transactions for the invention. A patent requires that an invention be novel, or recent and original, and not previously known. The product or process should not be a trivial extension of what is already known. When a patent is granted, the inventor is given a private monopoly for a fixed duration to restrict others from making, using, or selling the invention. The applicant for a patent must include a full written description of the invention. In exchange for the patent, the patent's subject matter should be published. The TRIPS agreement stipulates that the term of patent protection should be no less than 20 years from the filing date of the patent application (IUCN, 1994; Kameri-Mbote, 2000).

Utility Patents and Plant Patents: Utility Patents provide protection for agricultural research products such as herbicides, insecticides, fungicides, transgenic plants, plant cells, plant genes, plant DNA sequences, plant tissue cultures, transgenic seeds, plant varieties, host vector organisms and many other products of agricultural research. Within Utility Patents are Plant Patents that apply to single variety of plants. However biologists are not happy with single plant patents arguing that they do not provide protection for broad inventive concepts especially with biotechnology where new traits such as for insect resistance cannot be confined to a single plant variety (Duffey, in Weaver 1993).

THE CONVENTION ON BIOLOGICAL DIVERSITY (CBD)

The CBD is the only major international convention that assigns ownership of biodiversity to indigenous communities and individuals, thereby giving them the right to protect this knowledge. Two articles of the CBD outline how member states are to treat their indigenous communities, and to develop relations among each other.

Article 8 (j) declares that State Parties are required to "respect, preserve and maintain knowledge, innovations and practices of indigenous and local communities embodying traditional lifestyles relevant for the conservation and sustainable use of biological diversity and promote the wider application with the approval and involvement of the holders of such knowledge, innovations and practices and encourage the equitable sharing of the benefits arising from the utilisation of such knowledge, innovations and practices."

Article 18.4 states that Contracting Parties should "encourage and develop models of co-operation for the development and use of technologies, including traditional & indigenous technologies."[15]

INDIGENOUS KNOWLEDGE (IK)

Indigenous Knowledge refers to the local knowledge by indigenous people that is unique to a given culture or society. It forms the basis on which local decisions on fields such as agriculture, education, health, natural resources management and others are made. Such people depend on specific skills and knowledge that have been influenced by internal creativity and experimentation for their livelihoods over a long period of time (Warren, 1991; Flavier et al. 1995, in World Bank Website for Sub-Saharan Africa). Indigenous knowledge has gained prominence of late as people realise the role it has played over time in preservation of biodiversity. Mariam Mayet (mimeo) describes traditional knowledge as any knowledge, innovation, or individual or collective practice of an indigenous population or local community, having real or potential value, associated with a biological resource, protected or not by intellectual property legislation.

The term Indigenous or sometimes Traditional Knowledge seems to refer to that body of knowledge held by people who are not regarded as "developed" as far as modern science and civilisation is concerned. Wherever this term is mentioned it is usually in relation to natives of a country or region whose history involves some kind of marginalisation at one point or another from "modern civilisation". The knowledge is constructed in relation to history, culture, economics, politics and most importantly power relations. Those who are politically, socially and economically disadvantaged, the powerless, are forced to accept without question the knowledge of the powerful. What the powerful know then becomes the yardstick against which all other knowledge is measured.

The packaging of knowledge into what is called "indigenous", "local" or , "modern scientific/formal" influences the value that will be attached onto such knowledge. It is quite apparent that traditionally, intellectual property rights regimes did not attach any value to indigenous knowledge to warrant its protection as property. This is one reason why globalisation poses dangers of impoverishing traditional or cultural societies if their knowledge is not accorded a status befitting any other body of knowledge. Gupta (mimeo) points out that people's knowledge system need not be considered informal just because the rules of the formal system fail to explain innovations in another system.

In developed countries resources, biological or intellectual property, are defined and controlled in terms of either individual or corporate ownership. Most resources can be traced down to either of the above entities. Traditional communities such as those found in India do/did not keep their knowledge documented in written form. Their knowledge is oral based, passed on from one generation to another. This shows how developing countries can take a unified stance as a way of making their knowledge accepted as property.

TRANSFORMATION OF LOCAL INSTITUTIONS INTO CURRENT IPR REGIMES

Since some traditional communities still have ethics prohibiting acceptance of compensation for knowledge or for granting access to biological diversity there is need for mental overhaul. This can be done through raising awareness programmes on the realities of globalisation and its implications on their resources and livelihoods. Given that most communities are now dependent on the cash economy one does not expect much resistance from them.

On the issue of knowledge and resources, whose ownership and management responsibility is the community, it is recommended that communities be assisted to register as companies. This makes the community eligible as a legal owner of resources under it as far as the current IPR regime is concerned.

PIRACY OF INDIGENOUS KNOWLEDGE

There are several incidences which show that indigenous knowledge is being pirated by the developed nations with their highly developed and sophisticated research laboratories whilst the developing countries are lagging behind still trying to make a case for their knowledge. The contribution of indigenous knowledge to the development of products through what is regarded as formal modern science is quite astounding.

There are three quarters of the plants that provide active ingredients for prescription drugs came to the attention of researchers because of their use in traditional medicine (Nijar, 1996). He states also that of the 120 active compounds currently isolated from the higher plants and widely used in medicine today, 74% show a positive correlation between their modern therapeutic use and the traditional use of the plant from which they were derived. Traditional knowledge is said to have increased the efficiency of screening plants for medicinal properties by more than 4000%.

The current value of the world market for medicinal plants derived from leads given by indigenous and local communities is estimated to be US$43 billion (ibid). Nijar (1996) further states that the value of crop varieties improved and developed by traditional farmers to the international seed industry is estimated to be US$15 billion. One wonders whether all such contribution from the traditional knowledge was ever acknowledged. Classification of indigenous knowledge as unpatentable by the North is just a strategic gimmick meant to guarantee them free access to it as a product of the commons.

Chitsike (1997) (ed) highlights biopiracy involving Quinoa, a high protein cereal which forms an important part of the diet of millions of indigenous people in Andean countries of South America, and turmeric,–an orange rooted plant found in India. In the Quinoa case, he reports how the Andean Countries people have cultivated and developed different varieties of this plant. Because of its nutritional value, which has twice the protein content of maize or rice, quinoa has started to enter the US and European markets. Every year Bolivia is reported to get US$1 million from the sale of this product. In 1994 two researchers from the US received a patent which gave them exclusive monopoly control of male sterile plants of the traditional Bolivian "Apelawa" quinoa variety. The researchers are said to have admitted that they did nothing to create the male sterile variety. It was " just part of the native population of plants". The patent covers any quinoa hybrid derived from Apelawa male sterile cytoplasm including 36 traditional varieties. Once the patent finds its way into corporate hands, Bolivian exports of quinoa to the US can be prevented and quinoa can be grown commercially elsewhere with the permission of patent holders.

On the turmeric case it is reported that this plant is a magic cure-all for many people in India. The turmeric plant, which is orange rooted is an ancient component of ayurdermic medicine, is native to the subcontinent and has been used for thousands of years in the treatment of sprains, inflammatory conditions and wound healing. In 1995 two US scientists from Mississippi were granted US patent on the use of turmeric for healing wounds. Though the government of India filed a challenge to the patent, the appeal can be upheld if India provides proof that turmeric has been used in India specifically for healing wounds. This proof should be in the form of an academic paper which predates the patent application. The US researchers are said to have acknowledged in the application for the patent that turmeric has long been used in India as a traditional medicine for treatment of various sprains and inflammatory conditions, but, they argued that there was no research done to that effect. So, if the patent could be granted on the basis that the process that had led to its discovery and use by the people of India could not be regarded as research, this means that all traditional based knowledge can not be patented. The implication is that any scientific researcher who can take traditional knowledge, verify it through a recognised scientific research process, without adding anything more, can apply for a patent to his/her benefit.

The Neem tree which is found in India has now more than 35 patents on it in the US and in Europe for its pesticidal properties (Chitsike,1997). Local communities who have been with this plant and have preserved it for generations are already marginalized because of reduced access to this resource due to high market demand. If the 35 patents were for Indian nationals or corporations nobody would raise questions of biopiracy but probably the distributional aspects within the country.

Some research techniques used in rural development initiatives facilitate expropriation or pirating of indigenous local knowledge.

Some research agendas and programmes carried out in the context of development institutions such as universities, NGOs and other rural development oriented institutions through various bilateral and multilateral co-operative programmes are flow channels through which Indigenous Knowledge is siphoned to developed countries where it is used to develop commercializable products. Dery, Otsyina, and Ng'atigwa (eds.) (1999) highlighted that knowledge of traditional medicine is a treasured secret of some individuals. This means given the chance such individuals could patent such knowledge. In order to extract this treasured information from people from local communities in developing countries special extractive tools were and are being developed commonly referred to as Participatory Research Methods. This is not to say these methods are bad but, they can be misused. These methods have inbuilt mechanisms to tease out valuable information from local people. No payment is made for this knowledge implying that such knowledge is common heritage. Publications from such acquired knowledge is patented by the authors. The communities supplying the knowledge may receive acknowledgments.

The often revealed objective of wanting to better understand the local communities so as to be able to come up with appropriate development programmes is quite novel but the knowledge derived from such efforts has far more beneficial consequences to the developed countries sponsoring such programmes.

When developed countries use such indigenous knowledge as input to their research processes and develop commercializable products, they have the capacity to alternatively develop synthetic substitutes to what they will have found through indigenous knowledge.

CONCLUSION

At this backdrop, it is clear, that the rights of indigenous and local communities need protection because without such protection, biological wealth cannot continue to exist. Moreover, as it is generally accepted, that biodiversity survives through the conservation and sustainable use strategies employed by indigenous and local communities. It should be remembered that the key to unlocking the nature and extent of the protection required for indigenous and local communities, is the appreciation and understanding of the relationship between collective ownership of biological resources and the traditional knowledge associated with such resources. In this regard, the developing countries like India really need to craft their way in order to prevent their resources from being siphoned to the developed countries.

NOTES AND REFERENCES

1. Darrel A. Posey & Graham Dutfield, Beyond Intellectual Property: Toward Traditional Resource Rights for Indigenous Peoples and Local Communities 60 (IDRC 1996).
2. Moore, Behring Sea Fur Seals Arbitration, 1 Intl. Arbitrat. Awards 755 (1898), (cited in P.W. Birnie & A.E. Boyle, International Law and the Environment 141 (2nd ed., Oxford U. Press 2002).
3. Birnie & Boyle, Supra N. 29 at 141.
4. United Nations Convention on the Law of the Sea pt. XI (Dec. 10, 1982) http://www.un.org/Depts/los/convention_agreements/texts/unclos/unclos_ e.pdf.
5. Patricia Marchak, M., Who Owns Natural Resources in the United States and Canada? Working Paper No. 20, N. Am. Series, Oct. 1998. http://www.wisc.edu/ltc/wp20.html.
6. Herman E. Daly & Kenneth N. Townsend eds., Generally Valuing the Earth: Economics, Ecology, Ethics, The MIT Press 1993, 127-151.
7. The Third United Nations Conference on the Law of the Sea (Dec. 10, 1982) http://www.un.org/Depts/los/convention_agreements/convention_overview_convention.htm (accessed Feb. 25, 2004) [hereinafter UNCLOS III]. UNCLOS III orchestrated the debates on ownership of the seabed. By virtue of Articles 136 and 137 of the 1982 UNCLOS, the resources of the deep seabed beyond national jurisdiction (the Area) have been pronounced the "common heritage of mankind" vested in mankind as a whole.
8. Martin O'Connor, Introduction: Liberate, Accumulate–and Bust?, in Is Capitalism Sustainable?: Political Economy and the Politics of Ecology 1-19 (Martin O'Connor ed., The Guilford Press, 1994)); see also Wolfgang Sachs et al., Greening the North: A Post-Industrial Blueprint for Ecology and Equity (Zed Books 1998).
9. Martin O'Connor, Introduction: Liberate, Accumulate–and Bust?, in Is Capitalism Sustainable?: Political Economy and the Politics of Ecology 1-19 (Martin O'Connor ed., The Guilford Press, 1994)); and Wolfgang Sachs et al., Greening the North: A Post-Industrial Blueprint for Ecology and Equity (Zed Books 1998).
10. Birnie & Boyle, *supra* n. 29, at 143.

11. Judge Shigeru Oda, NIEO, Law of the Sea and Common Heritage of Mankind: Some Commentsin Legal Aspects of the New International Economic Order 171-173 (Kamal Hossain ed., Francis Pinter 1980).

12. Wolfgang Sachs, Planet Dialectics: Explorations in Environment and Development 87 (Zed Books 1999).

13. Birnie & Boyle, *supra* n. 29 at 141.

14. James M. Buchanan, *Symmetric Tragedies: Commons and Anticommons*, 43 J. of L. & Econ. 1-13 (U. of Chicago Press 2000).

15. Kameri-Mbote P. (2000). Community Rights, Farmers and Breeders Rights in Africa : Towards a Legal Framework for Sui Generis Legislation. African Centre for Technology Studies, Nairobi. Draft Working Paper Presented at the FAO/IUCN Regional Workshop on Community Rights, Farmers and Breeders Rights, Nyanga, Zimbabwe, October 29 – November 1, 2000.

16. George, J. and Van Staden, J. (2000) Intellectual Property Rights: Plants and Phyto-medicinals – past History, Present Scenario and Future Prospects in South Africa. South African Journal of Science. Vol. 96 (8) :433-444.

17. Swinson, J.V. (2000). Intellectual Property. Australian Science Teachers' Journal. Vol. 46, 3:36-40.

18. Opcited, 16.

19. Opcited, 16.

20. Nick Middleton (1999). Intellectual Property Rights: a battleground for trade and biodiversity? IUCN, Gland, Switzerland. 16 pp.

21. Mayet Mariam, Freelance environmental lawyer, based in Johannesburg South Africa, Securing sustainable livelihoods: Imperatives underpinning the development of an appropriate regime to protect community rights to biodiversity. mmayet@global.co.za.

22. Opcited, 16.

23. Opcited, 18.

24. Opcited, 16 & 18.

25. Mpofu B. (undated). Farmers and Breeders' Rights. 12 pp.

26. Opcited, 16.

27. Duffey, W.H. (1993). Intellectual property laws and their impact on agricultural research. In: Weaver R.D. (ed.) U.S. Agricultural Research: Strategic Challenges and Options. Agricultural Research Institute, 9650, Maryland.

28. United Nations Convention on Biological Diversity (1993) *at http:// environment.* harvard.edu/guides/intenvpol/indexes/treaties/ CBD.html (last visited Apr. 8, 2003).

29. World Bank (Sub-Saharan Africa Region), (2000). What is Indigenous Knowledge System. World Bank Web Site.
30. Opcited, 22.
31. Gupta, A.K (undated) .Rewarding Creativity for Conserving Diversity in third world : Can IPR Regime Serve the Needs of Contemporary and Traditional Knowledge Experts and Communities in Third World. Indian Institute of Management, Ahmedabad. 6 pp.
32. Nijar G. S. (1996) In Defence of Community Knowledge and Biodiversity. A Conceptual Framework And The Essential Elements of a Rights Regime. Third World Network. Penang.
33. Nijar G.S. (1996b) TRIPs and Biodiversity. The Threat and Responses: A Third World View. Third World Network. Penang.
34. Chitsike L.T. (ed.) (1997). Report on Indigenous Knowledge Workshop held in Madrid–Spain: November 1997. Convention on Biological Diversity.
35. Ibid.
36. Dery, B.B., Otsyna R., Ng'atigwa C. eds. 1999. Indigenous Knowledge of Medicinal Trees and Setting Priorities for their Domestication in Shinyanga Region, Tanzania. Nairobi: International Centre for Agricultural Research.

15

THE TRADE RELATED INTELLECTUAL PROPERTY RIGHTS (TRIPS) AGREEMENT AND THE DEVELOPING COUNTRIES

Lakshmi Narasaiah

The Basic norms of free competition established in the nineteenth century induced legislators to provide relatively weak forms of intellectual property protection. Often innovators could rely only on such factors as lead time. Reputation for quality and continuing technical improvements to maintain their foothold in the market.

Undermining this outlook were two developments that led to the inclusion of intellectual property issues in the World Trade Organisation (WTO). First, the rise of knowledge–based industries radically altered the nature of competition and disrupted the equilibrium that had resulted from more traditional comparative advantages. Second, the growing capacity of manufacturers in developing countries to penetrate distant markets for traditional industrial products forced the developed countries to rely more heavily on their comparative advantages in the production of intellectual goods than in the past. Market access for developing countries thus became a bargaining chip to be exchanged for greater protection of intellectual goods within a restructured global market place.

Since 1986 the developed countries drive for extraterritorial protection of intellectual property rights has largely ignored the competitive capabilities of developing countries with respect to intellectual goods, and it has also downplayed these countries' rights to preferential treatment under existing rules. At the same time, the logic of multilateral trade negotiations skews the pre-existing North–South conflict over intellectual property rights by introducing the prospects of trade concessions in unrelated fields. Intellectual property rights constitute but one of many variables that bear on competitive capacity and the transfer of technology in general.

PRIMARY INTELLECTUAL PROPERTY REGIMES

Patents

The extension of patentability to virtually all types of technology recognized by developed patent systems, the prolongation of patent protection to a uniform term of twenty years, and legal recognition of the patentee's exclusive rights to import the relevant products could adversely affect developing countries whose existing patent laws fall below these standards. In practice, however, the competitive status of any given developing country in a post-TRIPS world will depend in part on the level of foreign direct investment it attracts and on the benefits that strengthened intellectual property rights bring to domestic innovators.

Competition under stronger patent regimes requires developing countries to adopt legal means of narrowing the scope of foreign patent monopolies and of encouraging local entrepreneurs either to work around the claimed inventions or to develop improvements suited to local conditions. To this end, local entrepreneurs should exploit technical information in disclosures published abroad; patent authorities should exercise all of the claims limitations practiced abroad; and domestic courts should strictly interpret the doctrine of equivalents. Legislative enactment of utility model laws would provide additional incentives to adapt foreign inventions to local conditions and to improve them further.

Moreover, unpatented traditional technologies will often remain suitable for local needs, and the resulting products may be sold at lower prices than imported products of patented technologies. Entrepreneur in developing countries should also be prepared to exploit unpatented applications of applied scientific know-how in such advanced technologies as biogenetic engineering and computer programme–related innovation.

In time, increased direct investment by foreign patentees could enable developing–country licensees who exploit their natural advantages, especially low labour costs, to succeed on both domestic and export markets where non-licensees were unable or unwilling to venture in the past. Familiarization with the benefits of the patent system should stimulate greater investment in domestic research and development and in technological innovation.

The gradual extension of patents to new technologies such as computer programmes and bio–genetic engineering without the emergence of agreed international minimum standards creates both opportunities and risks for the developing countries. While the developed countries enjoy unique advantages in biotechnology that only become available to developing countries as a consequence of stronger patent systems, some developing countries may find their own competitive status enhanced by the provision of proprietary rights, including plant breeders' rights, though others may not. The patenting of biogenetic advances decreases the scope for reverse– engineering and could also increase the costs of doing business in key sectors of some developing economies, notably agriculture. As regards information technologies, reliance on copyright and trade secrets at the international level appears less unfavourable to the developing countries' prospects than patents, for reasons that are set out below. However, the tendency to patent software could diminish these prospects by posing limits to reverse engineering and to the attainment of the interoperability, and this trend adds to the overall costs of disseminating information goods.

To the extent that patented technology is not made available on reasonable terms or that un–wholesome economic dependencies actually arise, developing countries will have to consider measures to restore the competitive balance that are consistent with the TRIPS Agreement. For example, the agreement allows compulsory licenses when the rights holders fail to licenses patented technology "on reasonable commercial terms". It also provides other bases for defensive regulatory action by emphasizing "the transfer and dissemination of technology, to the mutual advantage of producers and users" and the need "to promote the public interest in sectors of vital importance to socio–economic and technological development".

Measures to restrain abuse of intellectual property rights as authorized by the Paris Convention also remain available under the TRIPS agreement, which expressly empowers developing countries to deal with licensing practices that adversely affect the international transfer of technology".

Finally, the agreement specially preserves the right of all states to "adopt measures necessary to protect public health and nutrition and to promote the public interest in sectors of vital importance to socio–economic and technological development, provided that such measures are consistent with the provisions of this agreement.

Trademarks and Geographical Indications

The TRIPS provisions give pre–existing norms greater specificity while softening the use requirement and eliminating both compulsory licenses and local linkage requirements. These provisions also subject the international regime of trade–marks and unfair competition to more stringent enforcement measures, including border controls against imports of counterfeit goods.

As a result, developing countries will need to reassess the pro–competitive functions of trade marks in open economies while addressing question of abuse in a more direct fashion. They should insist on receiving the technical cooperation and aid that the TRIPS agreement envisages for the purposes of defraying administrative and enforcement burdens.

Governments should consider policies and incentives that encourage enterprises to established their own market identities through appropriate trademarks and foreign firms to allow licensees to adapt more of the licensed products for both domestic and export needs under local trademarks.

Copyrights

Authors in many developing countries are very active in both domestic and foreign markets. It nonetheless remainstrue that the balance of trade in cultural goods favours exports from developed countries. This imbalance could increase under the TRIPS agreement, which generally applies the international minimum standards of the Berne convention, plus selected standards from the Rome convention on neighbouring rights.

While efforts to implement these standards is mandatory, developing-country authorities should familiarize themselves with the extent to which the scope of copyright protection varies from country to country, in the absence of authoritative legal limitations recognized by international law. Carefully framed public–interest exceptions may further reduce the overall costs of a TRIPS

Agreement without violating international copyright norms. Moreover, the revised Berne Convention already provides compulsory licenses for educational and scientific test, and developing countries may wish to consider marking greater use of these concessions.

ANCILLARY PROPRIETARY REGIMES

Trade Secrets

In modern economies trade secret law regulates the pace of competition by endowing second comers with an absolute right to reverse–engineer. To operate successfully under such a regime, developing countries must realign the concept of "transfer of technology" with the nature of competition in open markets. Technology is transferred through self–help methods of reverse engineering. The potential benefits of reverse–engineering unpatented technologies increase when advanced technologies are involved, notably biogenetic engineering, computer programmes and computer–aided design. The unpatented, non–copyrightable know–how underlying these technologies is often embodied in tangible products available to the public, which renders classical trade secret protection of doubtful efficacy. By ignoring this problem, the TRIPS agreement provides entrepreneurs in developing countries with major opportunities, notwithstanding the extension of trade secret law under TRIPS, provided they are willing and able to master the art of reverse–engineering.

Other Proprietary Regimes

The TRIPS agreement mandates intellectual property protection for industrial designs, plant varieties and integrated circuit designs. Although the developed countries enjoy a clear advantage in advanced sectors of industrial design, more tradition sectors rooted in aesthetic appeal rather than technical efficiency remain accessible to firms in developing countries.

Need for Multilateral Policies

Global economic integration increasingly requires that intangible creations receive minimum international standards of legal protection. Purely territorial intellectual property rights will thus give way to international sovereignty. However, the norms, of that law represent a delicate balance between the interests of states at different stages of development, so that the evolution of international intellectual property law will have to accommodate these norms and that balance.

Efforts to implement higher intellectual property standards will put increasing strains on competition law, which is not directly covered by the TRIPS agreement. Identifying the parameters of healthy competition valid for all players in an integrated world market will become a pressing task for the international community in a post – TRIPS world. These issues will be complicated by the fact that innovators, users, and second comers all have different stakes in fashioning the rules of unfair competition law, and their interests will increasingly vary more with their economic roles than with the geopolitical affiliations of their respective national states.

Competition law must, become an integral part of international discussions of intellectual property rights, and there is a great need for multilateral cooperation to achieve a marketwide balance between incentives to create, and reasonable opportunities to imitate and improve upon, technological innovation. These discussions should lead to an internationally agreed framework for promoting a transfer of technology that is compatible with the drive for greater economic efficiency. To the extent that such cooperation succeeds, it will contribute a new perspective to the notion of fair competition that should strengthen the prospects of all participants in the global market place.

16

COMMERCILISATION OF NON-TIMBER FOREST PRODUCTS (NTFPs) IN INDIA UNDER THE IPR REGIME

S. Vaidehi, K. Raja Mohan Rao & T. Masha

INTRODUCTION

Non-Timber Forest Products (NTFPs) and Non-Wood Forest Products (NWFPs) are terms that are being widely used currently to denote what was termed Minor Forest Produce (MFP) earlier. The term NTFP as is used now broadly includes fuel and fodder, biomass, bamboo, cane, grass, fiber, oil, tannin and dyes, gums, resins, medicinal plants, barks, leaves, flowers, fruits, tubersel, mushrooms, seeds, mammals, birds, reptiles, fish and insects etc.,[1]

NTFPs AND POVERTY ALLEVIATION

For Centuries, people of the tropical rainforest have been collecting NTFPs either for their subsistence or in exchange for manufactured produce and money. An important question for science and development is to asses how far NTFPs presently do, or could, at local level, help alleviate poverty and improve the welfare and livelihoods of forest-dependent communities. In many parts of the world, subsistence gathering is still important. Hunting, fishing and plant gathering provide an important part of the diet and health system of rural people, and an essential part of plant material for household use. NTFP collection for trade ("extractivism") has been proposed as a promising strategy for poverty alleviation in forest areas. But how far does reality provide substantiating evidence for this premise? If " extractivism "- an old practice in the fortunes and social upgrading of forest product traders, the role of NTFPs in the success of economic or social strategies of local collectors is less obvious.[2]

NTFP commercialization, defined as increasing the value of an NTFP in trade, is expected to increase income and employment opportunities, especially for poor and otherwise disadvantaged people. This expectation is based on the well-documented importance of many NTFPs in rural livelihoods, the emergence of new markets for natural products, and the development of new marketing mechanisms (green marketing, fair trade) there has been much speculation that NTFP commercialization can provide opportunities for (relatively) benign forest utilization and even create incentives for conservation.[3]

MAGNITUDE OF NTFPs IN INDIA

NTFP plays a significant role in providing subsistence and cash income to a large part of the world's population. Studies from all tropical regions also indicate that the poorest households in rural communities are directly depending on NTFPs for their livelihood security. The challenges of managing forests for commercial NTFPs is to promote economic development by maintaining and even increasing production while simultaneously maintaining or improving ecological conditions.

NTFPs play a very important role in the countries' economy. They form the basic raw material for phytopharmaceuticals and various other industries. More than two thirds of the world's plant species–at least 35000 of which have medicinal value–originate in developing countries[4]. There are nearly 300000 and 750000 plant species are thought to exist in the world with much of the diversity found in tropical zones. And today's global food supply rests essentially on the biological diversity developed from wild plants and animals, savannas and the forests of the Third World. By and large these are raw materials for the North.[5]

The NTFPs provide raw materials for large number of industries processing, cater employment, to 40 per cent of poor artisans and contribute 54 per cent of forest revenue to state. NTFPs offer an excellent potential for international trade. NTFPs account for 70 per cent of India's forest product exports and the demand for phytochemicals is expected to increase in the future. Ahmed (1997) reported eight different categories of NTFPs; some are important for tribal indigenous groups. For example, in West Bengal tribal groups collect 27 plants for commercial products, 39 plants for food, and 47 for medicines. NTFPs could become a new frontier for trade and sustainable commercialization of biological resources at the international level if intellectual property rights are secured.[6]

A systematized mechanism for sustainable management, harvest and marketing of NTFPs from the grass roots level to the level of export to international markets does not exist. Looking at the magnitude of the NTFP resource and its potential for international trade there is a huge scope for strengthening and streamlining the existing market channels for profitable trade and export of these NTFPs to the international markets .In order to make these products internationally competitive, it is mandatory to ensure that these products are responsibly extracted from a sustainable managed and certified forest area. State governments receive around Rs.450 crs annually by way of royalty from NTFPs. It estimated provide about 40per cent of total official forest revenues and 55per cent of forest based employment. In India unemployment has always been a concern for planners and policy makers. The forestry sector, with 23per cent of the country's geographical area, provides 2.3 million person years of employment. Of this total 1.6 million person years is related to NTFP.

NTFPs AND RURAL LIVELIHOOD SECURITY

NTFPs as a source of livelihood and Poverty alleviation. Poverty in rural India is generally considered to be linked to inadequate arable land or its low productivity. Collections from forests such as fuel wood and non-timber forest products (NTFPs) and their contribution to household income in rural areas especially for communities living adjacent to forests are lonely unnoticed. There are an estimated 100 million people in the country who live in and around forests and another 275 million for whom forests constitute an important source of livelihood.[7]

LIVELIHOOD IMPLICATIONS OF NTFPs

The rationale for supporting NTFP commercialization is often to improve the livelihoods of poor people, especially NTFP producers.

By creating and capturing more value, it is hoped that poor people will gain from improved income and employment opportunities. However, there is a real risk that the benefits will not be captured by the intended beneficiaries. Indeed, there are many examples in which traditional producers and users of an NTFP have been made worse off by commercialization (e.g. Nepal cases cited by Krishna Gautam, e-dialogue).

Successful trade requires a minimum set of skills and assets, including business contacts and knowledge of the ways of doing business. Poor people typically do not have those skills and assets and so, when new commercial opportunities arise, they may be out-competed by local "elites", with more capital to invest, better connections, and better skills, or by competitors from other areas. Risks exist in terms of resource access and control and in terms of commercial competitiveness.

And, as discussed above, commercialization tends to lead to increased demand for raw material that is met by increased harvesting of wild resources and then, increasingly, from intensified management and cultivation. The poor are typically at a disadvantage. When a wild resource gains value, the most powerful actors are likely to capture control [8].And production of managed resources requires ownership or control over land and/or resources that the poor do not have.

Where external interventions are designed to support commercial development, particular attention needs to be addressed to how resource rights, information and prototype business opportunities are translated into action. Potentially more serious, many NTFPs represent important sources of "safety-net" (a resource that households can turn to in times of need), subsistence (for households own consumption) or cash. Increased commercial trade can quickly lead to reduced access through over-exploitation and/or changing property rights, such that poor local people are left worse off and more vulnerable. In the case of marula in north-central Namibia, for example, although the tree is widespread, one quarter of households do not have direct access to marula fruits and related products and rely on the goodwill of their friends and neighbours to share the resource. There is a risk; therefore, that commercialization will lead to the increased 'privatization' of the resource and the exclusion of certain groups from the benefits[9]. This situation was well described by May (19.)

with reference to the babacu palm kernel trade in Brazil. And where commercialized products have important local ritual or medical uses, increased exploitation to supply the market may lead to an erosion of cultural values and health.

There are also price effects of changing markets. Increased interest can lead to increased harvesting and reduced prices, once again with negative impacts on small-scale producers. The e-dialogue included several examples of negative impacts of this kind. [e.g Krishna Gautam Feb. 16).

Wealthier people are generally better placed to take advantage of new market opportunities, having land and/or capital, as well as better skills and connections. For example, research on the bamboo case in China showed that as opportunities in the bamboo sector increased and farmers intensified their management, better-off households gained the largest share of the increased earnings, and poorer households gained the least.

Other factors also contribute to this anti-poor bias. Intensified management, whether in a plantation system or in a managed forest system, requires security of tenure over the land/resource, some confidence that there will be a market for the product when it is harvested, and enough economic security that the grower can afford to wait for slow-maturing products. The poor, by definition, do not have these assets.

It is simplistic, and often wrong, to assume that because an NTFP is important to poor people, efforts to develop it will help the poor. In practice there may be severe constraints that make it difficult to move beyond the stage of wild gathering. Where the resources are treated 'de facto' as open access resources, over-exploitation and dissipation of rents prevail. Moreover, the "external conditions" such as transportation infrastructure, market access, property rights, education, and health care, and limits in terms of available capital, skills and connections, make it difficult for the poor to move beyond the current situation. Some of these products might be classified as "poverty traps", where even decreasing prices result in the need to increase harvesting to maintain a minimum income level. Others, under the prevailing institutional conditions, do not offer sufficient economic advantage. It is necessary to examine each case carefully to see where the real constraints operate and to identify solutions.

COMMERCIALISATION OF NTFPS AND MARKET ASPECTS

Commercialisation of NTFPs may prove to be a viable option for poverty reduction and reduction of deforestation, if their harvest from the forests is substituted by cultivation on village agricultural lands. The exceptional cases of medicinal plants: Shatavar (*Asparagus racemosus*), and *Safed Musali* (*Chlorophytum tuberosum*) (widely used in traditional Ayurvedic medicines) growing naturally in selective patches in the forests of Madhya Pradesh, are a paradigm. In the past few decades due to unsustainable harvesting practices and over exploitation, these plants became locally extinct in many parts of forests in Madhya Pradesh. But, after the JFM resolution of the Government of India in (1990), ready markets for the products (through involvement of the JFMC institutions) encouraged some communities to reduce their harvest from the forests and cultivate these medicinal plants on their agricultural farms. This saved a large amount of time and energy, provided higher monetary benefits per hectare from their agricultural lands and reduced the extraction load of these medicinal plants from the wild. Hence grassroots community-based involvement in commercialization of NTFPs can shift the load of extraction of products from natural forests and help in alleviating the problem of over-exploitation.

GLOBAL TRADE

Global imports of medicinal plants and parts were estimated to be over US$ 1 billion in 2002. Leading importers of medicinal plants were Hong Kong, USA, Japan, Germany, France, China, Korea, Italy and Canada, Hong Kong and USA together accounted for more than 30 per cent of global imports. Major exporters were China, followed by India, USA, Germany and Korea. Comparison of major Exporters and importers in World Trade of Medicinal plants indicates that China were the leading net exporter of medicinal plants.

EXPORT PERFORMANCE OF INDIA

Medicinal Exports from India in the year 2002–03 were US $124.5 million, as compared to US $ 133.28 million in the year 2001–02.

North America, especially USA is the major market for Indian medicinal plants accounting for over 50 per cent of exports. The exports to North America are also showing promising growth trends for Indian medicinal plants. Other major markets for India are Japan, France and UK.

Major Importers of Medicinal Plants–2002

Sl No.	*Country*	*US $ 000*	*% of share*
1.	Hong Kong	176720	65.41
2.	USA	147131	13.67
3.	Japan	118994	11.05
4.	Germany	76102	7.07
5.	France	51814	4.81
6.	China	48582	4.51
7.	Korea Rep.	43094	4.00
8.	Italy	42839	3.98
9.	Canada	35988	3.34
	Total above	741264	68.84
	World	1076662	100.00

Source: Compiled from India Traders.

Countrywise Export of Indian of Medicinal Plants

Sl. No.	*Country*	*% of share in total Exports*
1.	USA	50.74
2.	Japan	7.20
3.	France	3.53
4.	UK	3.00
5.	UAE	2.60
6.	Germany	2.22
7.	Spain	1.99
8.	Taiwan	1.83
9.	Australia	1.62
	Total above	74.73
	Grand Total	100.00

Source: Compiled from India Traders.

Major items of medicinal plans and extracts that are being exported from India included psyllium husk, saps and extract, Henna powder, senna leaves. Sandalwood chips and pods, and karaya gum. The export of top 10 medicinal plant products accounted for over 85 per cent of total exports. Until 2001–02 India exported mainly in the form of crude drugs and extracts. This accounted for nearly 70 per cent of total medicinal plant product exports. The remaining 30 per cent were exported as finished products in 2001–02.

While the trend in 2002–03 showed a decline in exports of medicinal plants and curde drugs. Exports of manufacturer products more than double, registering a better growth of over 200mn per cent in 2002–03; from US $ 50.4 million in 2001–02 to US $ 154.2 million 2002–03. The increase was particularly striking when exports of Ayurvedic medicines a (not put up for retail sale) shot up by more than four times from nearly US $20 million in 2001–02 to more than US $ 100 million in 2002–03. Thus, it may be concluded that the thorough exports of Indian medicinal plants have fallen. The increase in Ayurvedic medicines exports in 2002–03 indicates that the medicinal plants exports are being undertaken in value added from.[10]

INTELLECTUAL PROPERTY RIGHTS AND NTFPs

The commercial development of many NTFPs builds on indigenous knowledge of natural products and their use. There is growing concern about how to compensate the holders of that indigenous knowledge. Furthermore, given that product development often occurs far from where the plant originates, there is equal concern about how to avoid so-called 'biopiracy' and ensure proper compensation for the nation where the plant has been collected. The 1992 Convention on Biological Diversity (CBD) marked a milestone in how biological resources, and more specifically genetic resources, are viewed in today's global economy, providing a broad legal framework to structure access and benefit sharing (ABS) agreements.[11]

How the CBD is implemented nationally and regionally is critical to the development and certification of plants such as Sangre de drago (*Croton lechleri*), whose status as a biological or genetic resource is open to debate. Clear national biodiversity legislation may be a deciding factor both in terms of encouraging certain practices, as well as by encouraging companies to seek nations and regions offering more favourable conditions for purchasing natural products. Costa Rica's early start in dealing with these issues, for example, has led to a steady influx of benefits from bioprospecting agreements. In contrast, delays in the finalisation of relevant legislation in Ecuador meant that imports of Sangre de drago by the US-based company, Shaman, were put on hold in 1994.[12]

At the same time as recognizing indigenous rights, it is important to acknowledge the intellectual property rights of the researchers or companies that take a product forward to market (e.g. isolating its active ingredient). A good example of how this has been achieved is the development of a new appetite-suppressing drug based on the *Hoodia* plant in southern Africa. Although the active ingredient was isolated and patented by the South African Council for Scientific and Industrial Research, this was only possible because of the traditional knowledge of the San bushmen, who had long used the plant to stave off hunger. After an intense debate, agreement has now been reached so that both parties will share in the benefits of the drug being developed.[13]

VOLUMES ARE TYPICALLY SMALL

Many NTFP markets are small in scope and value, and therefore attract limited attention or investment[14]. When they do hit the big time, supply may be a serious problem. Clay (1996) emphasizes the importance of volume to NTFP marketing, stating that it is unlikely that any single producer could provide enough products to meet the needs of even a small company in North America. While this would not be a good marketing strategy in any production sector, it does seem to be a common problem among NTFP start-up enterprises in developing countries. Product development must include detailed planning of how to meet possible future demand, including looking into how different producers can collaborate through market cooperatives to provide adequate supplies of NTFPs to major markets[15]. Where products derive from threatened plant species, supply issues are complicated by conservation considerations. On the other hand, niche and fair trade-type markets may be small relative to potential production, as in the case of marula oil, the supply of which is far greater than can be absorbed by its current main international market, The Body Shop[16].

PRODUCT LIFECYCLES MAY BE SHORT

Getting products into the market is one problem, keeping them there is another. NTFP markets are notoriously vulnerable to substitution. The South American continent has a particularly high share of 'boom and bust' experiences to report including the classic case of natural chicle. Chicle fuelled the modern chewing gum industry and its extraction was the main industry in the Yucatan

Peninsula of Mexico in the mid 20th Century. But, by 1960, the development of much cheaper petroleum-based gum had almost eradicated demand for natural chicle[17]. In addition to substitution by synthetic products, NTFP producers may have to compete with large-scale cultivation in other countries as in the case of the Brazilian natural rubber harvesters, whose livelihoods were turned upside down by the massive production of plantation rubber from South-East Asia. In the case of cosmetics and herbal medicines, many products are considered 'luxury' items meaning that change in demand is particularly difficult to predict.

THE RISKS ASSOCIATED WITH NTFP COMMERCIALIZATION

We have considered the structure of natural products markets and recognized the increasing complexity of those markets in a global economy. And, we have looked at some of the constraints that limit the opportunities, especially of NTFP producers and poor people generally, to participate profitably in these markets. But what happens when commercial markets for NTFPs develop and demand increases? There are some clear lessons from theory and from experience regarding the risks that are associated with NTFP commercialization from both the conservation and livelihoods perspectives.

CONCLUSION

NTFPs are important in the livelihoods of forest dependent people and particularly women, who play a crucial role in their collection, processing and trade. Appropriate commercialisation strategies of NTFPs increase the opportunities for forest dwellers, increase their economic value and provide information that will raise the awareness of policy makers and donors of the importance of these forest products and the need to incorporate them in official statistics and poverty reduction programmes. To maximize the potential contribution of NTFPs to livelihoods, there is a need to explore local, national, regional and international markets. There are many challenges that need to be dealt with to enable rural dwellers to take more advantage of NTFP development. These are, among others, providing improved technologies to increase the productivity of NTFPs, helping organize local communities in group marketing and providing a cost-effective market information system. Finally governments and the private sector have an important role to play by reducing transaction costs (especially eliminating the unnecessary road controls) and improving road and market infrastructure (security, electrification, storage)[18].

NOTES AND REFERENCES

1. Satish Tiwari (2000),"Environment and forests", Anmol Published, New Delhi.
2. Genevieve Michon (2005), "NTFP Development and Poverty alleviation: Is the Policy Context favourable?" Workshop report of Non-Timber Forest Products between poverty alleviation and market forces.Ed. Jean-Laurent Pfund & Patrick Robinson.
3. Brian Belcher& Kate Schreckenberg (2003), "NTFP Commercialzation-A Reality Check".
4. Crucible Group (1994), "People, plants and patents: the impact of intellectual property on biodiversity, conservation, trade and rural society". Ottawa, ON, IDRC. 1994. xxii + 118p. :ill.
5. Nijar G.S. (1996), "In Defence of Community Knowledge and Biodiversity. A Conceptual Framework and the Essential Elements of a Rights Regime". Third World Network. Penang.
6. Katwall, R.P.S. et.al (2001), "Status of forest genetic resources conservation and management in India".
7. Prema Gera (2002) "Women's Role and contribution to Forest Based Livelihoods".
8. Dove, M.R. (1994), "Marketing the Rainforest: 'Green' Panacea or Red Herring? Analysis from the East-West Center" 13: 1-7.
9. Wynberg, R. (2003), "The management, use and commercialisation of marula: policy issues". Project report, DFID/FRP Winners and Losers project, Science and Technology Policy Research Centre, University of Cape Town.
10. Prahalathan, S.(2004), "Export Potential of Indian Medicinal Plants and Products" Financing Agriculture, July-September 2004.
11. Alexiades, M.N. (2002), Sangre de drago (*Croton lechleri*). Pp 136-155 in Shanley, P., Pierce, A., Laird, S.A. and Guillén, A. (eds) Tapping the green market: certification and management of non-timber forest products. Earthscan, London.
12. Ibid.
13. Kahn, T. (2003), "South African tribe seals benefit-sharing deal. Science and Development Network News", 10 January 2003. Available at:*www.scidev.net/News/index.cfm?fuseaction=printarticle& itemid=328&language=110/06/2003.*

14. Shanley, P., et.al., (2002), Introduction. Pp3-6 in Shanley, P., Pierce, A., Laird, S.A. and Guillén, A. (eds) Tapping the green market: certification and management of non-timber forest products. Earthscan, London.
15. Ervin, J.B. and Mallet, P. (2002), "The rise of certification, the current state of the playing field for NTFP certification programmes and future prospects". Pp 7-19 in Shanley, P.
16. Schreckenberg, K. (2003), "Appropriate ownership models for natural product-based small and medium enterprises in Namibia". Consultancy report for the Ministry of Trade and Industry, Windhoek, Namibia. Laird, S.A. and Guillén, A. 2002. Marketing issues. Pp 322-336 in Shanley, P., Pierce, A.
17. Laird, S.A. and Guillén, A. (2002), "Marketing issues". Pp 322-336 in Shanley, P., Pierce, A., Laird, S.A. and Guillén, A. (eds) "Tapping the green market: certification and management of non-timber forest products". Earthscan, London.
18. Ousseynou Ndoye (2005), "Commercial Issues Related to Non-Timber Forest Products" Workshop report of Non-Timber Forest Products between poverty alleviation and market forces. Ed. Jean-Laurent Pfund & Patrick Robinson.

17

IMPACT OF THE INTRODUCTION OF INTELLECTUAL PROPERTY RIGHTS PROTECTION ON DEVELOPING COUNTRIES

Mohd Izhar Ahmad

INTRODUCTION

I refer to is intellectual property rights and how protection of those rights can foster economic growth, provide incentives for innovation and attract investment that will create new jobs and opportunities for India. India fully realizes its incredible potential and takes it rightful place in the global economy. India's own self-interest and the welfare of the Indian people are at stake. Responding to the challenges of development will not only benefit India but also will provide an example of leadership for other developing economies throughout the world.

Business has changed during the past hundred years in a way that has emphasised the value of ideas and knowledge. Today, many companies find their most valuable assets being intangible and they are therefore dependent on functioning IPRs systems, but does the rigid protection of IPRs serve all people in our globalised world?

The purpose of this paper is to summarize and discuss the impact of the introduction of IPRs protection on developing and least developed countries in accordance with the Trade Related Intellectual Property Rights (TRIPS) Agreement. The question is whether developing countries will be able to catch up with their technological development if IPRs protection is extended.

THE IMPACT OF TRIPS ON DEVELOPING COUNTRIES

The developing countries have been forced to agree to TRIPS. The term 'developing country' is not clearly defined by the WTO. Basically, member-countries themselves declare their status as a developing country, of course, under observation by the other members.

In Asia, and much of the South, patents were never allowed on life forms because of ethics, colonial legacies and the threat that statutory monopolies in the health and food sectors pose to peoples' basic needs. Until recently, industrialized countries also excluded living organisms from intellectual property (IP) regimes. Unlike manufactured products, biological material was considered the realm of nature and therefore regarded as a "discovery", not an invention. Besides, living organisms reproduce themselves, so the tenets of IP law would need to be bent to suit their characteristics. But with the dawn of the hybrid seed industry and, later, the biotechnology-driven life sciences industry, plant breeding has become big business and those businesses want exclusive rights to their research results.

In a democratic society, all sectors must make their voices heard. It is especially important that those forward-leaning sectors of society, those with a vision for the future, work to make that vision a reality. Those of you here today comprise that forward-looking sector of India's society, and I am certain that working together, we can make the vision of a strong, dynamic and innovative Indian economy a reality. And intellectual property protection is key to that vision. India has the building blocks in place to create a vibrant, knowledge-based economy. But action is needed to create a legal system, infrastructure and enforcement mechanisms to bind those building blocks together so they may be used to their greatest advantage. I would like to share with you today the steps we believe India must take in order to raise its intellectual property protection to world class level, and in doing so, lay the foundation for further economic growth across all sectors of the knowledge-based economy.

It is a fact that valuable knowledge is primarily in the hands of enterprises in the developed countries and developing countries have to import this know-how. Developing countries are concerned that a strengthened, worldwide IPRs system may lead to anti-competitive tendencies with negative effects on welfare in these countries. Transnational corporations may abuse their monopoly-power, gained through their intellectual property, or the transfer of technology may be restricted. TRIPS Agreement's prime objective was not the battle against counterfeiting and piracy but "technological protectionism". Developed countries are regarded as innovators and suppliers of products whereas developing countries serve as markets. Especially in the US strong industrial lobbies such as the pharmaceutical, software, and returns on R&D.

The question is why developing countries finally agreed to TRIPS. Two factors have influenced this decision:

- The United States' threat of bilateral initiatives.
- Developing countries saw some advantages in tariff reductions of agricultural products, textiles and other products of their concern through WTO Agreements but under the 'single package' system they had to agree to all negotiated points including TRIPS.

Many countries of the developing world that do not have strong IPR regimes remain mired in economic stagnation and worse yet, have suffered the negative effects of the "brain drain." Talented scientists, engineers, artist and inventors leave their home countries where their work is unprotected and migrate to those countries where it is. While this is certainly a boon for those countries—like the United States—that receive these immigrants, this process does little to help the developing world. India itself provides an excellent example to share with the world of how the negative effects of lax IPR regimes can be reversed. Just a few years ago, India was losing a battle to retain the best and brightest of its engineers and computer scientists.

The lack of an effective copyright law forced those scientists and technicians to immigrate to countries where their hard work could be protected and kept safe from unfair exploitation by competitors seeking easy advantages. The Indian parliament finally passed a copyright law to protect the hard work and creativity of its computer scientists. The result: a burgeoning high tech industry producing some of the world's most advanced software and employing thousands of workers who might otherwise have left India for greener pastures in other parts of the world. The National

Association of Software and Service Companies estimates that software piracy in India has declined from a high of 89 percent in 1993 to 60 percent now, an impressive improvement.

THE PHARMACEUTICAL INDUSTRY AND TRIPS

The infectious diseases which are, from a scientific point of view, treatable, account for 14 million deaths each year, most of them in developing countries. A number of factors worsen the situation in these countries, e.g. poverty and lacking access to health services. Efficient and affordable medicines could cut down this death toll if people had access to such drugs. 25 million people out of the 36 million who are infected with HIV worldwide live in sub-Saharan Africa and the enormous share of infected people of the whole population has a dramatic impact on life expectancy in this region. Again, affordable medicines could help. In developed countries live-saving drugs have raised life expectancy of HIV infected people dramatically but this treatment is unaffordable for people in developing countries, where 95% of people who have AIDS are from.

Considering India's enormous resources in the pharmaceutical sector, the results it could see from proper patent protection could far surpass the examples we have seen in other countries, like Jordan pharmaceutical sector that employed reverse engineering to create generic drugs at low prices. But Jordan's generic companies had to compete with numerous generics from all over the developing world, not to mention those in the developed world. Facing severe economic difficulties, the Jordanian government came up with an economic development plan that included implementation of strong intellectual property rights to foster research and development and expansion of the knowledge-based economy. The result is a dramatic increase in foreign investment from major pharmaceutical firms, most of which have now opened offices or expanded their commercial and research activities in Jordan. Jordanian exports of pharmaceuticals increased from $150 million in 1999 to $200 million in 2001, a significant increase for a country with a population of 5 million.

India itself provides an excellent example to share with the world of how the negative effects of lax IPR regimes can be reversed. Just a few years ago, India was losing a battle to retain the best and brightest of its engineers and computer scientists. The lack of an effective copyright law forced those scientists and technicians to immigrate to countries where their hard work could be protected and kept safe from unfair exploitation by competitors seeking easy advantages. The Indian parliament finally passed a copyright law to protect the hard work and creativity of its computer scientists.

India is the fourth leading supplier of bulk pharmaceutical products and active ingredients globally. With some $2 billion in exports, India's pharmaceutical industry is recognized as a global player. India has the world's third largest pool of scientifically and technically trained personnel. Despite the lack of pharmaceutical patent protection, a small research and development sector is emerging. Stronger product patent protection will encourage the development. Knowledge-based industries have the potential to create thousands of jobs for Indian workers, tremendous revenues for the government and substantial increases in India's exports.

The Indian Patent Office is faced with a growing backlog of approximately 40,000 unexamined patent applications. Enforcement of IP protection is seriously lacking. Judicial delays mean that cases can take up to 10 years to see resolution and payment of damages on IPR violations

BIOPIRACY

By the mid-1900s, some industrialized countries began to offer limited forms of plant variety protection (PVP) to breeders of new crop varieties. PVP was constructed as a so-called "alternative" to patenting that would supposedly be attuned to the needs of agriculture. It guaranteed breeders a commercial monopoly on the use of their varieties while leaving loopholes open for farmers and other breeders.

Third World countries heavily rely on domestic agricultural production, which makes IPRs like patents and plant breeders' rights an important issue. Plant breeders' rights are applied in the case of the development of new plant varieties through conventional methods and they are a kind of sui generis protection, which does not include re-using of the seed and further research on the basis of the developed variety. Three criteria have to be fulfilled in order to obtain a 15-20 year protection: the variety has to be distinct, uniform and must keep its characteristics upon reproduction.

The export of agricultural products and biopiracy is a dangerous threat to farmers in these countries. Biopiracy describes the situation where someone, either an individual or a corporation, gains a patent on a plant variety already in use by someone else. The Rural Advancement Foundation International (RAFI) points out that in most cases the victims of such action will be farmers in developing countries and the perpetrators mostly are companies in industrialised nations. As a consequence, the titleholder may prevent importation of the product in question or demand royalty payments.

Patents and plant variety protection (PVP) are two different forms of intellectual property rights. Like any IPR, both patents and PVP provide exclusive monopoly rights over a creation for commercial purposes over a period of time. A patent is a right granted to an inventor to prevent all others from making, using, and/or selling the patented invention for 15-20 years. The criteria for a patent are novelty, inventiveness (non-obviousness), utility, and reproducibility. Although patents were designed for industrial application, with biotechnology, patent offices now grant patents on microorganisms and, in some countries, on all life forms.

PVP laws can provide exemptions for breeders, allowing them to use protected varieties for further breeding, and for farmers, allowing them to save seeds from their harvest. In plant breeding, PVP is the weaker sister of patenting mainly because of these exemptions.

In Asia, the seed industry and its allies have aggressively promoted the Union for the Protection of New Varieties of Plants (UPOV) as the appropriate system of *sui generis* protection. UPOV is a small intergovernmental organization that administers common rules for the recognition and protection of PVP internationally. Most of the 46 UPOV members are industrialized countries, which currently operate the UPOV Convention of 1978 or 1991. Accession to the Union is now confined to the 1991 Act. Through successive revisions of the Convention, the rights granted to breeders have become more and more similar to those granted under the patent system. While breeders get exclusive commercial control over the reproductive material of their varieties and the right to enforce licenses, farmers planting PVP-protected varieties are prohibited from saving seeds for replanting except under highly restricted conditions. And increasingly in many countries practicing PVP, the right of the breeder extends to the farmers' harvest and the direct products of that harvest. In the next few years, enormous pressure will be placed on Asian countries to take further steps to complete the legislative processes and tighten the laws in favor of corporate breeders. The pressure on Asian countries which adopt PVP systems based on UPOV to accede to further demands of global industry will only grow.

An Material Transfer Agreements (MTAs) is a contract between two or more parties specifying the conditions under which materials–say, a seed sample–are exchanged. The conditions may cover confidentiality, transfer to third parties, commercialization, and other issues. MTAs are often used when the materials in question hold commercial value and embody some form of intellectual property that the provider wishes to retain exclusive control over. Some MTAs define the materials, such as gene constructs, as the "technical property" of the provider, "taken to mean, without limitation, tangible property such as ... germplasm and the biological materials and derivatives thereof." In this way, an MTA can provide sufficient monopoly control over intellectual *property* in a country that does not provide statutory intellectual property *rights* on plants and animals. MTAs are thus a *de facto* form of intellectual property protection, governed by contract law, not IP law.

TERMINATOR CROPS

Another development in biological protection is Genetic Use Restriction Technology (GURT), more popularly known as "terminator" and "traitor" technologies. GURTs prevent farmers from saving seeds since the genetically engineered plants will not germinate in subsequent generations or will not express a particular trait (such as herbicide resistance) unless sprayed with specific chemicals that activate the right gene. Industry intends to use these technology protection systems to secure exclusive intellectual property control in the South, where laws and enforcement of IPRs on plants are weak.

Terminator or Traitor seeds are genetically modified to be sterile and not usable for replanting. As a consequence, farmers using these seeds would be forced to purchase new grain every sowing season. This makes quite clear how dangerous Terminator technology is, primarily for the 1.4 billion people worldwide who heavily rely on farm-saved seed and who could not afford to buy new seed every year. Moreover, this technology could be used to develop plants which may be dependent on chemical treatment in order to become fertile or healthy giving Gene Giants the power to control agriculture and thus food supply worldwide. The US ignores experts' warnings and is actively involved in the further development of a technology aimed at exploiting the poorest of the poor. The patentability of Terminator technology not only legitimates but also even fosters further research in this field, which one day will lead to the commercial application and unimaginable consequences for millions of people on earth.

RAFI pointed out that the researchers' fears were not justifiable. Of the 60 countries with Vitamin A deficiency–which golden rice is supposed to address–only 25 could possibly honor any of the patents involved. And in these countries, only 11 of the patents could constrain the project locally. Seven of those are held by four transnational corporations (Syngenta, Aventis, Monsanto, and DuPont), two of which have expressed their interest to make the technology freely available to the poor.

CONCLUSION

To summarise the situation, developing countries are in a serious situation if they try to comply with the obligations imposed on them by the TRIPS Agreement. I see the urgent need for a reform of TRIPS although in some cases a different interpretation of the regulations would be sufficient in order not to discriminate against developing countries, their economies and their people.

Intellectual property rights form the basis for scientific and economic development because they offer an incentive to someone, either individuals or organisations, to invest time and knowledge in research activities. Inventors are given the right to derive monopoly profits, which means that only they are allowed to exploit their invention during a certain period of time. As a consequence, this exclusive right has to be legally enforceable. The whole society should benefit from these works, as they drive economic growth and technological development. Admittedly, the effects of IPRs depend on various economic variables such as the social value or the existence of substitutes.

Consumption of a public good by someone does not influence someone else's opportunity to consume this good as well. To maximise welfare within a society it would be better not to price the use of know-how in order to keep the marginal cost at zero but nobody would then be interested in providing knowledge.

As India's knowledge based economy grows, it will benefit not only India, but the rest of the world as well, especially the developing world it leads. With Indo U.S. relations at an all-time high and India business becoming increasingly global, it is time for "new think" to prevail in the IPR debate. I look forward to seeing the fruits of this collaboration–a globally important Indian pharma industry, protection for Indian films and music, a healthier IT sector, and the further blossoming of India's already impressive creative energies. I am confident we will rise to the challenge.

BIBLIOGRAPHY

Correa, C. (2000), *Intellectual Property Rights, the WTO and Developing Countries: The TRIPS Agreement and Policy Options.* London: Zed Books.

Fink, C. (2000), *Intellectual Property Rights, Market Structure, and Transnational Corporations in Developing Countries.* Berlin: Mensch-und-Buch-Verlag.

Messner, Sophie (1997), "Implications of the TRIPS-Agreement under the GATT for Developing Countries".

Pass C., Lowes B. and Davies L. (1993), *Collins Dictionary of Economics.* 2nd ed. Glasgow: Harper Collins Publishers.

Rafi (2001a), *USDA Says Yes to Terminator.* Retrieved: 2 November 2001.

Rafi (2001b), *New Terminator Patent Goes to Syngenta.* Retrieved: 2 November 2001.

Rafi (2000), "Golden Rice and Trojan Trade Reps: A Case Study in the Public Sector's Mismanagement of Intellectual Property," *RAFI Communique,* Number 65, September/October.

UN (1996), The *TRIPS Agreement and Developing Countries.* Geneva: United Nations Publication.

Watal, J. (1999), *Intellectual Property Rights and Agriculture: Interests of Developing Countries.* Retrieved: 25 October 2001.

WTO (2001a) *The WTO in brief.* Retrieved: 27 October 2001.

WTO (2001b), *The Multilateral Trading System–Past, Present and Future.* Retrieved: 27 October 2001.

WTO (2001c), *Intellectual Property: Protection and Enforcement.* Retrieved: 27 October 2001.

WTO (2001d), *Who are Developing Countries in the WTO?* Retrieved: 27 October 2001.

18

INDIAN FOLKLORE–PROTECT ME! PROTECT ME!

Vaijayanthi & Vaheed Z. Ubaidullah

The term 'folklore' was first coined by William Thoms in 1846. According to the Model provisions of the World Forum on the Protection of Folklore, convened by WIPO and UNESCO in Phuket in April 1997 "Expressions of folklore" means productions consisting of characteristic elements of the traditional artistic heritage developed and maintained by a community of a country or by individuals reflecting the traditional artistic expectations of such a community and in particular:

(i) Verbal expressions, such as folk tales, folk poetry and riddles;

(ii) Musical expressions, such as folk songs and instrumental music;

(iii) Expressions by action, such as folk dances, plays and artistic forms of rituals whether or not reduced to a material form; and

(iv) Tangible expressions such as:

  (a) Productions of folk art, in particular, drawings, paintings, carvings, sculptures, pottery, terracotta, mosaic, wood work, metal ware, jewelry, basket weaving, needlework, textiles, carpets, costumes;

  (b) Musical instruments;

  (c) Architectural forms.

In such societies, where the masses are illiterate, and the oral traditions are the means through which propagation of the necessary elements of culture takes place scholars used the term 'folklore' to refer the language of the people, the system of their livelihood like hunting, agriculture, customs relating to marriages, deaths, etc., and the basic code of conduct, all of which are transmitted orally. According to scholars, all elements of learning that are passed through an oral tradition from generation to generation in a society belong to the domain of folklore.

Some forms of folklore are manifested and communicated almost exclusively in the written as opposed to oral form, such as autograph-book verse, book marginalia, epitaphs, and traditional letters.Indian literature has a sizeable share of folk songs, folk tales, poems, riddles and even many stories forming part of great epics like The Ramayana and The Mahabharata and the Panchatantra and Betal stories, all of which form part of the rich heritage of folklore. Yet another category of folklore is that which is neither oral nor written. Folk dances, folk arts and crafts, folk paintings, sculptures, etc., are transmitted not orally or through written medium, but through visual tradition, imitations, observations, through training and performances.

Some social scientists hold the view that folklore is the creation of a group of people who belong to the same contiguity of dwelling place and culture regardless of whether the location of residence is city, town or village.

Folklore, thus, is the product of human creativity, creation of people who live in a particular geographical area, sharing the same language, culture, mechanism of livelihood and living conditions. It is the product of the creative ideas of the people who express such creativity through verbal, artistic or material forms, and this in turn is transmitted orally or in written form or through some other medium from one generation to another, belonging to a literate or non literate society, tribal or non-tribal, rural or urban people.

THE ELEMENTS OF FOLKLORE

Folk Literature

These include myths, legends, fairy tales, anecdotes, short stories, etc. In addition, proverbs, riddles, ballads, songs, rhymes, etymologies, folk titles,metaphors, chain letters, poetry, etc.Most of these elements which form part of folk literature have been created and passed on by word of mouth, some of them have been essentially oral literature now preserved in script and some have been traditionally preserved in written form.

Folk Practices

Folk beliefs, customs, superstitions, rites and rituals, folk festivals, etc., are folk practices forming part of a community's daily life.

Folk Arts or Artistic Folklore

Folk dances, folk theatre, folk gestures (examples are They yam, Parayanthullal, Kootthu of India) are all performing arts. Non-performing arts like painting, sculpture, embroidery, weaving, carpet making, costumes designing, and archery are also forms of folklore.

Folk Science and Technology

Methods of folk treatment, folk medicines, preparation of dairy products, fertilizers, and methods of agriculture and seed technology fall under folk science. folk technology, folk architecture, tool making, ornament making, pottery, etc., are some examples of the common forms of Folk Technology.

Thus, to conclude based on the characteristics that have been associated with it, 'folklore' can be defined as the sum total of human creativity. It encompasses the customs, games, beliefs, festivals, and practices which human societies have owned through tradition from generation to generation. It includes literature, performing and non-performing arts, paintings, sculptures, arts and crafts, embroidered quilts, alpanas and their related mechanisms and designs, which have been handed down by tradition to the societies from previous generations through word of mouth or traditionally by non-oral means. The patterns of houses, fences, tools, and many other materials being used by the societies, as well as those materials, their traditional manufacturing techniques and architectural designs, which the human societies have inherited from their forefathers; the medicines and other objects invented through experimentation and traditional scientific methods, which passed on as heritage to the societies through generations. The process of creation, making, designing and construction of these elements, as well as their sustenance in the societies, which has been in operation since ancient times and in a similar manner their transmission, diffusion, creation of variants, reshaping and renewal which have also been a continuous phenomenon since long past.

FOLKLORE IN INDIA

India is a citadel of rich and diverse cultures and religions. It is a country of great contrasts where big cities, atomic power plants, sky scrapers, super computers, and hi-tech cities serve as a window to the tremendous potential for modern technology and co-exist peacefully with small village settlements and tribal communities. The villages and tribal settlements of India are living proof that it is possible for a culture depicting the essence of simplicity, rich artistic creativity, with a proud and historic past to not only exist, but also flourish along with a life style dominated by fast changing, complex technology and highly competitive commercial system. Tribal culture is one of India's proudest symbols of heritage. Tribal art and crafts, languages, religious beliefs, scientific ideas, agriculture technologies, architectural designs, and medical practices all have had profound impact on India's past history and constitute a major component of the composite culture of India. There are millions of tribes in India including the Lepcha, Daflas, Mikir, Naga, Khasi, Garos, Kuki and so on. The Central region tribes include the Santhals, Oraons, Hos, Juang, Gonds, Baiga Bhil. hench us, Todas, Kadars, Kanis and Badaga, among others. The tribal communities in India are the primary source of folk culture and folk tradition- folk literature and handicrafts, handlooms, folk painting, etc., contributed by these communities are significant components of Indian folklore.

Handicrafts are a major element of folklore developed in India. These are objects made by the skill of the hand and depict the ingenuity of the creator and cultural heritage evolved over centuries. Created primarily to serve the ritual and personal needs of the community, these handicraft objects have entered the market for commercial trade. The variety of objects created by the deft hands of the tribal villagers cover large segments like textiles, floor coverings, pile carpets, pottery and terracotta, wood work, metalware, jewelry, stone carving, cane furniture, ivory and horn carving, basket making, mat weaving and many other festival and ritual crafts and wall decorations such as 'alpanas' (alpanas are flowing linear patterns made on the floor of beaten clay by rice paste).

There are rich traditions under each of these categories of handicrafts, contributed by the folk communities through rigorous and regular practices. For example, there are different styles of textiles that have developed over the past centuries in different parts of the country and are being woven even today, like cotton fabrics and handlooms, silk weaves and brocades, tie and dye such as bandhani and patola, hand painted, dyed and painted fabrics, folk embroideries, shawls and woolen weaves and tribal weaves.

Folk agriculture practices again cover a wide spectrum of activities leading to the development of the most important occupation of India. The practices cover a range of sciences from appropriate weather forecast devices, seed development, animal husbandry to water management technologies, agricultural tools and pesticides, and fertilizers. There are well-developed cultivation practices like the jhoom and terrace cultivation patterns in the North East, and plantation cultivation programs in the South. These are vast resources contributed by the tribal communities transmitted through the generations.

The entire Indian subcontinent, stretching from the Himalayas in the North to the Western Ghats in the South West, is rich in biodiversity. The flora and fauna of the subcontinent developed over a period of time is an inseparable part of the folk tradition and heritage.

Many of these tribes have in their treasures some secret medical cures against diseases and calamities, acquired over a period of experimentation based on trial and error and form part of the collective wisdom of the community. Besides the two advanced medical systems of Indian origin, i.e., Ayurveda and Sidha, the tribal and folk medical systems also have a long history. They are still in vogue in the forest and rural areas. The potential of their being exploited commercially by pharmaceutical entrepreneurs, both Indian and foreign companies, is growing day by day. The tribes of the respective areas know the medical properties of the herbs and vegetables that grow in the region and have, therefore, become the repository of a large traditional knowledge base or a living database whose exploitation is resorted to on a large scale resulting in depletion of a rich resource.

The various languages dialects and sub languages spoken in different parts of the country are rich in literature. Collections of folk tales, myths, fairy tales, legends, animal tales, anecdotes, short stories, dramas, proverbs, riddles, ballads, songs, lullabies, rhymes, chants, charms, speeches, etc., form a major part of the literary treasure that each language or dialect can feel proud of.

Similarly, folk arts, both performing and non-performing categories like folk dances, drum beats, folk dramas, folk gestures, folk caricature and folk painting, and sculpture, have influenced the cultural image of the country drastically. The renewed interest among the modern urban culture to appreciate and to enjoy the folk creations is a recent phenomenon. This factor is reflected not only in urban art centers and homes, but also in music, film and architectural industries. Costumes, jewelry and household appliances are designed after the ethnic models in order to address the unprecedented demand for such creations by the sophisticated urban societies. Many of the music companies specialize in folk music albums or portfolios. Film industries are also keen to incorporate folk dances, martial arts, and folk rites and rituals to enhance realism and add ethnic flavor to their products taking into account the popularity these elements have acquired of late. Irrespective of all these developments, it is unfortunate to note that there is as yet no legislation providing specific protection for folklore in this culture-rich country.

THE NEED TO PROTECT TRADITIONAL KNOWLEDGE AND FOLKLORE:

- Equity considerations–the custodians of traditional knowledge should receive fair compensation if the traditional knowledge leads to a commercial gain.
- Conservation concerns–the protection of traditional knowledge contributes to the wider objective of conserving the environment, bio-diversity and sustainable agricultural practices.
- Preservation of traditional practices and culture–protection of traditional knowledge would be used to raise the profile of the knowledge and the people entrusted with it.
- Prevention of appropriation by unauthorized parties or avoiding "biopiracy".
- Promotion of its use and its importance to development.

Unique Problems In Protecting/Patenting Folklore

The nature and unique features of folklore render it difficult to recognize , protect and provide the IP rights to the indigenous people and communities looking forward to protect their traditional knowledge. A single all-encompassing system of protection for traditional knowledge may be too specific and not flexible enough to accommodate local needs.

Some of the issues include:

1. How might indigenous peoples attempting to claim IP rights establish a spokesperson/ collective bargaining entity to make decisions regarding utilization of IP resources.
2. Is TK and folklore better protected as prior art (by publication/ establishment of searchable database) or trade secret (by limiting access to the information), or by a sui generis protection scheme (by enactment of new laws)?
3. If TK is known "by others" for more than one year prior to date of invention, it is not novel. Who might "others" be, for consideration of public disclosure, if for example an invention is patented by a community collective?
4. When more than one community shares a common resource, or when communities share aspects of TK and folklore, which is considered the "owner" for considerations of property and compensation for use.
5. Absence of any accessible written record for the patent examiner to decide or determine the status of the TK or FL– Whether it is a prior art or is the knowledge under question already under public Domain.
6. Inability of the patent examiner to access documentation that would challenge the novelty or inventiveness of an application based on traditional knowledge or folklore.
7. The nature of traditional knowledge is such that more of it is transmitted orally than written down. This poses particular problems when parties not authorized by the holder of that knowledge seek to obtain IPRs over it.
8. Local communities, or individuals within such communities, have found the intellectual property system, particularly the patent system, to be unattractive, both due to ignorance and sometimes due to lack of very high benefits.

Controversial Patent cases involving Traditional Knowledge and folklore

Turmeric: Turmeric (Curcuma longa) is a plant of the ginger family yielding saffron-coloured rhizomes used as a spice for flavouring Indian cooking. It also has properties that make it an effective ingredient in medicines, cosmetics and as a colour dye. As a medicine, it is traditionally used to heal wounds and rashes. The University of Mississippi Medical Centre were granted US patent No. 5,401,504 on "use of turmeric in wound healing".

CSIR argued that turmeric has been used for thousands of years for healing wounds and rashes and therefore its medicinal use was not novel.Their claim was supported by documentary evidence of traditional knowledge, including an ancient Sanskrit text and a paper published in 1953 in the Journal of the Indian Medical Association. USPTO upheld the CSIR objections and revoked the patent. The legal costs incurred by India in this case have been calculated by the Indian Government to be about at US $10,000.

Neem: Neem (Azadirachta indica) is a tree from India and other parts of South and Southeast Asia It is now planted across the tropics because of its properties as a natural medicine, pesticide and fertilizer. Neem extracts can be used against hundreds of pests and fungal diseases that attack food crops; the oil extracted from its seeds is used to treat colds and flu; and mixed in soap, it is believed to offer low cost relief from malaria, skin diseases and even meningitis.

In 1994 European Patent No. 0436257was granted to the US Corporation W.R. Grace and USDA for a "method for controlling fungi on plants by the aid of a hydrophobic extracted neem oil". The patent was later revoked by the EPO in 2000 after a group of international NGOs and representatives of Indian farmers filed a legal opposition against the patent.

Ayahuasca: For generations, shamans of indigenous tribes throughout the Amazon Basin have processed the bark of Banisteriopsis caapi to produce a ceremonial drink known as "ayahuasca" (which means "vine of the soul") in religious and healing ceremonies to diagnose and treat illnesses, meet with spirits, and divine the future.

An American, Loren Miller obtained US Plant Patent 5,751 in June 1986, granting him rights over an alleged variety of B. caapi he had called "Da Vine". The Coordinating Body of Indigenous

Organizations of the Amazon Basin (COICA)–an umbrella organisation representing over 400 indigenous groups fought to protect this exploitation.

Hoodia Cactus: The San, who live around the Kalahari Desert in southern Africa, have traditionally eaten the Hoodia cactus to stave off hunger and thirst on long hunting trips. In 1995 CSIR patented Hoodia's appetite-suppressing element (P57). In 1997 they licensed P57 to the UK biotech company, Phytopharm. In 1998, the pharmaceutical company Pfizer acquired the rights to develop and market P57 as a potential slimming drug and cure for obesity (a market worth more than £6 billion), from Phytopharm for up to $32 million in royalty and milestone payments. The San People threatened legal action against the CSIR on grounds of "biopiracy" and claimed as stakeholders and original discoverers and users and obtained a share of future royalties.

PROTECTING FOLKLORE-THE MODUS OPERANDI

The issue of protection of traditional knowledge (TK), innovations and practices of indigenous/local communities is currently on the agenda of different inter-governmental bodies, including the WIPO, WTO/TRIPS and the CBD. Since the existing IP regime is not found to be adequate to protect the holistic character of TK, a predominant view is emerging, mainly supported by developing countries, to devise a sui generis regime for its protection.

MAKING USE OF THE EXISTING IP SYSTEM TO PROTECT AND PROMOTE TRADITIONAL KNOWLEDGE

The current intellectual property system can be utilized to commercialize traditional knowledge or prevent its misuse. For example, Aboriginal and Torres Strait Islander artists in Australia have obtained a national certification trademark. Like any other trademark, this certification mark or Label of Authenticity is intended to help promote the marketing of their art and cultural products and deter the sale of products falsely claiming to be of Aboriginal origin.

The use of copyright protection in Canada to protect tradition-based creations including masks, totem poles and sound recordings of Aboriginal artists; the use of industrial designs to protect the external appearance of articles such as head dresses and carpets in Kazakhstan and the use of geographical indications to protect traditional products such as liquors, sauces and teas in Venezuela and Vietnam are growing examples of IP tools that can protect TK and folklore.

The ability to extend the life of trademarks indefinitely and the possibility of collective ownership of such rights suggest that they may be especially suitable for protecting traditional knowledge. This is also the case with geographical indicators, which may be used to protect traditional products or crafts if particular characteristics of such products can be attributed to a particular geographical origin.

Practice of traditional medicine is an area that has the potential to be quite well documented. In Lao People's Democratic Republic, for example, the Government established the Traditional Medicines Resource Centre (TRMC) which is working with local healers to document details of all traditional medicines with a view to promoting a sharing of practices within Laos. Any benefits or royalties realized from knowledge recovered during the collaboration will be shared with all the communities involved.

However, trademarks and geographical indications can only prevent the use of the protected marks or indications; they do not protect the knowledge, or the technologies embracing that knowledge, as such.

Other IP rights, especially those requiring some form of novelty or those with fairly limited periods of protection seem less appropriate for protecting traditional knowledge and folklore.

Thus the existing IPRs do have a role to play in protecting traditional knowledge. Whether that role is a significant one remains to be seen. Experience would suggest that the impact may not be great, not least because of the high cost of obtaining and enforcing rights. If the majority of small companies in developed countries have found the intellectual property system, particularly the patent system, to be unattractive, then it seems unlikely that local communities in developing countries, or individuals within such communities, will derive much benefit.

Until an acceptable international regime is adopted, bilateral agreements based on reciprocity and mutual recognition may be considered as a viable mode for extra-territorial recognition of TK at the international level and a comprehensive system may be devised at the national level for its holistic protection.

SUI GENERIS-THE ALTERNATIVE TO PROTECTING TK AND FOLKLORE

There is a lot of debate on the systems of protection that can be adopted to provide legal protection to the intellectual property of indigenous people and communities. Most of these discussions have tried to adapt the existing forms of IPRs like patents, trade secrets, copyrights etc. to the field of IK and folklore. This is not likely to work because of the inherent mismatch between the protection that was created for finite, inanimate objects coming out of industrial activity and the flowing, mutable and variable properties of biological materials.

How can a patent, with its life of 20 years be applied to an intellectual property that has existed for a few hundred if not a few thousand years! Case law in India has shown that Copyrights are not adequate to protect IK. Rulings have said that the idea is not important, just the mode of expression of the idea. The court has ruled to say that even if the defendant in a suit has used a common stock of knowledge, no action can be brought.

A pragmatic approach that has been strongly advocated by some academics and NGOs is the development of a *sui generis* regime, that is, a legal regime "of its own kind" which is specifically adapted to the nature and characteristics of TK. Though this approach has received considerable attention in the literature, little progress has been made in terms of actually implementing this kind of protection.

The *sui generis* protection of artistic expressions of folklore is necessitated by the fact that:

(i) Such expressions are being continuously transformed by their community of origin, whereas works created by individual authors are as a general rule completed in a form that is unique to their authors;

(ii) Artistic expressions of folklore do not, as a general rule, have any known creator. They pertain to the entire community, which incorporates them into its social life, whereas the works protected by copyright belong to one or more known authors, who created them;

(iii) Works were protected in order to encourage authors to create new works, whereas artistic expressions of folklore are protected in order to preserve important features of the identity of national communities in danger of dying out;

(iv) Works are protected for a limited duration, whereas expressions of folklore require unlimited protection if the features of folklore wherein the specific nature of national identity is located are to be stratified in the social fabric.

It is these features of the artistic expressions of folklore that determine the *sui generis* approach to protection in respect of its scope, the ownership of the rights to be recognized, the procedures for exercising them and the penalties imposed on any violations to which they might be subject.

Moreover, expressions of folklore, time-honoured and hallowed by social tradition, form part of the cultural heritage as a whole. As such, they can be protected by the full arsenal of public law provisions governing the preservation of this heritage against the different violations to which it may be prey.

CONCLUSION

The legal protection of folklore and traditional knowledge demands a *sui generis* system both at the national level and internationally; though the 1982 UNESCO/WIPO Model Provisions remain a good starting point for national provisions there need to be adaptations to the requirements of the various local environments. There is a need to consider whether the protection of folklore and traditional knowledge can be incorporated into a single legislative item that takes account of their specific nature, of whether such protection should be instituted in two distinct texts. It is recommended that the search for an appropriate framework for protecting artistic expressions both of folklore and of traditional knowledge be treated as matters of equal urgency.

RECOMMENDATIONS

(i) The States of the region should

(a) Develop their interests and the financial and organizational resources devoted to protecting folklore and traditional knowledge;

(b) Alert the communities concerned, the specialists and the general public, to the cultural and economic benefits of protecting this cultural heritage;

(c) Develop regional cooperation in this field and adopt a regional policy in regard to conservation and the provision of protection of folklore and traditional knowledge;

(ii) WIPO and UNESCO should

(a) Establish a standing committee on the protection of traditional knowledge and folklore in order to explore the adaptations that protection requires;

(b) Develop their cooperation in order to provide developing countries with the desired legal and technical assistance, training of specialists in the field of identification, documentation and conservation of folklore and traditional knowledge, and the necessary equipment and other financial resources.

(iii) Universities and Research Institutions should

(a) Develop digital databases to facilitate the patent examiners.

(b) Document after through research the various statuses of traditional knowledge.

(c) Collaborate with private NGOs to sensitise the indigenous communities to protect and utilize appropriately the traditional knowledge.

ACKNOWLEDGEMENTS

The articles compiled have been obtained from the following sources. The authors profusely acknowledge the authors and their organization:

http://www.wipo.int/tk/en/studies/cultural/expressions/study/kutty.pdf.

http://www.who.int/medicines/organization/trm/factsheet271.doc.

http://www.biodiv.org/convention/articles.asp.

http://www.unctad.org/trade_env/test1/meetings/delhi/statedebateTK.doc.

http://www.wto.org/english/thewto_e/minist_e/min01_e/mindecl_e.doc.

http://www.wipo.int/globalissues/tk/report/final/index.html.

http://hostings.diplomacy.edu/quaker/new/doc/tkcol3.pdf.

http://www.iprcommission.org.

http://www.niaaa.com.au/label.html.

http://www.wipo.org/eng/meetings/2002/igc/doc/grtkfic3_7.doc.

http://www.wipo.org/eng/meetings/2002/igc/doc/grtkfic3_10.doc.

http://hostings.diplomacy.edu/quaker/new/doc/OP4.pdf.

19

INTELLECTUAL PROPERTY RIGHTS AND BIODIVERSITY CONSERVATION IN INDIA

K. Raja Mohan Rao, S. Nirmala Mary & B.D.Ranjitha Kumari

INTRODUCTION

Biodiversity is defined as variability and variety in life forms including genes, species and ecosystems. Biodiversity conservation seeks to maintain life support systems provided by nature. Adding to the impact of natural processes, human intervention has had an adverse effect on these life support systems and thereby on biodiversity. Therefore much attention has been focused internationally on formulating policies towards the conservation of biodiversity over the past few decades. Biodiversity is an example of global public goods because natural ecosystems and the impacts of their degradation cut across man-made boundaries. The highest concentration of biological diversity in the globe is in developing countries. Poorest countries are the most threatened by biodiversity degradation for two reasons: firstly, high population dependence on natural resources for livelihoods, food security and health; secondly, inability to adapt to change due to rapid population growth, absence of markets, weak institutional capacities, and use of inappropriate or obsolete technologies.

DISTRIBUTION OF BIOLOGICAL RESOURCES

The structure of the world's biodiversity shows a distribution pattern which is not uniform. G. Egziabher (2000) states that biodiversity increases towards the equator and decreases towards the poles. Industrialized countries are characteristically located in biodiversity poor regions in the North whilst developing countries are found in biodiversity regions mostly within the tropics. This characteristic distribution of developed and developing nations on the surface of the globe has led to the use of the terms North and South in describing these nations respectively. The industrialized countries of the North, with their highly developed research facilities, see themselves as the hub of modern biotechnology. They are however biodiversity poor. The South are biotechnology deficient but are rich in biodiversity. Because of that, developing countries remain poor whilst developed countries enrich themselves from biological resources found in developing countries.

More than two thirds of the world's plant species–at least 35 000 of which have medicinal value–originate in developing countries (Crucible Group, 1994). Nijar (1996) also points out that between 3,00,000 and 7,50,000 plant species are thought to exist in the world with much of the diversity found in tropical zones. He also indicates that today's global food supply rests essentially on the biological diversity developed from wild plants and animals, savannas and the forests of the Third World. By and large these are raw materials for the North.

BIOLOGICAL RESOURCES IN INDIA

India is one of the 12 mega diversity countries globally recognized. Its geographic position, extent–both land and sea, and the resultant varied climate and topographies have given rise to 10 biogeographic zones namely the Trans-Himalayan, Himalayan, Indian Desert, Semi-arid, Western Ghats, Deccan Peninsula (including the Eastern Ghats), Gangetic Plain, Northeast India, Coasts and Islands. Each of theses biogeographic zones is characterized by unique ecosystems and species of organisms. Around 127,000 species of micro-organisms, plants and animals have been described till date. Estimates by experts suggest that there could be another 400,000 species yet to be identified. A large number of these would be micro-organisms and invertebrates. (GOI, 1998). It shares 2.4% of land area but 8% of the global bio-diversity and is rich in floral wealth having 16,000 species of flowering plants of which 33% are endemics. About 1500 species are considered RET category in India (roughly it comes to about 10% of the floral), 10% of India flora i.e., 1600 species are restricted in distribution are present only in Western Ghats. The Western Ghats is one of the 18 "hotspots" of the world. (in India we have 2 "hotspots" namely Eastern Himalayas and Western Ghats). Western Ghats holds about 4000 flowering plants of which 1600 species are endemics. About 10% of the Western Ghats floras are considered medicinal plants.

ISSUES IN BIODIVERSITY

The United Nations Convention on Biological Diversity provides the legal framework to address this type of environmental threat and to reverse the present trend. While the Convention on Biological Diversity (CBD) was signed in December 1992 with 177 signatories to date, there are the major issues are relating to the translation of Convention on Biological Diversity (CBD) tenets into the national governance systems. As widely acknowledged since Rio, multisectoral implications need to be a part of planning and development at the local, regional and national level.

Each signatory has started working on, and some countries have already completed their National Biodiversity Strategy and Action Plans which attempt to address the main tenets of the CBD which are: (1) conservation (2) sustainable use and (3) equitable sharing of benefits arising out of Biodiversity utilisation. However the ground reality is that the concerns of the CBD have not yet been mainstreamed because biodiversity is affected by market valuation as well as by the fact that there are concerns related to its conservation, sustainable use and equitable sharing of benefits with regard to subsistence, livelihoods, development, governance and other issues. It is pertinent to mention that the 1990s has been characterized by contentious debate about how to reconcile the protection of biodiversity and intellectual property rights. The Two international treaties, (1) the Convention on Biological Diversity (CBD) and (2) the Trade Related Intellectual Property Rights (TRIPs) agreement of the World Trade Organisation (WTO) have significant implications for the nexus of Intellectual Property Rights (IPRs), biodiversity and associated knowledge systems. The CBD requires parties to safeguard biodiversity and the traditions and knowledge of those indigenous and other local communities associated with this biodiversity, and lays down the basic elements for access to biodiversity resources and associated knowledge systems. The TRIPs Agreement obliges party states to modify their national IPR regimes to meet much-enhanced international standards, which could have significant implications for biodiversity and the associated knowledge systems. In addition, the World Intellectual Property Organisation (WIPO) and other international institutions are becoming increasingly active on the subject. The singular advantage that the WTO process has for ensuring compliance arises from the fact that it can use the instrument of trade sanctions against an erring member, while the CBD has no enforcement mechanisms.

In response to the debate at the international level, there is considerable activity at the national level. Several countries (Costa Rica, Eritrea, Fiji, India, Mexico, Peru, Philippines) are developing legislation, or other measures, which respond to the above treaties or in other ways address the relationship between IPRs and biodiversity. Nations are seeking to achieve the following objectives:

- Protection of indigenous knowledge (traditional and modern) from being "pirated" and used in IPR claims by industrial/ commercial interests;
- Regulation of access to biological resources so that alleged historical "theft" of these resources by the more powerful sectors of the global society can be stopped, and communities/ countries are able to gain control and benefits from their use.

Several countries are considering a range of incentive measures to achieve the conservation of biodiversity and the sustainable use of biological resources, as mandated by Article 11 of the Convention on Biological Diversity (CBD). To some extent or the other, a number of such measures were already in place in many countries even before the CBD, but the latter has given an additional impetus, and in some cases, a new direction, to the thinking and practice of incentives. Some of these aspects have been dealt with in the CBD Secretariat's relevant papers (UNEP 1996; 1998) and in the decisions regarding this agenda item at the third and fourth Conference of Parties to the CBD (Decisions III/18 and IV/10A).

BIODIVERSITY VS. INTELLECTUAL PROPERTY RIGHTS

The CBD has two interesting provisions relating to IPRs. Article 16.5 states that Contracting Parties shall cooperate to ensure that

IPRs are "supportive of and do not run counter to the CBD's objectives." However, this is "subject to national legislation and international law." Article 22 states that the CBD's provisions will not affect rights and obligations of countries under "existing international agreements, except where the exercise of those rights and obligations would cause a serious damage or threat to biological diversity." Read together and in the spirit of the CBD, many people have concluded there is a basis for countering the seemingly inexorable march of the IPR regimes described above.

But in order for this argument to hold, the actual impacts of IPRs on biodiversity need to be examined. In this regard the following must be considered:

- Current IPR regimes have allowed industrial and commercial interests to appropriate the resources and knowledge of resource-rich but economically poor countries and communities, further impoverishing them and denying them the benefits of technological innovation;
- IPRs are likely to greatly intensify the trend of homogenization of agricultural production and medicinal plant use systems.
- Having to pay substantial royalties to industrial countries and corporations could greatly increase the debt burdens of many countries. This could further intensify the environmental and social disruption that is often caused when debt repayment measures are taken up, such as the export of natural products;
- The patenting of life forms is abhorrent to many traditional societies and modern conservationists because of the underlying assumption that nature exists apart from, and solely for the use of, humans. The privatisation of knowledge is also repugnant to many societies that hold knowledge to be largely, though by no means solely, in the public domain.

CHANGING IPR REGIMES

A combination of the relevant clauses in TRIPs and the CBD can be used as justification for modification to existing IPR regimes that can help to safeguard the public interest. Many people have argued, for instance, that apart from the usual criteria of novelty, etc. that are required of an IPR application, the following information should also be required:

- Source (country/community/person) of the material or information that has gone into the produce/process for which an IPR is claimed;
- Proof of prior informed consent from the country and community of origin (Articles 15(5) and 8(j) of the CBD);
- Details of the benefit-sharing arrangements entered into with the community of origin, wherever applicable (Article 8(j) of the CBD).

Countries like India have also suggested that all IPR applications that are related to biodiversity and biodiversity-related knowledge should be posted on the Clearing House Mechanism web site (set up under the CBD), giving concerned government, communities or individuals an opportunity to object if they feel that their rights have been violated. These suggestions have not yet been accepted at the international level, but are being incorporated into some domestic legislation.

INTELLECTUAL PROPERTY RIGHTS OVER BIOLOGICAL MATERIALS

The essential element of the TRIPS Agreements related to agriculture and food security is the requirement for WTO members to make patents available for any technological inventions, whether products or processes. One reason for greater interest in patents is the rapid development of biotechnology in agriculture. There are four options within Article 27.3(b). First, to allow patents on everything. This would include all materials and all forms of technology. Second, to exclude plants, animals, and biological processes, but not plant varieties. This means that whereas naturally found plants, animals, and the natural biological process by which they are created could be excluded from patents, crop varieties could not. The third option is to exclude plants, animals, and biological processes from patenting and to introduce a special *sui generis* for the protection of plant varieties. A *sui generis* system allows a country to create a system of its choice which would enable the minimum protection agreed to in the WTO. The final option is to exclude plants, animals, and biological processes from patenting but not plant varieties, and to provide a *sui generis* right. This would mean that plant varieties could be patented or protected by an independently created *sui generis* system (Leskien and Flitner 1997).

Most developing countries have chosen the third option. A *sui generis* system of protection is one adapted to particular subject matter; it allows countries to make their own rules for protection of new plant varieties. One possible *sui generis* system likely to be recognised is the International Union for the Protection of New Varieties of Plants (UPOV) system. This was initially developed in Europe and has now been adopted by the industrialised countries. The UPOV system has undergone several changes after its formulation in 1961, but these have resulted in almost no concessions for farmers and plant breeders in the South (Balakrishna, 2000). Article 27.3(b) of TRIPS is perhaps the most controversial clause of the entire WTO agreement (Sahai, 2001). It requires members to provide for the patenting of 'non-biological and microbiological processes', and WTO members are now in the process of defining their positions regarding the future of the provisions. There are indications that a few members, like the USA, would like the *sui generis* option to be eliminated altogether, while most developing countries are preparing national legislation to implement it. There are proposals to treat UPOV as the only *sui generis* option for plant varieties. The problem is that UPOV is not in the interests of developing countries, since it does not contain any rights for farmers. There is only the right granted to the breeder, which in today's context is increasingly 'the company'. Patents on seeds would severely restrict farmers access to them, since they would have to buy fresh seed for every sowing.

There are potential conflicts between the TRIPS patenting regime and the Convention on Biological Diversity (CBD), as well as the International Treaty on Plant Genetic Resources (ITPGR) of the FAO. These conflicts are widely seen as more political than legal in nature, and the US government has made early implementation of TRIPS a top priority of its foreign policy (Mulvany 1999). These matters are likely to emerge as matters of dispute under the WTO's dispute settlement system in the coming years.

UPOV 1991 conditions will significantly diminish the farming community's capacity to be self-sufficient in seed and self-reliant as agricultural producers (Sahai, 2002). UPOV requires plant varieties to be 'distinct' from other varieties, produce genetically 'uniform' progeny, and remain genetically 'stable' over generations. After the 1991 UPOV amendment, a new quality 'novelty'–has been added to the minimal characteristics required. The uniformity requirement has potential to contribute to genetic erosion. In addition, the cost of maintaining UPOV certification is beyond the means of most farmer/breeders. Although peasant farmers have also cultivated plant varieties expressing desirable traits over time, their varieties rarely meet the UPOV requirements. These conditions for a 'Plant Breeders Right certificate' under UPOV run contrary to the goal of enhancing genetic diversity. Furthermore, the kind of protection that it grants is an exclusive monopoly right. This contrasts sharply with the broader goals of collective remuneration and benefit sharing that are expressed in a number of other global agreements.

IMPACT OF IPRs ON BIODIVERSITY, GENDER RELATIONS, AND COMMUNITIES

Biodiversity is the basis of food and livelihood as well as human and animal health for poor and marginalized communities. To alter the dynamics of control and usage of biodiversity through IPR rules will further impoverish and marginalise local communities, and women will be disadvantaged, in terms of both their economic and decision-making roles.

The case of the Canadian farmer Percy Schmeiser and his dispute with Monsanto over an alleged violation of IPR shows the way in which IPR regimes are being implemented by corporations to establish monopolies. Monsanto sued Schmeiser for huge damages for violating its patent on 'Roundup' Ready canola, after specimens of the proprietary canola were found on Schmeiser's property. Canola is a crosspollinating crop, so the likely source of the offending canola was pollen from a nearby 'Roundup Ready' field, but the case demonstrates the extent to which multinational companies will go to establish monopolies on bio-resources. Such actions would have grave consequences in developing countries, since denying rights over vital resources would affect the communitys ability to survive.

Commercial interests that target bio-resources on a large scale for the market will threaten the bio-resource base, and the knowledge base associated with it. The impact on women, and through them families, will be immediate. There is a steady depletion of rare medicinal flora from the hill regions, because of collections being conducted by pharmaceutical companies. A sub-species of *Taxus baccata*, the Himalayan Yew tree in the Himalayan region, is facing near extinction as a consequence of over-exploitation for its cancer-curing properties. Large areas of the Kumaon and Garhwal Himalayas in India have been stripped of medicinal plants by head loaders collecting for foreign and Indian companies. This devastation of flora means that women lose the resources they need for use in home remedies to treat their families and their livestock (Sahai 1996).

Patents on seeds would limit women's ability to breed new, locally adapted varieties for food, healing, and rituals. This would strike at nutritional security for families and also at the socio-cultural identity of communities, as women have bred varieties integral to local food habits and cultural and religious practices.

When patents are permitted, there is currently no requirement for disclosing the source of the plant material, nor the key information lead for the claimed invention: that is, the indigenous knowledge of the characteristics, say of the particular medicinal plant. Bio-piracy constitutes a misappropriation of the intellectual property of local communities. In the case of the patent on turmeric, or *neem*, the knowledge of the wound-healing property or the bactericidal property of the respective plants was the basis of the invention that was granted a patent by the US Patent and Trademark Office. The consequences could be two fold. Exercise of the patent in India could lead to corporate control over wound-healing or antiseptic products derived from turmeric and neem. On the other hand, if such products had the potential for export to the USA, such an opportunity could be denied, because the existing US patent could be used to block any imports.

Whether in the field of medicinal plants or in agriculture, women will be excluded from the decision-making process. They will have less say in what will be planted in the field, because seed availability will increasingly shift to crops with a single dominant trait. Women are likely to have fewer options and less flexibility to use bioresources for multiple uses. Since participation in the cash economy to make up the loss in these sectors will either not be possible for women or will place additional burdens on them, it is also likely that the ensuing deprivations will become permanent (GTZ 2001).

IMPACT OF IPR ON BIODIVERSITY IN INDIA

Traditional and substantial dependence on the biodiversity resources for fodder, fuel wood, timber and minor forest produce has been an accepted way of life of the rural population that accounts for nearly 74% of India's population. With the radical demographic changes, the land to man ratio and forest to man ratio has rapidly declined. From about 0.20 ha. in 1951, the per capita forest area had been reduced to 0.11 ha in 1981 (Lal, 1989) with further trends of reductions in subsequent years. The lifestyles and the biomass resource needs having remained unchanged, the remnant forests have come under relentless pressures of encroachment for cultivation, and unsustainable resource extraction rendering the very resource base, unproductive and depleted of its biodiversity. Coupled with these incongruities and aberrations in landuse, the unsound development strategies have led to increasing threats to biodiversity resources by way of illegal encroachment of 0.07 million ha of forest, cultivation of 4.37 million ha and diversion of forest for river valley projects (0.52 million ha), industries and townships (0.14 million ha), transmission lines and roads (0.06 million ha) and an additional 1.5 million ha for miscellaneous purposes (TERI, 1999).

The unabated pace of development of hydraulic structures to harness hydropower driven by necessity to meet the growing requirements of water for inputs to irrigation, domestic use and industrial purposes has led to the construction of over 4000 dams in India. The creation of valley bottom reservoirs in wilderness areas has brought the destruction of some of the finest forests and biodiversity-rich unique ecosystems. The biodiversity losses due to deforestation for hydropower and mining projects are perhaps the greatest threats to biodiversity in India.

The other important factors that have contributed to staggering loss of biodiversity are pollution of rivers, destruction of mangroves and fragile mountain systems, loss of wetlands due to land reclamation, poaching and hunting. Apart from the primary loss of biodiversity due to development, there are numerous other problems contributing to the loss and endangered status of several floral and faunal species. These include habitat losses and fragmentation leading to the formation of isolated scattered populations becoming increasingly vulnerable to inbreeding depressions, high infant mortality, susceptibility to environmental stochasticity and in the long run, possible extinction. According to the Red list of Threatened Plants (IUCN, 1997), 19 species are already extinct and 1236 species are threatened. Of these, threatened 41 taxa are possibly extinct in the wild, 152 are endangered, 102 are vulnerable, 251 are rare, and 690 are indeterminate.

BIODIVERSITY STRATEGIES IN INDIA UNDER IPR ERA

Biodiversity is an umbrella term covering the variety and variability of all living organisms. It includes the variety of living organisms, the genetic difference among them, and the communities and eco – system in which they occur. Biodiversity is recognized at three levels. Species diversity, genetic diversity and eco–system diversity.

National Biodiversity Strategy and Action Plan (NBSAP) Project

Currently the process of preparing a National Biodiversity Strategy and Action Plan is going on in the country. One of the major strategies of this project is to link the biodiversity conservation with the on going other related processes and projects. JFM is a major on going project in the country and as such as biodiversity conservation strategies has to be linked with the JFM projects.

The Approaches Statement of the NBSAP Project

Biological diversity is the central tenet of nature, one of its key defining features. Evolution has produced an amazing variety of plants, animals, and micro-organisms, intricately inter-connected, and worthy of respect and conservation in their own right. Biodiversity is also the basis for the continuous evolution of species. This diversity is also the backbone of human societies and cultures, in terms of the ecological functions it provides, and the myriad survival and livelihood needs it meets. A national biodiversity action plan should therefore be able to protect these critical characteristics and functions. It is proposed that the National Biodiversity Strategy and Action Plan(NBSAP) will take the following as its basic tenets:

Scope of Coverage

The term 'biodiversity' is being taken in its holistic sense to encompass all levels of biodiversity, ecological and evolutionary processes, including:

Natural ecosystems: e.g. forests, grasslands, wetlands, deserts, mountains, coastal and marine areas, including the historical changes taking place in such ecosystems.

'Wild' species and varieties: species of plants, animals, and micro-organisms existing in their natural state, and the genetic variation within each of these species.

Agricultural Ecosystems: e.g. farmlands, pastures, capture fisheries, aquaculture, including historical changes in land-use patterns.

Domesticated species and varieties: species of crops, livestock (including poultry), captive-bred fish, and micro-organisms in ex-situ collections, and the genetic variation within each of these species.

Aspects of Coverage

Biodiversity has several aspects that need to be looked at. It is proposed that the NBSAP will cover the following:

Conservation of biodiversity at ecosystemic, species, and genetic levels (through) in–situ, ex-situ, in vitro, and other measures), and of the associated ecological functions, with a special focus on endemic, threatened, and otherwise critical elements;

Sustainable use of biological resources, implying their use in such a manner as will not imperil their long-term existence, or will not in other ways threaten biodiversity;

Social, economic, political and inter-generational equity, including in decision-making with regard to conservation and use, in sharing of benefits, in access to and protection of knowledge and information relevant to biodiversity, and soon.

Ethical, cultural, scientific, and economic dimensions, including:

(i) the right of species and ecosystems to survive;

(ii) the primacy of survival and livelihood based on biodiversity, and of creating a stake for people in conservation and sustainable use;

(iii) various cultural ways of relating to nature; and

(iv) the role of biodiversity in economics and technology.

Micro level strategies and action plans

The national strategy also involves preparation of micro level strategies and action plans for biodiversity conservation. Already micro plans are prepared for the JFM implementation. Local Biodiversity Conservation should form a part of the JFM micro plans.

CONCLUSION

Since biodiversity is the basis of food and livelihood as well as human and animal health for poor and marginalized communities, IPR rules should not be allowed to further impoverish and marginalized local communities. In this regard what should be done is all IPR applications that are related to biodiversity and biodiversity–related knowledge should be posted on the clearing house mechanism website (set up under CBD) so that concerned government, communities or individuals can have the opportunity to object if they feel that their rights have been violated.

REFERENCES

Ashish Kothari, & R.V. Anuradha (1999), "Biodiversity and Intellectual Property Rights: Can the Two Co-Exist?" Cites as: 2(2) Journal of Int'l Wildlife L & Pol'y (1999).

Suman Sahai (2004), " TRIPS and Biodiversity: A Gender Perspectives", Gender and Development, Vol. 12, No. 2, July.

Manvel Ruiz (2003), " Intellectual Property Rights and Biodiversity: Process and Synergies", Workshop on TRIPS and CBD Global Biodiversity Forum, Cancun, Mexico, September 5-7.

Annamalai.R. (2000), "Joint Forest Management concepts, policies, and guidelines" Tamil Nadu Forest Department, Government of Tamil Nadu, Chennai.

Biodiversity Support Foundation (1993), "African Biodiversity: Foundation for the Future. A Framework for Integrating Biodiversity Conservation and Sustainable Development".

Gupta, A.K. (undated). "Compensating Local Communities for Conserving Biodiversity: How Much, Who Will, How and When". 20 pp.

Morris Mudiwa (1999), "Global Commons: The Case of Indigenous Knowledge, Intellectual Property Rights and Biodiversity".

Nijar G.S. (1996a) In Defence of Community Knowledge and Biodiversity. A Conceptual Framework And The Essential Elements of a Rights Regime. Third World Network. Penang.

Nijar G.S. (1996b), TRIPs and Biodiversity. The Threat and Responses: A Third World View. Third World Network. Penang.

G/Egziabher T.B. (2000), Intellectual Property Rights in Biological Diversity and Trade Agreements. The Institute for Sustainable Development, Addis Ababa.

Crucible Group (1994), People, Plants and Patents: The Impact of Intellectual Property on Biodiversity, Conservation, Trade and Rural Society. Ottawa, on, IDRC. 1994. xxii + 118p. : ill.

Kothari, A., P. Pandey., S. Singh and D. Variava (1989), Management of National Park and Sanctuaries in India: Status Report. Indian Institute of Public Administration, New Delhi.

Lal, J.B. (1989), India's Forests, Myth and Reality. Natraj Publishers, Dehradun, India.

TERI (1999), TERI Energy Data Directory & Yearbook 1999/2000. Tata Energy Research Institute, New Delhi.

IUCN, (1997), Red List of Threatened Plants. IUCN. Gland, Switzerland.

Vinod Mathur and Asha Rajvanshi, (2001), "The Integration of Biodiversity into National Environmental Assessment Procedures" National Case Studies, India, September, Produced for the Biodiversity Planning Support Programme UNDP/UNEP/GEF.

Sahai, S. (1996), How do we Protect our Genetic Resources?. Economic and Political Weekly, New Delhi.

Gene Campaign and CEAD (1998), Convention of Farmers and Breeders (CoFaB), A Draft Treaty Presented as an Alternative to UPOV, New Delhi.

GTZ (Deutsche Gesellschaft für Technische Zusammenarbeit GmbH) (2001) Gender Relations and Biodiversity., Issue Papers BIODIV, www.gtz.de/biodiv.

20

INTELLECTUAL PROPERTY RIGHTS AND COOPERATIVES

Samwel Kakuko Lopoyetum

INTRODUCTION

Cooperative sector plays a significant role in uplifting the socio-economic status of the weaker sections (strata) of most of the developing Economies such as India and Kenya. In India, there is huge diversities of a sub-continent which has thousand of cooperative organizations covering large geo-economic and geo-political ramification of the country. The weaker section of the economy can utilize natural resources which are available in their own regions by forming cooperative organizations such as multi-purposes cooperative societies. They can become members of these cooperative organizations whose rights are to procure natural resources like minor forest produce (MFP), plantation, land, irrigation, fisheries, natural forest, salt production, herbal medicines, and protection of environment, water resources management etc. The performance of these Cooperative Organizations would require through revamping, rejuvenation, rehabilitation, re-engineering and making them to become more productive, profitable and sustainable in the 21st Century. Cooperativisation is the best method to protect the natural resources, environment, IPR and transmit the property rights to the members and the community. This is contrary to nationalization, privatization, quasi-government, and corporatisation of natural resources. Cooperativisation would give direct benefits through equal sharing strategies and improvement of the entire socio-economic conditions of the members and weaker sections of the society. It involves open and voluntary local people participation in the management and administration of the natural resources and environment. The natural resources management cooperative organizations are facing numerous difficulties as stated in this paper. There are innumerable problems and barriers hampering the growth of natural resources management by cooperative organizations. Suitable suggestions and strategies for enhancing effectiveness and efficiency of cooperative organizations in natural resources management and administration are highlighted in the paper.

In the wake of WTO regime with their rules and regulations and accompanied by LPG's, it is highly essential to transfer management of natural resources, Common Property Rights (CPR), etc to cooperative sector/organizations. This can lead to cooperativization of Natural Resources and Environment Even the patent rights, Intellectual Property Rights (IPR) can be transferred to cooperative organizations/institutions for the overall protection of natural resources and bio-diversity. Many developing countries such as **India** and **Kenya** are bio-technologically backward and highly rich in bio-diversity and natural resources. Therefore, co-operativisation of natural resources are highly imperative in the 21st century. Exploration and Exploitation of natural resources cum bio-diversity can be left to cooperative organizations because they are the only institutions, which are mainly concerned socio-economic growth and welfare of the for the community as stipulated in the **Cooperative Principles (No. 7), which is being emphasized as "the concern for the community"**. It is pertinent for the community through cooperative approach to protect the natural resources, Environment, and common property through cooperative approach to protect the natural resources and common property by organizing viable and profitable cooperative ventures, Infact, side-by-side they can undertake fullfledged research and development programmes that can be undertaken by cooperative sector to evolve suitable methods of utilization and exploitation of natural resources in the long-run. There is extremely very huge relevance of designing and implementing successful cooperative organizations for managing common property resources (CPR's) and natural resources which are very indispensable in the 21st century and New Millennium, to protect and even add-value to the natural resources and carryout all IPR Educational Programmes. Cooperative organizations can acquire appropriate technology from within and outside India to effectively and efficiently manage the natural resources and bio-diversity and enhance IPR Education in the New Millennium.

Subsequently, the Higher level cooperative organizations such as the role of Indian Fertilizers Farmers Cooperative Ltd (IFFCO's) involvement in agriculture and rural development for the last two decades prompted to launch a pilot project in pursuance of the national policy on farm forestry in 1986-87. The objective was to provide fuel and fodder to the village community, farmers and farmwomen. The project was also emphasizing on the social and economic aspects of the forest management by empowering farmers. The farmers are motivated to form the village level primary farm forestry cooperative societies. The society takes up the activities as a nodal agency for securing various funds. The IFFCO provides necessary technology, guidance and training facilities to the members and cooperative personnel to make the society a viable unit. Participatory Rural Appraisal programmes can be organized and participatory planning, monitoring and evaluation can be undertaken by the cooperative organizations to improve the Efficiency and Effectiveness of the Natural Resource Management Cooperative Organizations.

The sustainable exploitation and utilization of natural resources can be undertaken at higher level of cooperative organizations and involvement of almost all members of the Natural Resources Cooperative societies. The use of land and environment and the deforestation activities for constructing buildings and houses is extremely high in this century, therefore, proper mobilization of available human resources in the best available methods and the use of scientific system to safeguard the highly depleted natural resources which mainly lies in the top corner of today's environmental management concerned activities. The Cooperativisation of natural resources and IPR Education is the only solution to these problems. The role of cooperative organizations in this regard is highly solicited. These cooperative institutions and organizations might take steps to restore the powers of natural resources and encourage (motivate), activate appropriate technological oriented approach in their utilization and exploitation of Natural Resources and provide IPR Education and Patent Right.

Secondly, the menace of ever growing population has attracted the attention of many cooperative organizations/institutions and the society/communities are encouraged to go in for the framing of very practical approaches to control the population in relationship to the available natural resources. Population studies in the form of research and developmental activities would be very paramount in the 21st century through cooperative approach. The mushroom growth of industries (small, medium, large) and various chemical factories are providing a tougher challenge to many environmental oriented organizations. Moreover, the Activities such as deforestation, exploitation of water resources and pollution of land, water (land, water, ocean) and air will boost the unsolicited and dangerous consequences in the delicate environment in this particular century. We all are aware of the fact that, the enormous growth of population is the very major negative contributor for the ill health of the environment and natural resources; therefore the only remedy would be Cooperativisation of the natural resources management (POSTCORB) and providing Cooperative Education and Extension Services to the community. Various NGOs, self-help groups can combine their efforts and strength with the cooperative organizations in solving the natural resources problems, IPR problems, patent rights, and help to mobilize human resources through Effective and Efficient training and development and initiate other allied activities to achieve the main goal and mission of sustainability of development in the 21st century and New Millennium.

So far, the cooperative institutions are doing well in almost all the states and exceptionally well in the field of Banking and Agricultural lending activities, but none of the cooperatives has excellent dent in the field of proper and sustainable management and administration of natural resources and IPR Education. Even all other trades, business and commercial activities are becoming profitable day by day. Why not the IPR Education and Patent Rights Education? Again, they are not oriented towards proper management and administration of the natural resources, protection of Environment, Bio-diversity, and Patent Rights Education. They are concerned with exploitation and unsustainable utilization of Natural Resources. These Cooperative institutions can obtain patent rights, copyrights, and IPR for their contributions in protecting the natural resources, environment, forestry, water management etc. By way of implanting the need for safeguarding the natural resources into the minds of common people,members, changing the exploitative nature of entrepreneurs and private organizations in their trading activities. Therefore, all the bad practices will diminish in the near future if cooperative organizations are made more active and profitable in the future. Through cooperative principles, cooperative practices, cooperative approach and cooperative ideology, Cooperative Education and Extension Services, Training accompanied by many collaborative activities and integrative approaches can be undertaken with the regional, local, National, International NGOs, governmental agencies and common participation of people to install effective and efficient management and administration of natural resources and bio-diversity in the 21st century.

India is blessed with abundant natural resources and bio-diversity, in fact from Himachal Pradesh in the north to Kerala in the south and from Nagaland in the east to Gujarat in the west, there is a wide variety of agro-climatic and geo-economic conditions which have ensured availability of equally wide range of natural resources and varieties of products are produced by the tribal population (tribals constitutes 8% of the country's population). The tribal are the natural guardians of the natural ecological heritage, therefore, their multi-dimensional development and socio-economic up-liftment of tribal would depend on the sustainability of the development of natural resources and bio-diversity. The market forces are exploiting the tribal products; they must be protected, modernized and sustained to ensure multi-dimensional transformation of tribal communities. This is only possible through cooperativization of the Tribal affairs and products. The formation of the Tribal Cooperative Marketing Development Federation of India (TRIFED) to provide assured market, remunerative prices for tribal produce, provide price support operations, provide marketing and financial supports to forest organizations engaged in collection and marketing of tribal produce, quality up-gradation of tribal products, export of tribal products, provide scientific exploitation of the forest products, storage, transportation, and maximization of unit realization of produce. The TRIFED is an apex level federation of state tribal development cooperative federation and state forest corporations, which have provided and ensured higher earnings and large employment opportunities for the tribal community. It is making a break through in the procurement and marketing of rare medicinal products and herbs. This particular products must be given IPR and Patent Rights. The Tribal Cooperative Societies must be given the rights to own the IPR of these Medicinal Products and Medicinal Plants. The medicinal herbs find use as tonics, digestive cures etc. Some of the medicinal herbs are Terminalia Chebula, Asparagus adscendens, cassia tora, Emblica officinalis, Rauwolfia serpentina, Amla, bahera, Aswagandha Bibibing, Chirayata, Giloy, Harar, Kalmengh Nirmali, Salam Panja etc. All these types of medicinal herbs and plants must be protected and the patent right, IPR, copyright and ownership must be given to the tribal community through cooperative organizations.

Even in the neighbouring, Sirumalai Hills-a discontinuous of shoot of the eastern ghats near Gandhigram University do have very rich vegetation and bio-diversity which are very distinct. The natural resources and bio-diversity and vegetation includes many valuable medicinal plants, which are used by the tribal and villagers as folklo medicine for diabetics. Even today, Diabetics has no real treatment but can be managed with reasonable results by using medicinal plants like Gymnema Silvestre and Geleganus of the family clepiadecea. Plants like Curculigo Orchioides is being administered for asthma, adhatoda vasica for bronchitic, Catharanthus roseus for leucamia, withania somnifera for cancer, gloriosa superba for leprosy and phyllathus emblica for giving relief to AIDS. Thus, the cooperative institutions/organizations can take advantage of natural and floral resources and move towards forming viable cooperative institutions and even initiating research departments to make additional research in Ayurvedha or indigenous system of medicine in the neighbouring region and obtain all the copy rights, IPR, Patent Rights for the best benefits of the members and community.

The New Generation Cooperatives (NGCs)must undertake people-friendly ventures, eco-friendly ventures and enterprises which can be organized, put into practice and mandatory geared to obtain copyrights and IPR in the long-run and even face the competitiveness created by New Economic Environment. Thus, the role of cooperative institutions/organizations will be imperative and significant in obtaining copyrights and IPR Education and management of Natural Resources. By providing Patent Right and IPR Educational Services to the Community in the whole of the 21st century shall be the mission and vision of cooperative movement.

21

NEED FOR MANAGEMENT OF INTELLECTUAL PROPERTY RIGHTS IN AGRICULTURAL SECTOR

S. Nehru & K. Raja Mohan Rao

INTRODUCTION

Intellectual property rights are of major economic importance. They are the basis of reward for invention, can act as a spur to innovation, provide a mechanism for technology and commercial transfer, and play a key role in the protection of commercial goodwill. Intellectual property law in essence provides a deterrent against copying or taking unfair advantage of others' work and also remedies should it happen. It is important in artistic areas (e.g. music, painting, literature) as well as in the industrial and service sectors.

There are several forms of rights and several areas of law which provide rights, which, together, are known as intellectual property rights. The main ones are:

Patents }	A requirement for registration —
Trade marks }	Registration function
Registered Designs }	Policy responsibility with Patents Office
Copy rights }	No requirement for
Rights in Performances }	Registration—policy
Design Right }	Responsibility with Patents Office

Other laws, in particular, those on breach of confidence, trade descriptions, theft, forgery and deception, may also be relevant to the protection of intellectual property rights, depending on the circumstances.

Companies will usually need to use a combination of different rights to protect a given product or process from the first idea to the end of its marketed life.

By the mid 1900s, some industrialized countries began to offer limited forms of plant variety protection (PVP) to breeders of new crop varieties. PVP was constructed as an "alternative" to patenting that would supposedly be attuned to the needs of agriculture. It guaranteed breeders a commercial monopoly on the use of their varieties while leaving loopholes which have now been plugged up drastically and the industry is pressuring governments to provide full scale patent rights against any form of tinkering with the very stuff of life. Today, with the breeding sector dominated by a few mega corporations, patents on plants and livestock, and draconian restrictions on farmers are the norm in most industrialized nations. Asia has followed a different path: but it appears increasingly likely that it will meet the same end.

THE GREEN REVOLUTION: LAYING THE BASIS FOR PRIVATISATION

In Asia, the foundation for the emergence of IPRs on life was laid by the Green Revolution of the 1960s and 1970s, when a package of credit, chemicals and most importantly, high-input responsive semi-dwarf varieties of staple crops such as rice and wheat were introduced in the region's farms. The Green Revolution spread rapidly and far. By the early 1990s, just five of these 'super varieties' accounted for 90 per cent of the rice grown area of both peninsular Malaysia and Pakistan, nearly half the rice lands of Thailand and Burma, and around a quarter of the rice area of China and Indonesia. These were the heartlands of tremendous genetic diversity of rice only a few decades ago. The "Super" wheat variety called sonalika has taken over half the wheat growing area in northern India and 70 per cent in Bangladesh and Nepal. Other crops followed a similar trend. Green Revolution varieties now dominate most of India's most important crops, accounting for 65 per cent of the rice area, 94 per cent of wheat, 64 per cent of spiked millet, 61 per cent of great millet, 52 per cent of maize, and 46 per cent of finger millet. The Green Revolution engineered the framework for the private sector's entry into Asia's agricultural sector. First, it established dependency on external seeds— the basis for a private seed market. As Green Revolution seeds stormed through the rural areas, Asia lost much of its abundant crop diversity. In the Indian state of Andhra Pradesh, one study found that the incursion of the Green Revolution had led to a loss of 95 per cent of traditional rice varieties without documentation. Centuries of farmer innovation were abandoned as the Green Revolution institutions–the International Agricultural Research Centres of the Consultative Group on International Agricultural Research (CGIAR), plus their national counterparts–entrenched themselves as the new "leaders" of agricultural progress. And even as the early gains of the Green Revolution did not last, most farmers, with limited access to pre-Green Revolution seeds or knowledge, remain dependent today on the off-farm breeding programs of the CG and national scientists, not without problems. In the words of one CG scientist, Tom Mew, from the International Rice Research Institute (IRRI) in the Philippines, the new varieties spawned by the Green Revolution lead to "sharp increases in the use of fertilizers and pesticides (that are) needed to ensure bumper harvests", which means that farmers planting them need cash or, more accurately, credit. With the Green Revolution, western capitalism came deep into the countryside, the traditional diversity was replaced by large scale cash crop farming, supported by a system of banks, pesticide merchants, middlemen and millers. The seed industry has taken a little longer, but it is now stepping in for its piece of the pay-off.

From the Green Revolution, the creation of a private seed industry was an easy step. Still, in the eyes of most corporations, the Asian seed market is vastly under-penetrated. Asia consumes one third of the world's agricultural seeds, nearly 40 million tonnes a year. But it accounts for less than a quarter of the $32 billion annual commercial seed market, with the bulk of sales currently concentrated in Japan and China. By and large, Asia's seed supply still remains the domain of farmers and the public sector. Farmers in India are responsible for at least 60 per cent of the annual seed supply, while farmers in the Philippines produce 80 per cent. But this situation is fast changing.

> "Seed companies have a 20 year timeline for rice.
> By then, the rice seed market
> Will look like the corn seed market today".

Sam Dryden, Emergent Genetics, 2000
(Personal Communication, October, 20)

The private sector stepped into Asia's seed supply in the 1980s when the World Bank and US supported seed programs and hybridization of new crops converged. F1 hybrids give high yields but they lose this advantage the following generation, so that farmers have to buy new seed regularly. Hybrids now exist for maize, rice, pigeonpea, millets, sorghum, oilseeds, rape seeds, sunflower and many vegetable crops. Markets for hybrid seed are starting to swell in many countries as in the Philippines, where the area of yellow corn planted of hybrid varieties surged from 10 per cent in 1991 to over 60 per cent in 1997.

Ultimately, the TRIPS Agreement has no appropriate solutions to offer in response to the demand that indigenous and local communities be granted protection rights for the agricultural varieties developed by them (farmer's rights). Many developing countries fear that the enforcement of intellectual property rights, most of which are held by multinationals, will hamper domestic development of agricultural bio technology. They fear that their own research efforts could be hampered or wrecked by the limitations placed on their freedom to choose certain technologies protected by patents. Patents held by multinational companies would only be released at monopoly prices, which would cause serious earnings problems for indigenous producers. Moreover, there would be an incentive for patent holders to export their products rather than to produce in developing countries and possibly lose control over the transfer of technology.

The companies argue that the protection of intellectual property rights creates the very incentives necessary to investment in research and that it is not possible to build monopoly positions when product innovation is so dynamic. Industrial scientific research sees a danger of monopolies arising only if complementary policies, such as competition policy and industrial policy, encourage monopolies by protecting established companies from competition. That, so they argue, applies also to the link between intellectual property rights and a country's ability to attract direct investment. The protection of these rights could be an important incentive to private capital flows. Under these circumstances, based on the ground realities of the Indian economy, the following steps are to be taken.

- There must be distinction between domestic use and trade-related uses of property rights.
- Broad non-specific patents should not be granted.
- We should concentrate on applying, developing and protecting technique in the domestic industry, instead of importing techniques.
- We should modernize our patents offices.
- State-supported research, both international and national, should form a strong counterweight to purely private-support-oriented research.
- Creation of seed banks
- Maintenance of Location specific Germplasm
- Awareness creation regarding bio-diversity conservation
- Promotion of collective organic farming.

CONCLUSION

From the economic point of view, the advantage to developing countries of introducing intellectual property protection in the agricultural sector in very clear. The associated incentives to technological innovation can make locations in developing countries more attractive to foreign investors, reduce the cost of agricultural inputs, improve the domestic food base, raise the competitiveness of domestic production and strengthen research capacities in advanced developing countries. These countries could then advance to become competitive net exporters of agricultural inputs as well as end products. In this regard India has already succeeded.

RERFERENCES

Pardey. G.P. and Wright D.B. (August 2001), "Intellectual property Rights and Agricultural R & D".

Basant R. (1998), "Intellectual Property Rights: A Note", II MA, MMCO.

Khoury S. (1998), "Valuing Intellectual Properties", in P.H. Sullivan (1998), profiting from intellectual capital: Extracting value from innovation, John Wiley and Sons, 335-356.

Sullivan S.P. (1996), "The importance of contex in the Derivation of Royalty Rates" in R.L. Par & P.H. Sullivan (1996), Technology Licensing, Corporate Strategies for maximizing value, John Wiley & Sons, 177-186.

Gupta A.K. (2002), "Strategies of NIF, and GIAN in Technological and Entrepreneurial Networking", IIMA.C.

Fox S.P. (1998), "Intellectual Property Management", in P.H. Sullivan (1998), Profiting from intellectual capital: Extracting value from innovation, John Wiley & Sons, 142-156.

Gupta A.K. (1998), "Strategic opportunities in Managing IPRS: Biodiversity, Drug Industry and Emerging Options", IIMA Working Paper No. 98-12-11.

Gupta A.K. (2002), "Framework For rewarding Indigenous knowledge in Developing Countries: Value Chain for Grass Roots Innovations.

Gupta A.K. (2002), "Competitive Strategy for Agricultural Export Through Value Addition: The Intellectual Property Rights Perspectives.

John H. Barton, (1999), "Intellectual Property Management".

Websites

www.grain.org/publications/asiaipr-en.cfm.

www.bestr.org/library/index2.html#pr.

22

IMPACT OF TRIPS ON INDIAN AGRICULTURE IN WTO REGIME

M. Mohsin Khan

By the end of 1950s most of the colonies which had underdeveloped considerably under the colonial rule became independent and launched massive programmes of industrialization. Within three or four decades these developing nation not only became self-sufficient in many respects but also emerged as net exporters of a large number of items. Import-substitution and export-promotion programmes adopted by these nations, particularly during the 'Seventies: helped them a lot'. It adversely affected the interests of the developed nation. Developed nations witnessed the worst recession of the twentieth Century. While the rate of growth in developed countries came to a standstill, in developing countries it ranged between 3-8 per cent per annum. Under the circumstances, the developed nations were left with no choice but to pressurize the Third World countries to open up their markets through liberalization, privatization and globalisation. Not being satisfied with GATT type rules which were applied on a provisional basis and that too only to trade in merchandise. They set up World Trade Organization (WTO) with permanent secretariat which will ultimately replace the GATT. The agreements which constitute WTO are almost all multilateral and involve commitments for the entire membership.

The multilateral trade negotiation at Uruguay covered broadly 15 areas which were subsequently regrouped into seven areas including Agriculture and Trade Related Intellectual Property Rights (TRIPs). While the agricultural trade liberalization was justified by the argument that Northern agricultural markets would open upto developing nations, only the reverse has happened. This is because of the fact that high levels of subsidies and protectionist barriers are still largely maintained in the North. More than six years of experience with WTO regime has shown that agricultural trade liberalization has become, in effect a unidirectional phenomenon that opens markets in the South for Northern business corporation but closes markets in the North for trade from the South.

TRIPs also favours the developed nations and goes against the interests of the developing nation. As per TRIPs Agreement, living resources can now be patented and 'owned' as private property. The age-old right of the farmers to save and share seeds has been done away with. Now it has been redefined from a right to a criminal offence of stealing property. More ever, the 'Terminator Technology', used by Monsanto or any other seed corporation makes seeds sterile after one crop. Thus, the farmers will be forced to buy seeds from these corporations every year which majority of Indian farmers cannot afford. The need of the hour is to remove food and agriculture from the free trade WTO regime. Or, the developing nation must have the option of imposing QRs in case they visualize a threat to their food and agriculture systems. They must present themselves as a united front as they did at Singapore in 1996 and at Seattle in 1999 if they really want to safeguard their interests.

By the end of *1950's* most of the colonies-which had underdeveloped considerably under the colonial rule became independent. After attaining independence these countries are launched massive programmes of rapid industrialization. Within three or four decades these countries, including the two biggest Asian countries (India and China) made, tremendous progress. They not only became self-sufficient in many respects but became net exporters of a large number of items so much so that by the end of *1980's* economic conditions became quite favourable for the developing and unfavourable for the developed nations. The OECD countries (including the G-7 nations)-witnessed worst economic recession of the 20th century. While the rate of growth in the developed world came to standstill, in developing countries it ranged between 3-8 per cent per annum. Thirty per cent of the youth is Spain, twenty per cent in France, Italy, Finland, Ireland etc. became unemployed-while the total number of unemployed in developed countries of the world amounted to 3.6 crores. The starting of Neo-Nazism movement in Germany in the beginning of the 'Nineties' and ethnic riots of Los Angeles in 1992 were the outcome of widespread recession and unemployment in these countries.

In Europe as a whole, car production went down by 18-20 per cent. In Italy in 1992, the Fiat Car company reduced its production of cars by 5 lakhs in comparison to 1989 and suffered a loss of 36 crore dollars. European production units of Ford Motor Company suffered a loss of 128 crore dollars. American computer giant IBM suffered a loss of 280 crore dollars in 1991, 690 crore dollars in 1992 and 800 crore dollars in the second quarter of 1993. Eastman Kodak Company, the World's largest photographic company, by the end of 1991, retrenched 15,000 of its -workers, further in January 1992, the company announced another scheme of retrenchment of ten thousand workers. Procter and Gamble, a U.S. Multinational Company had to close thirty out of its 147 production units and retrenched 13,000 workers. In the second quarter of 1993, the company suffered a loss of 122 crore dollars. Not only this, the company also had to reduce prices of its products by 15 per cent because of the severe recession. Similarly, Dale Computer Corporation, Digital Equipment, etc., also suffered heavy losses and reduced prices of their computers by 12 per cent.

One of the main reasons for the above state of affairs is the fact that the developing nations, over the years, set up almost all types of industries and provided them protection through a number of tariff and non-tariff measures. This was undoubtedly to the detriment of all developed countries. These countries were left with no choice but to pressurize the developing countries to 'open up their markets through liberalization, privatization and globalisation'. The pressure came through the IMF and the World Bank whenever the developing nations approached them for financial assistance. The Uruguay Round of Multilateral Trade Negotiations of GATT, which lasted for eight years also gave serious thought to the aforementioned state of affairs. The most important outcome of these negotiations is the birth of the World Trade Organization, which, in effect, is the substitute of GATT.

Before the World War Second many countries, in order to protect their industries, had imposed restrictions on international trade which considerably reduced its volume and left adverse effects on all the countries. For removing these artificial restrictions on international trade, the General Agreement on Tariffs and Trade (GATT) was born in 1947. Ever since the GATT was set up eight rounds of negotiations have been held on trade matters at Havana (1947), in France (1949), in Britain (1950-51) in Geneva (1955-56, 1960-62 and 1964-67) in Tokyo (1973-79) and Uruguay (1986-93).

The eighth round (Uruguay Round) covered a period of eight years. It was here that the Dunkel Draft came into being. When the Uruguay Round of negotiations was on, some member nations sought to include new items like agricultural products. Textiles & Clothing, Services etc. on the agenda. This initially led to some confusion; there also being disagreement on other new items like Intellectual Property Rights which included the controversial issues of patents. Arthur Dunkel, the Director General of the GATT, presented a package of proposals as a compromise formula which was later on signed by all member nations on December 15,1993. The Ministers of Member Nations accorded further political backing to the Dunkel Draft by approving it at Marakkesh on April 15, 1994. The meeting at Marakkesh also affirmed that the results of the Uruguay Round would strengthen the world, economy and lead to more trade investment, employment and income growth throughout the world. The World Trade Organization (WTO) is the embodiment of the Uruguay Round results and successor to the GATT.

World Trade Organization: The WTO is not a simple extension of GATT. It completely replaces it and has quite different character. While GATT was applied on a provisional basis, WTO commitments are full and permanent. Secondly, GATT rules are applied to trade in merchandise goods whereas WTO covers a number of trade–related issues. Though originally a multilateral instrument, by 1980, the GATT had become quite selective through various new plurilateral agreements. The agreements, which constitute the WTO, are almost all multilateral and involve commitments for the entire membership. Finally, WTO is a permanent institution with its own Secretariat and its dispute settlement system is faster and more automatic and less susceptible to blockages.

The multilateral trade negotiations at Uruguay covered broadly 15 areas which were subsequently regrouped into the following seven areas: (a) Agriculture (b) Market Access (c) Textiles & Clothing (d) Trade-Related Intellectual Property Rights (e) Export Subsidy & Tariffication (f) investment Measures & institutional Matters and (g) Trade in Services.

Agribusiness Giants: Allover the world Structural Adjustment Programmes of the IMF and the World Bank, which include trade liberalization also, have already shattered the economies of many developing nations because of the rising costs of production and collapsing prices of commodities. The Multinational Corporations of the Industrialized World for quite sometime have started to play the role of 'State Monopolies'. The 'Agribusiness Giants', in their efforts to gain control over the world's agricultural economy, tiave played a crucial role in the process of globalisation of agriculture. Right from selling seeds and other agricultural inputs, to trading commodities and to processing of food, they want to exercise complete control over the world's agriculture*.

During the last decade, there has been a merger of chemical, pharmaceutical, biotechnology and seed companies to create 'Life Science Corporations'. Monsanto is the -World's largest biotechnology corporation. It has acquired seed companies like Dekalb, Agracetus, Asgrow, Calgene, Holden, Delta, Pine Land, Mahyco, Rallis and Seed Division of Cargill. Similarly, U.S. based Cargill, already the -world's largest grain trader, has merged–with the–world's second largest grain trading corporation–Continental Grain. Cargill also processes and distributes agricultural, food, financial and industrial products and has approximately 80,600 employees in more than 1,000 locations in 65 countries and business activities in 130 more. It controls over 70 per cent of the world's trade in cereals.

In India also Cargill's presence is extensive. In 1998, it became the biggest exporter of protein meals from India–having exported 3,00,000 tons of such meals. It also exported 10,000 tons of non-basmati rice. In 1999, it procured 10,000 tons of–wheat. It has entered into an agreement–with the Punjab Government to procure-wheat and rice, develop grain handling and storage facilities and carry out contract farming of-wheat. It already has its own pier in Jamnagar.

W.T.O. Agreement on Agriculture: As mentioned above, the MNCs, over the years have become so powerful that the governments of the industrialized countries have to work in accordance with the wishes of these business giants. It has been rightly remarked that the aims of the industrialized nations have not changed and that the major trading powers are changing tactics to pursue their objective of capturing the economic (and trade) space and markets of developing countries for their corporations. Even the policies of the World Bank and the IMF are influenced, to a great extent, by the business interests of the MNCs. In fact, at the Uruguay Round of GATT the interests of the Agribusiness Giants were pushed by the U.S. Delegation led by Clay ton Yeuter, a former Cargill employee. The Agreement on Agriculture of the WTO is the rule based system for trade liberalization in agriculture. But these rules go against the food security, biodiversity and culture of the developing nations. India has started facing a host of, internal and external threats** including the 'unequal trade bargain inherent in the WTO agreement of 1994'.

The structure of WTO is supposed to be like UN General Assembly—one member one vite–with no Veto Powers–but in more than six years of its operation there has not been-a single vote taken. Instead, decisions are taken by so-called 'concensus' wherein small and less powerful nations are browbeaten into accepting the decisions taken by the powerful countries which continue to ignore the trading rules when convenient. The Seattle Round of WTO which aimed at further liberalization of trade in food and agriculture totally excluded from the negotiations the countries of Africa and the Caribbean. Similarly the Dispute Settlement Body (DSB) of the WTO deliberates in private even though its judgements are binding on disputing countries.

The WTO regime ensures corporate control over the food and agriculture systems. For instance, Agreement on Agriculture (AoA) rules apply to countries even though it is not countries or their farmers that engage in global trade in agriculture but global agribusiness giants like Cargill and Monsanto. And they gain from every rule that marginalizes farmers by removing support from agriculture or any rule that deregulates international trade, liberalizes exports and imports or renders restrictions on exports and imports illegal. The following three are components of Agreement on Agriculture:

(a) *Market Access,* that is, the disciplines on import restraints and tariffs.

(b) *Domestic Support,* that is, subsidies by governments to domestic producers.

(c) *Export Subsidies.*

(a) Market Access: The WTO agreement on the import of food is entitled 'Market Access' and is covered by part III, Articles 4 & 5 and Annexure -3. All signatory countries must convert quantitative restrictions and other non-tariff measures into ordinary customs duties. This is known as 'tariffication'. In other words, non-tariff barriers such as quantitative restrictions (quota, import restrictions through permits, import licensing etc.) are to be replaced by tariff to provide the same level of protection and the progressive reduction of the tariff levels is to be made. The member countries have to' provide minimum market access, beginning with one per cent of the domestic consumption in the first year of the implementation period, to be increased, in equal annual installments, to two per cent at the beginning of the fifth year. After that, it has to be increased to four per cent. 'Market access opportunities are defined as 'imports as a percentage of the corresponding domestic consumption'.

The reduction commitments on import tariffs for all agricultural products (on an average) is 36 per cent for Developed Countries (1995-2000), 24 per cent for Developing Countries (1995-2004) and minimum cut per product line is 15 per cent for the former and 10 per cent for the latter, Customs and other duties-will be calculated on the basis of the difference between the import price and the 'trigger price' (the average of 1986 to 1988 prices) and shall not exceed one-third of that level. Thus, removal of quantitative restrictions on imports of agricultural commodities is a major goal of trade liberalization in agriculture. India had quantitative restrictions on import of 825 agricultural products as on April 1, 1997 -which it had been justifying on balance of payment considerations. These quantitative restrictions have now been completely phased out (April, 2001).

The tariff levels have been bound by India for primary agricultural products, processed agricultural products and edible oils-with a few exceptions, at 100%, 150% and 300% respectively for end period of the Agreement. Within these Bound tariff levels, there is considerable flexibility for imposing appropriate tariffs on import of agricultural commodities for protecting the interests of farmers. The agricultural products generally attract a maximum slab of 35% applied import tariff. Under GATT Article XXVIII, negotiations were conducted during the period December 1999 and January 2000 and on a number of agricultural items, the tariffs have been increased. However, past more than six years of working of Agreement on Agriculture *(AoA)* shows that, on the whole, it has gone against the interests of the developing nations. According to the FAO, as a result of trade liberalization measures; Africa's food import bill will go up from $ 8.4 billion to $ 14.9 billion. For Latin America and the Caribbean, the value of increased imports is $ 0.9 billion. For the Far East, the imports bill will increase by $ 14.1 billion. For the Near East, the import bill will increase to $ 27 billion and the trade gap will widen from US $ 11 to US $ 19 billion by the year 2000.

(b) Domestic Support: The WTO clauses on 'Domestic Support' have two main objectives: (a) to identify acceptable measures of support to farmers and (b) to discipline trade distorting support to farmers. Through the extremely complicated and confusing system of 'amber box', 'blue box' and 'green box' labeling the WTO regime makes it difficult for the citizens, policy-makers and the government of developing nations to figure out as to what is really happening, there are three categories of support measures that are not subject to reduction under the Agreement. These three categories of exempt support measures are:

(i) *Green Box Measures:* Policies that have the minimum impact on the patterns of production and flow of trade are classified as 'Green Box Measures' and include the following types of assistance:

(a) Government assistance on general services like research, pest and disease control, training, extension and advisory services.

(b) Public stock holding for food security purpose.

(c) Domestic food aid.

(d) Direct payment to producers, such as government financial participation in income insurance and safety nets, relief from natural disasters.

(e) De-coupled income support.

(f) Government financial participation in income insurance and income safety net programmes.

(g) Payments (made either directly or byway of government financial participation in crop insurance schemes) for relief from natural disasters.

(h) Structural adjustment assistance provided through producer retirement programmes; resource retirement programmes and investment aids.

(i) Payments under environmental assistance programmes.

(j) Payments under regional assistance programmes.

It should be noted here that these 'green box' policies, for the most part, with affect farmers only 'in affluent countries whose governments are more able to pay for the producer retirement and resource retirement programmes etc! As per AOA terms and conditions, the subsidy on producer retirement must be conditional on total and permanent retirement of the recipients from marketable agricultural production. Similarly, subsidy for resource retirement must be conditional on retiring land from marketable agricultural production for atleast three years, and in the case of livestock, on its slaughter or permanent disposal. Thus, the farmers can get assistance for leaving farming or livestock but not for staying active as producers. Moreover, the farmers tiave no say in what happens to the land left by them.

(ii) Blue Box Measures: These measures include direct payment to the farmers for production limiting programme and are relevant from the point of view of the developed countries alone. These policies are allowed as long as the supports are 'de-coupled' from production supports. It implies that direct payments can be provided to support incomes of farmers and that the overall cost of production will not be reflected in the price of commodities. In effect, these exclusions imply that incomes of farmers in industrialized countries will be directly paid by the governments and will not be influenced by trade. On the other hand, since incomes of Third World farmers are derived from production and trade and not from direct income support from the governments they will be totally vulnerable to change in global trade patterns and international prices of agricultural commodities.

There is some Special and Differential Treatment for Developing Countries as far as certain support measures are concerned. They mainly consist of (a) investment subsidies which are generally available to agriculture in developing countries and (b) agricultural input services generally available to low income and resource poor producers in developing countries.

(iii) Amber Box Measures: These are the most important measures from the point of view of the producers in developing countries which demand commitment to reduce support to be achieved by quantification of domestic support, that is, the Aggregate Measure of Support (AMS) and then by progressive reduction of the AMS. It consists of two parts: (1) product specific subsidies, that is, the difference between the administered prices (minimum support prices in India) and external reference prices (c.i.f. prices of imports of f.o.b. prices of exports), times the quantity which gets such support (ii) non-product specific subsidies, that is, subsidies on inputs such as fertilizers, electricity, irrigation, etc. The AMS, net of exempted categories of support measures, is subject to reduction commitments. The support is to be reduced by 20% of the country's 1986-88 level in case of developed countries and 13% in case of developing countries over a period of six years (1995-2000) and ten years (1995-2004) respectively. It is to be noted here that the domestic support given to the agricultural sector within the specified permissible level, that is, upto 10% of the agricultural produce in developing countries and 5% in developed countries is allowed. In other words, AMS within this limit is not subject to any reduction commitment. Presently, in India, the minimum support price provided to commodities is less than the fixed external price (1986- 88 average) determined under the agreement. The product specific support is, thus, negative. The subsidies on agricultural inputs (non-product specific support), such as power, irrigation, fertilizers, etc., are well below the minimum permissible level of 10% of the value of agricultural output. Therefore, India is under no obligation to reduce domestic support currently extended to the agricultural sector.

It has already been mentioned that the policies that do have a substantial impact on the patterns of production and flow of trade are classified as 'amber box , policies and are subject to reduction. For example, they include budgetary outlays, foregone revenues and payments at the national and sub-national levels.' There is a wrong assumption that these commitments regarding domestic support are primarily aimed at containing the high levels of subsidies for industrial agriculture and global trade of making small farmers of the developing nations more competitive and leading to prices that would reflect the true cost of production. But, in fact, it may not happen because reduction of 'amber box' policies under AMS addresses prices at the first point of sale. Additional subsidies enjoyed by the global agribusiness and trading interests such as subsidies for investment, fertilizer, marketing and infrastructure are all exempted. Thus, the WTO rules support corporate industrialized agriculture but not the farmers. Again, though India is under no obligation to reduce product specific and non-product specific subsidies according to the AOA, Indian agricultural subsidies related to water and power are being removed under the World Bank Structural Adjustment policies, it means that while support to the farmers has been declining, support and subsidies for industries providing agricultural inputs have been going up. For example, the subsidies for urea increased from Rs. 16.7 billion in 1996-97 to Rs. 20 billion for 1997-98. Thus, the politics of subsidies of WTO favours industry and Northern agribusiness and goes against farmers of the developing nations.

(c) Export Subsidies: Articles 8-11 of the AoA deal with export subsidies. The official justification for the AoA is the removal of export subsidies that have facilitated the sale of large EU and US surpluses on the world market. The main features of export subsidy commitments are as follows:

(i) Export subsidies, measured in terms of both the volume of subsidized exports and budgetary expenditure on subsidies, based on 1988-90 average price, have been capped.

(ii) Developed countries are committed to reducing the volume of subsidized exports by 21 per cent and the expenditure on subsidies by 36 per cent, both over a six year period (1995-2000).

(iii) Developing countries are committed to reducing the volume of subsidized exports by 13 per cent and the expenditure on subsidies by 24 per cent, both over a ten year period (1995-2004).

It should be noted here that export subsidies of the kind listed in the AoA which demand reduction commitments are non-existent in India. For example, exemption of export profits provided in India from Income Tax under section 80 HHC of the Indian Income Tax Act is not among the listed subsidies. Moreover, developing countries are free to provide certain subsidies, such as reduction of export marketing costs, internal and international transport and freight changes. India is making use of these subsidies in certain schemes of Agricultural and Processed Food Products Export Development Authority (APEDA), specially for facilitating export of horticulture products.

Implementation of AoA: While the agricultural trade liberalization was, justified by the argument that Northern agricultural markets would open up to India, India's exports to Europe have actually declined from 13 per cent to 6 per cent. This is because of the fact that high subsidies and protectionist barriers are still largely maintained in the North. More than six years of experience-with WTO regime has shown that agricultural trade liberalization has become, in fact, a unidirectional phenomenon that opens markets in the South for Northern business corporations but closes markets in the North for trade from the South. Global threats to our agriculture could be faced if a 'livelihood box' was included in the re-negotiated WTO agreement which would permit developing countries to impose quantitative restrictions on the import of agricultural commodities, when such imports are likely to destroy livelihood opportunities for resource poor farming families and landless agricultural labour.

It was anticipated that due to the reduction of domestic support in developed countries, cereal production would shift from developed to developing countries. But it has not happened. At best the policies in many developed countries have only been cosmetically altered by shifting the support from one box to another. In absolute terms, the total farm support in OECD countries has increased by 8% to 363 billion US dollars in 1998. The US congress, in view of the collapse of commodity prices during the last two year's, has approved a total of $15 billion worth of emergency farm aid during the last three years. Since the Uruguay Round of GATT., US subsidies have doubled instead of declining-while direct payments to US farmers have gone up from $ 9 billion to $ 15.3 billion. Thus, continuation of the high domestic support to agriculture in developed countries is a cause of concern as they encourage overproduction in these countries leading to low levels of international prices of agricultural products.

In a recent study conducted by the FAO, it has come to the conclusion that there-was little change in the volume exported or in diversification of products and destination. Tariff peaks continue to block exports from Third World countries to the developed countries. They still remain very high in certain sectors like cereals, sugar and dairy products.

During the Uruguay Round the developing nations were led to believe that distortions in agricultural trade would be reduced and scope of exports of agricultural products from the developing countries would increase. But neither the anticipated gains in exports of agricultural products from these countries have been realised nor the contemplated fair trading regime (free of distortions) has helped efficient producers in realising higher prices for their products. On the contrary, prices of most of the agricultural commodities are declining in the world markets. Without substantial reduction in export subsidies and domestic support in developed countries, benefits to developing countries, in terms of increased exports, can not exports, can not accrue.

Infact, subsidies pose a major obstacle to exports from developing countries. During the Uruguay Round, for the first time on effort was made to establish effective disciplines on industrial subsidies and a distinction between prohibited, actionable and non-actionable subsidies was also made. Although, the Uruguay Round resulted in limits being set to agricultural subsidization, total annual levels of support for agriculture in OECD countries averaged $ 350 billion in 1996-98. The impact of this agricultural support either in the form of direct export subsidies, processing subsidies or direct payments to farmers, is to allow agricultural products to be sold on domestic and world markets at below production cost. This not only precludes the entry of producers of developing countries into northern markets but also results in an unfair competition in their own markets. In dairy production, for example, subsidies in EU countries range from 40 per cent to over 100 per cent of the world market price of the products. Consequently, although EU producers are among the world's highest cost producers of dairy products, they have a 50 per cent share of the world market.[2]

Agriculture is important segment in India's exports. Therefore, food security of OUI people, protection of the interests of domestic farmers and finding greater market access in developed countries for our exports should be our guiding principles in negotiation tariff reduction during the next round.

Trips-A Threat to Farmers' Rights: In addition to Agreement on Agriculture, introduction of Trade Related Intellectual Property Rights (TRIPs) at the Uruguay Round of GATT also threatens the majority of population of the Third World countries. It sets enforceable global rules on nine types of intellectual property-copyright, trademark, trade secrets, geographical indications, industrial designs, integrated circuits, patents, micro-organisms and plant varieties. TRIPs rules extend to living resources, so that genes, cells, seeds, plants and animals can now be patented and 'owned' as private property. Living organisms and life forms that are self-creating were, thus, redefined as machines and artifacts made and invented by patentee which ultimately give the patent-holder a monopolistic right to prevent others from making, using or selling seeds. The age-old seed saving and sharing by farmers has now been redefined from a right to a criminal offence of stealing property. In addition to this, the Life Science Corporations are engaged in the production of genetically engineered and herbicide tolerant seeds that lock farmers into dependence on chemical inputs and render agriculture more vulnerable.

The 'Terminator Technology' used by these corporations make seeds sterile after one crop and the farmers cannot save them. They will, infact, be forced to buy seeds from these corporations every year which majority of Indian farmers cannot afford. As already mentioned, chemical companies of the world have bought up seed and biotechnology companies and recognised themselves as 'Life Science Corporations'. Ciba Geigy and Sandoz have combined to form Novartis, Hoechest has joined with Rfwne Paulenic to form Aventis, Zeneca has merged with Asia, Dupont has bought up Pioneed Hi Bred. Eighty per cent of all genetically engineered seeds planted are now Monsanto's Intellectual Property. It also owns broad species patents on cotton, mustard and soyabean crops which were not 'invented' or 'created' by Monsanto but have been evolved over centuries of innovation by farmers of India arid East Asia working in close partnership with bio-diversity gifted by nature.

As a matter of fact, there are many perversions inherent in patents on living material. The first is the ethical perversion which refers to the claim that plants, seeds, cows, sheep or human cell lines are nothing but products of mind created by Monsanto, Novartis, lan Wilmut or any other MNC. Living organisms have inherent quality of self-creation, they make themselves and as such, cannot be reduced to the status of 'inventions' or 'creations' of patent-holders. Secondly, recognition of MNCs as 'owners' of seed through Intellectual Property Rights (IPR) converts farmers into 'thieves ' when they save seed or share it with neighbours. Again, IPRs and patents give the patent-holder a monopolistic right to prevent others from making, using or selling seeds. According to the recent decision of the Canadian Federal Court even, if inadvertently patented seeds come to the field of a farmer tie will have to pay penalty to the Seed Company. Thirdly, it encourages biopiracy. It is the theft of biodiversity and indigenous knowledge through patents.

The above state of affairs adversely affects the developing nations in many ways. It diverts the scarce biological resources to monopoly control of MNCs which means resource theft from poor two-thirds of humanity who depend on bio-diversity for their livelihoods and basic needs. Bio-piracy is, in fact, intellectual theft, which robs Third World people of their creativity and their intellectual resources. Moreover, by creating market monopolies for the MNCs, bio-piracy excludes original innovators from their rightful share of local, sub-national, national and international markets. It appears as if the WTO regime is there to protect the powerful and punish the victims. In a dispute initiated by the USA against India, WTO forced India to change its patent laws and grant exclusive marketing rights to foreign companies on the basis of foreign patents. Thanks to the vehement criticism in Parliament that none of these Bills has so far been passed and two of them have been entrusted to the Select Committee.

Finally, bio-piracy creates a false claim to novelty arid invention even though the knowledge has evolved since ancient times. The recent US Government grant of patents for antidiabetic properties of Karela, Jamun and brinjal to two NRIs Onkar S. Tomer & Kirpanath Borah and their colleague Peter Gloniski is a case in point. The use of these substance for controlling diabetes is every body's knowledge and practice in India since ancient times. Their medical use is–well documented in authoritative trealises like the 'Wealth of India', 'Compendium of Indian Medicinal Plants' and the 'Treatise on Indian Medicinal Plants '. It also refutes the claim of so many that Indian knowledge is not documented. Had there been one or two cases of such false claims to invention on the basis of bio-piracy there would not hoe been much hue and cry. It has actually taken the form of an epidemic. Neem, Haldi, Pepper, har, bahera, amla, mustard, basmati, ginger, castor, Jaramla, amaltas and now Karela and Jamun have all been patented. The problem is not, as was made out to be, in the case of turmeric, an error made by a patent clerk. The problem is deep and systematic and it calls for a systemic change and not a-case-by case challenge.

As a matter of fact, globalisation of trade in agriculture means forced imports and exports which ultimately implies genocide by destroying local agriculture and food systems through subsidized dumping. Agriculture and food must, therefore he removed from the free trade discipline of the WTO.

If this is not done nobody will be able to produce or reproduce patented agricultural, medical or animal products freely, thus eroding the livelihood of small producer and preventing the poor from using own resources and knowledge to meet their basic needs of health and nutrition.

We need to build a movement to allow countries 10 exclude food and agriculture from free trade arrangements, so that ecological and social justice concerns become the basis of how food is produced, distributed and consumed. Or, special provisions for imposition of Quantitative Restrictions under specified circumstances should be made available to all developing countries irrespective of tariffication in the event of a surge in imports or a decline in prices for ensuring the food and livelihood security of their people.

NOTES

* The new export-oriented policies as part of agricultural globalisation have led to shift in India from the production of food crops to commodities for exports. Such policies, to begin with, reduce our food security and secondly, capital-intensive corporate controlled agriculture cannot be sustained by the small farmers. It requires increased use of pesticides resulting in increased debt, despair and sometimes suicides among small farmers.

** Agriculture is still the primary livelihood for three-fourrtisofhumanity. It is as much a cultural activity as an economic one. It is threatened by 'trade liberalization 'driven both by the Srtuctural Adjustment Programmes of the World Bank and the IMF and by the WTO's Agreement on Agriculture. The globalisation of food and agriculture systems means the corporate take over of the food chain, erosion of food rights, destruction of cultural diversity of food, biological diversity of crops and displacement of millions from the rural-based livelihood. If not checked, it will complete the project of colonisation that led to the conquest and ownership of lands and territories.

REFERENCES

For Further Details refer to the *Economics Times,* New Delhi, January 25, March 13, April 19, May 29, July 15, August 12, 12 and 19, 1993 and March 10. 1994.

UNCTAD Trade & Development Report-1999, Geneva, page 137.

23

PROSPECTS AND MARKETING POTENTIAL OF MEDICINAL PLANTS

S. Ganesh, M. Sundaramari & G.S. Kannan

INTRODUCTION

India has an amazing collection of plants. Of the total number of flowering plant families in the world, nearly 72% grow here. The herbal and medicinal plant industry has a history of over 5000 years. These plants have a diverse market and encompass crude drugs as starting materials for extraction and semi synthesis of modern pharmaceuticals. Herbs are used for the preparation of both traditional and orthodox medicines throughout the world. Currently, the procurement and marketing arrangements of these plants are highly unorganized. Herbal plants have global market worth about US $62 billion per annum and India's share is only 0.2 %. However, the Indian herbal industry is at blooming stage. Planning Commission of Government of India in June 1999 has established a task force to study the export market, which has suggested to fix up the target of medicinal plant export to the tune of Rs. 3000 crores by 2005 A.D. and Rs.10,000 crores by 2010 A.D. Medicinal plant industry commands a multi million dollar trade and has tremendous potential throughout India and abroad.

I. Problems in the Medicinal Plants' Cultivation

- Identification of herbal species is difficult even for the botanists. Differentiating the plant parts such as roots, barks etc. is also a difficult task since the resembleness is very high. This paves way for adulteration.

- Improved scientific cultivation for some of the medicinal plants is not remunerative due to the unorganized and erratic production and marketing.
- Gestation period for some of the perennial herbs is long e.g. Nutmeg, Neem, Bael, Arjun, Asoka.
- Yield potential is highly influenced by biotic and abiotic factors.
- Quality and the amount of chemical or alkaloid available in the plant parts also varies.
- Lack of agro techniques for many medicinal plants.
- Inadequate availability of quality planting materials.
- Due to the monopolized supply of raw materials to the drug manufacturers, the producer gets very low price. The market prize is largely decided by buyers, forest contractors and sellers. Market fluctuation is also high.
- Many produces are highly perishable in nature. The produces can not be stored under ordinary condition for a long time and to be used or sold fresh.
- Lack of cold storage facilities and transportation facilities.
- For most of the medicinal plants, the economic part is roots and entire plant, which leads to destructive harvest and thereby causes species' extinction.
- Lack of long term strategy for conservation of biodiversity of the forest area.
- Lack of alternate support for the ethnic communities which depend upon forest resources for their livelihood.
- Urbanization of tribal and forest areas.
- Since the demand for medicinal plants is increased, their survival in their natural habitats is under growing threat. It is presumed that around a thousand species of medicinal plants are facing threat to their existence in the wild, and some of them have become extinct.
- Lack of documentation of traditional knowledge on medicinal plants.

The knowledge of the people associated with the traditional folk practices using wild plants are now depleting/fast disappearing due to modernization and gradual migration.

- Lack of post harvest technologies like production of value added products/derivatives.
- Lack of buy back policies and financial support.
- No idea of what medicines are made from the plants taken out of our country.
- Little research knowledge than the developed countries.

II. PROSPECTS OF MEDICINAL PLANTS' CULTIVATION

Medicinal plants constitute a segment of the flora, which provides raw material for use in the pharmaceutical, cosmetic, fragrance and flavour industries. Most of the medicinal plants extensively used in traditional systems of medicines are obtained from wild source leading to dwindling of populations of numerous plants. Some of the important medicinal plants have become threatened in their natural habitat e.g. *Rauvolfia serpentina.*

One of the major difficulties being experienced by the Indian System of Medicine (ISM) is that of obtaining sufficient quantities of genuine medicinal plants for the manufacture of genuine medicine. Under such circumstances, measures are to be taken to promote the cultivation of medicinal plants.

In our country, there are only few herbal drugs under large scale cultivation that are used in indigenous systems of medicines as well in modern systems of medicine. These are listed below:

Sl. No.	*Common Name*	*Botanical Name*
1.	Isabgul	*Plantago ovata*
2.	Senna	*Cassia angustifolia*
3.	Poppy	*Papaver somniferum*
4.	Periwinkle	*Catharanthus roseus*
5.	Glori Lilly	*Gloriosa superba*

There are others that are cultivated on a very small scale exclusively used in Indian systems of medicine are as follows:

Sl. No.	Common Name	Botanical Name
1.	Val milagu	*Piper longum*
2.	Turmeric	*Curcuma longa*
3.	Ginger	*Zingiber officinale*
4.	Amukkara (Ashwagandha)	*Withania somnifera*
5.	Sarpagandha	*Rauvolfia serpentine*

Tamil Nadu is under strategic geographical location and possesses an invaluable treasure of medicinal plants holding a major share in cultivation and export of many medicinal plant species.

In Tamil Nadu, cultivation of medicinal plants has gained momentum in the last two decades. Cultivation of senna, a popular laxative herb has acclaimed commercial significance in the southern districts of Tirunelveli and Ramnad where the soil is sandy alkaline. The cultivation of glory lilly is confined to red and black soils of Salem, Erode and Dindigul districts. Similarly the cultivation of medicinal bitter gourd (Mithipahal) is confined to Cuddalore district.

With increased awareness among farmers, commercial cultivation of *Aloe, Phyllanthus niruri, Centella asiatica, Withania somnifera, Acorus calamus, Gymnema sylvestris* and even stevia have gained momentum in the recent years.

In the dry tracts with limited irrigation facilities crops like Ashwagandha and Aloe can be introduced. In coconut and arecanut gardens, herbs like Geranium, Patchouli and Acorus calamus can be grown. In the hilly tracts, cultivation of Geranium, Patchouli, Thyme Rosemary have gained popularity. In coastal and deltaic districts like Thanjavur, Trichi, Nagapattinam, Cuddalore and Thiruvarur, there is ample scope to diversify from the present rice based cropping system to medicinal and aromatic plants cultivation at least partially.

Hundreds of species available under the natural eco-system are gathered and exported to many countries. The state now is a potential supplier of herbal raw materials, phyto chemicals, herbal medicines, essential oils, floral concrete etc. Considering the export market, a few species having the commercial significance are cultivated in large area. The area and production of major herbal plants in Tamil Nadu are tabulated hereunder:

Sl. No.	Common Name	Botanical Name	Area Ha.	Production M.T.	Bio-chem compound
1.	Senna	Cassia augustifolia	3000	5000	Sennosides
2.	Periwinkle	Catharanthus roseus	1000	4500	Vincristine Vinblastine
3.	Glory lily	Gloriosa superba	500	450	Colchicine Colchicoside
4.	Coleus	Coleus forskohlii	250	500	Forkohlin
5.	Gallnut	Terminalia chebula	NA	45000	Tannin
6.	Annatto	Bixa orellana	50	150	Bixin
7.	Aloe	Aloe vera	20	300	Aloe gel
8.	Keezha nelli	Phyllanthus amarus	50	125	Phyllanthin
9.	Dhavanam	Artemesia pallens	200	3 tons oil	Essential oil
10.	Atmagupta	Mucuna pruriens	50	100	Beans

III. OPPORTUNITIES FOR MEDICINAL PLANTS' CULTIVATION

Among the estimated source of 3.6 lakhs plant species spread over the earth, 40 per cent is available in our country. Recent survey indicated that about 7,195 plant species are being used in various Indian systems of medicines. But only 800 species of medicinal plants are being used by 7,800 herbal product industries for manufacturing 25,000 effective plant based formulations.

Medicinal Formulations for ISM

Sl. No.	Botanical name	Part used	No. of formulations
1.	Saraca asoca	Bark	55
2.	Withania somnifera	Root	109
3.	Aegle marmelos	Leaves and fruits	60
4.	Tribulus terrestris	Whole plant	65
5.	Tinospora cordifolia	Stem	88
6.	Cyperus rotundus	Rhizome	102
7.	Piper longum	Spike	135
8.	Acorus calamus	Rhizome	51
9.	Tripala: Terminaliachebula, T. belerica, Phyllanthus emblica	Fruits	219
10.	Glycyrrhiza glabra	Root	141

In addition to the formulations for ISM, approximately 25 per cent of the active compounds of drugs prescribed in modern system of medicine have their origin in higher plants.

Plant Drugs Obtained from Higher Plants

Sl. No.	Drug	Clinic action/use	Primary Bot. origin
1.	Atropine	Anticholinergic	Atropa belladonna
2.	Codeine	Analgestic/antitussive	Papaver somniferum
3.	Colchicine	Anti-gout	Colchicum autumnale Gloriosa superba
4.	Digitoxin	Cardio tonic	Digitalis purpurea
5.	Digoxin	Cardio tonic	Digitalis lanata
6.	Methoxsalen	Psorasis / Vitiligo	Ammi majus
7.	Quinine	Antimalarial	Cinchona ledgeriana
8.	Reserpine	Antihypertensive	Ravolfia serpentina
9.	Sennoside A & B	Laxative	Cassia angustifolia
10.	Vinblastine	Anticancer	Catharanthus roseus

In modern system of medicine, drugs are not available for tropical diseases like immuno-modulators as chemotheraphy, adaptogen, diabetes, rheumatic disease, cardio vascular diseases and bronchial asthma. Plant based drugs for curing and healing of these diseases are being screened from herbals used in ISM based on the traditional knowledge. Probable plant based drugs.

Sl. No.	Botanical Name	Therapeutic claims
1.	Tinospora cordifolia	Anticancer
2.	Commiphora mukul	Anticancer
3.	Rubia cordifolia	Blood purifier
4.	Hemidesmus indicus	Blood purifier
5.	Glycyrrhiza glabra	AIDS
6.	Hypericum perportum	AIDS
7.	Coleus forskohlii	Cardio-vascular diseases
8.	Boswellia serrata	Anti-inflammatory
9.	Ammi visnaga	Bronchial asthma
10.	Pterocarpus marsupium	Anti diabetics

USE OF MEDICINAL PLANT IN WEED MANAGEMENT

The enthusiasm among weed scientists and agricultural chemists to evolve new herbicides from naturally occurring allelo-chemicals is on the increasing trend. The list of different donors and target receptors are listed below:

Weeds contribute for an annual loss of 20 million tones of food grains with an estimated cost of Rs.10,000 crores besides the losses in vegetables, fruits and plantation crops. Managing the weeds by mechanical methods is labour intensive and expensive. Use of herbicides results in a shift in the weed flora, builds up toxic residues in the soil and depresses micro flora in the rhizosphere.

Allelopathic Donors Reported to Interfere with Target Receptors

Sl. No	*Donor*	*Receptor*
1.	Coleus amboinicus	Water hyacinth
2.	Water melon	Amaranthus caudatus
3.	Calapogonium muconoides	Desmodium adscendeus
4.	Cassia fistula	Parthenium hysterophorous
5.	Azadirachta indica	Parthenium hysterophorous
6.	Eucalyptus globules	Cyperus rotundus
7.	Delonix regia	Parthenium hysterophorous
8.	Saraca indica	Parthenium hysterophorous
9.	Aegle marmelos	Parthenium hysterophorous
10.	Zizyphus jujube	Parthenium hysterophorous
11.	Argemone mexicana	Cyperus rotundus

USE OF MEDICINAL PLANTS AGAINST PESTS AND DISEASES

Use of pesticides and fungicides for the management of crop pests and diseases is to be dispensed due to their inherent ill effects like residual toxicity, development of resistance by pathogens (resurgence) environmental pollution etc. Due to the increasing awareness about pesticide hazards, we are forced to use botanicals for control of plant diseases and pests.

Sl. No.	*Herbal source*	*Target- Pest/disease*
1.	Pongamia glabra	Basal stem rot of coconut (*Ganoderma*)
2.	Turmeric extract	Onion leaf blight (*Alternaria palendul*)
3.	Solanum nigrum	Inhibit the mycelial growth of various fungi
4.	Neem products	Anti fungal & insecticidal properties
5.	Eucalyptus extract	Fusarium wilt of tomato
6.	Datura stramonium	Sclerotium rolfsii of betel vine
7.	Kundumani leaf extract (*Aperus precatorius*)	Sugarcane red rot (Colletotrichum sp.)
8.	Henna (Lawsonia inermis)	BPH Nilaparvata lugens
9.	Tulsi (Ocimum sanctum)	Spodoptera litura
10.	One big garlic + 5g. onion + 10 g chilli powder	Bhendi leaf hopper *Amrasca biguttula biguttula*
11.	One big garlic + 5g. onion + 10 g chilli powder	Bhendi fruit borer Earias vitella

Sl. No.	*Herbal source*	*Target- Pest/disease*
12.	5 kg Agave leaf + 5 kg. Etti leaf + 5 kg neem leaf + 10 lt. Cow urine + 1 kg pungam cake	Brinjal fruit bever (*Lucinoides orbonalis)*
13.	5 kg Agave leaf + 5 kg Etti leaf + 5 kg neem leaf + 10 lt. Cow urine + 1 kg pungam cake	Brinjal leaf beetle

IV. DEMAND PATTERN

In Tamil Nadu, about 50 species are identified to possess a trade value and demand. Whether the demand, which has seen a quantum jump, will continue to remain at this level is a questionable point. The demand pattern can be classified into three i.e. steady, increasing and erratic.

Steady

Species which are used in traditional medicines like Siddha, Ayurveda, Unani and Homeopathic formulations are reported to have a steady demand. The species are as follows:

1. Sarbagandha — *Rauvolfia serpentina*
2. Amukkara — *Withania somnifera*
3. Perunelli — *Phyllanthus emblica*
4. Vallarai — *Centella asiatica*
5. Kadukkai — *Terminalia chebula*
6. Thandrikkai — *T.belirica*

Increasing

With the aggressive sales promotion by the herbal cosmetic industry, the demand is likely to gradually increase for species used in soap, hair oils, shampoos, facial creams etc. Some examples are listed below:

1. Semparuthi — *Hibiscus rosasinensis*
2. Marthani — *Lawsonia inermis*
3. Karisalankanni — *Eclipta prostrata*
4. Poochankottai — *Sapindus trifoliatus*

Erratic

Most of the species that have found a temporary export market fall under this category. The demand fluctuates violently depending upon the foreign market.

1. Nithyakalyani — *Catharanthus roseus*
2. Kanvalikizhangu — *Gloriosa superba*
3. Medicinal coleus — *Coleus barbata*

On the account of the fact that derivatives of medicinal and aromatic plants are non-narcotic having no side effects, the demand for the herbal medicines is on the increase in both developing and developed countries. Currently, most of these herbs are commercially cultivated and marketed by countries like France, UK, Canada, Turkey and USA. It is estimated that Indian Consumption alone of these herbs is about 200 tonnes per year and only about 60 tonnes are produced indigenously.

V. WORLD TRADE IN MEDICINAL PLANTS

World over the medicinal and aromatic plant materials are processed into pharmaceuticals, phyto-pharmaceuticals, herbal remedies, homeopathic, medicinal and herbal teas, cosmetics, sweets, dyes, essences, varnishes, detergents etc. The botanical drugs are required and purchased by many different industries. Understanding such herbal trade is an essential feature.

Herbal Trade in UK

The surveys conducted clearly indicated the positive attitude of the public towards complementary medicines. 74 per cent of public favoured its inclusion in the National Health Insurance Scheme. The UK is one of the fastest growing markets in the herbal products. At least one million pounds are spent per annum on alternative medicines.

Herbal Market in USA

The herbal market in USA is estimated at US$ 3.24 billion a year. Recent survey conducted revealed that the major importers of herbal medicines of indigenous system of medicine are USA and Europe .The herbal medicine in the form of Ayurvedic formulation or drugs popular in USA and Europe are furnished below:

Herbal Medicines Popular in USA and Europe

Sl. No.	*Botanical Name*	*Formulation/Effective Compound*	*Therapeutic Claims*
1.	Allium sativum	Allicin and other related compounds	Hypocholesterolemic Hypolipemic
2.	Hypericum perforatum	Flavoroides	Treatment of mild depression and nervousness
3.	Aloe barbadensis	Hydroxyanthra cenederivative	Laxative treatment of skin diseases
4.	Valeriana officinalis	Sesqueterpene	Sedative
5.	Silybum marianum	Flavonolignans	Hepato protective inflammation
6.	Emblica officinalis	Formulations	Hypocholestew lemic
7.	Zingiber officinale	Formulations	Improve digestion, Arthritis, ulcers
8.	Withania somnifera	Formulations	Promote energy and vitality
9.	Bacopa monneri	Formulations	Stimulate mental function
10.	Glycyrrhiza glabra	Formulations	Ulcers, Eczema, Psoriasis

Herbal Trade in Japan

In Japan, during 1975-1990, a 15 fold increase was reported in herbal product sales as compared to only less than 3 fold increase in the sales of other pharmaceutical products.

Herbal Trade in China

The Chinese herbal industry requires 4,60,000 tons of plant materials to produce plant based medicines each year. Nearly 200 medicinal plants are cultivated in 4,40,000 hectares with an output of 3,00,000 tons, more than 700 farms are engaged in cultivating high quality medicinal plants. The traditional medicines have a 40% share in the total pharmaceutical products.

Herbal Trade in Germany

In the last 3 years, Germany had imported 40,000 tons of botanicals to the tune of $109 millions from 109 countries. One third of the material was re-exported as finished products to Western Europe and USA.

Global Market

Currently, global market for herbal products which includes medicines, health supplements, herbal beauty and toiletry products is estimated at around US$ 62 millions. Global market for herbal medicine alone is estimated to be around US$ 5 billions growing at the rate of 30-40 % annually and is expected to reach US$ 16 billions by 2005. It is estimated that China accounts for over 40% of this trade while India's share is estimated to be less than 2 per cent. Market research in Europe conducted during 1999 indicated that products that give energy are highly desirable in UK, France and Germany. Other popular claims are:

Lowering cholesterol (UK & France), Promoting healthy bones (UK & Germany) and Boosting immune system (Germany & France).

Herbs used for health care

Sl. No.	*Health Claims*	*Herbals of Traditional Medicine*
1.	Give energy	*Withania somnifera, Asparagus racemosus, Mucuna pruriens*
2.	Lower cholesterol	*Emblica officinalis, Commiphora mukul*
3.	Promotes healthy bones	*Cissus quadrangularis*
4.	Boosts immune system	*Azadirachta indica*

INDIAN SCENARIO

In India, the traditional systems of medicine such as Ayurveda, Unani and Siddha have a share of 70% of the pharmaceutical market corresponding to the population of the country. Export of crude drugs and essential oils in 1995 from India was US$ 53 millions and US$ 123 millions respectively, altogether bringing revenue of US $ 66 millions. Though we are ranking number two in terms of export medicinal plants, we rank only sixth position in terms of value. This indicates that we have not capitalized the market and so far only neglected the export of finished crude drugs or the processed extracts.

EXPORT OF MEDICINAL PLANTS FROM INDIA

Among the exported items Isabgol or Psyllium (*Plantago ovata*) husk and seeds was the foremost foreign exchange earner leaving behind opium. Export of Psyllium husk and seeds during 1992-93 was to the extent of Rs.77.41 crores. Senna leaves and pods rank second with an earning of Rs.12.30 crores. Pseudo-ginseng (*Withania somnifera*) and zeodovary roots have earned a foreign exchange of Rs.8.38 and 2.16 crores respectively.

Nuxvomica (*Strychnos nuxvomica*) seeds, poppy (*Papaver somniferum*) seeds, poppy flower tops and poppy husk, periwinkle roots, Belladona leaves, Chirayta (*Andrographis paniculata*) asafoetida (*Ferula asafoetida*) etc, constitute the other items of export. In addition, export of medicinal plants under the name 'Crude drugs' and others fetches about Rs.24.40 crores annually. India is the second largest producer and exporter of Jasmine and tuberose concrete. Indian perfume production is for Rs.318.50 crores which is less than 2% of the total world market.

Instead of exporting the raw herbs, the manufacturers and exporters should try to move up the value chain by exporting either extracts or products based on these medicinal herbs so as to exploit the huge opportunities for export.

List of plant portions and their derivatives banned for export from India (By ministry of commerce)

1. *Cycas beddomei*
2. Vanda coerula (Blue vanda)
3. Saussurea costus
4. Phaphiopdilum sp.
5. Nepenthes khasiana
6. Renanthera inshootiana
7. Rauvolfia serpentina
8. Ceropegia sp.
9. Fererea indica
10. Podophyllum hexandrum
11. Treeferns- Cyatheaceae sp.
12. Dioscorea deltoidea
13. Euphorbia sp.
14. Orchidaceae sp.
15. Pterocarpus santalinus
16. Cycadaceae (Cycads)
17. Taxus wallichiana
18. Aquilaria malaccensis (Agarwood)
19. Aconitum sp.
20. Coptis teeta
21. Coscinium fenestrum
22. Dactylorhiza hatagirea
23. Genetiana kurroa
24. Gnetum sp.
25. Kampheria galanga
26. Nardostachys grandiflora
27. Swertia chirata
28. Picrorhiza kurroa

IMPORT OF MEDICINAL PLANTS IN INDIA

In order to meet the domestic requirement and also for export, India has been importing certain medicinal plants accounting for Rs.2.74 crores during 1992-93. Among the major items imported were ginseng, Pyrethrum flowers, liquorice roots, agar wood, chirayata etc.

INTERNATIONAL PRICES OF CERTAIN ALKALOIDS

• Tropane alkaloids	Annual market valued US $100 millions
• Hyoscyamine/ Scopolamine	$ 350-1400 per kg. i.e. Rs.14000 to 56000/kg
• Digtoxin	Rs. 45000/kg
• Digoxin	Rs. 70000/kg
• Vincristine (0.0005-0.0003 %)	Each gram valued US $ 1500 (Rs.60000/g)

- 1g Vincristine could be extracted from 500 kg of leaves in a processing cycle of16 weeks.

Major Medicinal Plants Under Cultivation in India

Sl. No.	*Crops*	*Area (ha.)*	*States cultivated*
1.	Psyllium	50,000	Gujarat, Rajasthan
2.	Senna	12,000	Tamil Nadu, Gujarat
3.	Poppy	18,000	M.P., Rajasthan, U.P
4.	Aswagandha	4,000	Neemuch – M.P.
5.	Cinchona	6,000	West Bengal
6.	Ipecac	100	Darjeeling
7.	Glory lily	700	Tamil Nadu, A.P., Karnataka
8.	Coleus forskohlii	300	Tamil Nadu, Karnataka, Maharashtra
9.	Periwinkle	3,000	A.P., Tamil Nadu, Karnataka
10.	Aloe vera	200	Maharashtra, Tamil Nadu
11.	Hops	100	Kashmir-Kullu, H.P.
12.	Japanase mint	10,000	U.P., Punjab, Tamil Nadu
13.	Lemon grass	20,000	Kerala
14.	Palmorosa	2,000	U.P., Karnataka, Tamil Nadu
15.	Celery	5,000	Punjab, Western U.P.
16.	Basil	500	U.P.
17.	Saffron	3,000	Palampore (Kashmir)
18.	Davanam	500	Karnataka, A.P., Tamil Nadu
19.	Vetiver	200	For oil – U.P.
20.	Damask rose	3,000	Aligarh – U.P., Udaipur
21.	Rose geranium	2,000	Tamil Nadu, Karnataka
22.	Jasmine	2,000	Tamil Nadu, Karnataka

CONCLUSION

The use of medicinal plants in pharmaceutical industry continues to be strong and has grown in recent years. Medicines derived from plants in US today accounts for approximately one fourth of all prescriptions written. Now, the world is witnessing an unprecedented growth in herbal usage. Major lacuna in Indian herbal sector is quality aspect. No farmer or corporate farming groups follow the good manufacturing practice for herbs. It is necessary to remember that quality assurance does not begin and end with the preparation of the final dosage form. It also involves selection of plant material, good cultivation and harvesting, post harvest practices, proper extraction and production of final dosage form. Another threat is competitive countries like China, Brazil etc., which are going in a big way in export of medicinal plants.

Patents and biopiracy are big threats to our Indian herbs sector. Already the patents have been obtained for *Azadirachta indica, Emblica officinalis, Curcuma longa, Momordica charantia, Aloe barbadensis, Bacopa monnieri, Punica granatum, Piper nigrum* etc. by mostly American, European and Japanese companies. Some of the above patents have also been revoked by the efforts taken by the Indian government. There is a danger of foreign companies walking away with Exclusive Marketing Rights (EMR's) on the basis of their patents obtained abroad.

Lack of proper marketing set up, dwindling prices of the produces and lack of value addition of herbs are also the weakness of our Indian herbal industry in addition to the rules and regulations of WTO and WHO.

Considering all these points, some urgent, comprehensive measures are to be taken to sustain and uplift the Indian herbal industry in World trade arena.

It is here that our scientists, pharmaceutical industries, practitioners of ISM and associates should take initiatives to protect the Indian medicinal plants to avert the threat produced by world's developed countries and pharmacy giants. Utilizing the tremendous opportunities available in this sector, proper policy initiation and implementation can be taken up to overcome many weaknesses and threats.

REFERENCES

Gautam, Sushilkumar and S.K.Sharma (2005), Cultivation, Use and Economic Value of Most Valuable Medicinal Plant-Shatavari. Agrobios, Vol. 4, No. 4: 30-30, Sep' 2005.

Kumar, N. *et al.* (1993), Introduction to Spices, Plantation Crops, Medicinal and Aromatic Plants. Rajalakshmi Publications.

Ravikumar, V.R. (2004), Medicinal and Aromatic Plants. Agro India, Bangalore.

Sundar, A. (2002), India's Role in Export of Medicinal Plants. *UZhavar Thunaivan*, Vol. 7, No. 1: 8-12, Jan' 2002.

Thamburaj, S., (2003), Production and Utilization of Medicinal Plants. In: Abstract of the National Seminar on Production and Utilization of Medicinal Plants Organized by Dept. of Horticulture, Annamlai University on 13-14 March, 2003, p. 1.

24

NO MORE NEEM, NO MORE TURMERIC !

B.R. Dwaraki

INTRODUCTION

India is one of those countries in the world known for a rich biodiversity. Our villages are also known for a panorma of a wide range of arts–both fine and performing. And the range of colourful handicrafts of India has already reached and appreciated in all nooks and cranny in the world. The medicinal value and the real work of neem and turmeric, for example, which our rural-folk knew for generations, reached the American continent who went in for their own research on them and only when the patent was sought on them, the Indian government woke up. Fortunately India could wage the fight in time. Let us not have any more neem or turmeric drama!

INTELLECTUALS

The revolution sweeping away the world the realm of Information Technology should make everyone to sit up and revisit the term 'intellectual'. A term which has been smartly "usurped" by the highly literate strictly speaking, no dictionary will readily line up the term with literacy. Even total illiterates can be intellectuals based on their rational performance of a challenging task. The IT revolution has brought into the game of "Intellectualism" two more distinguishable terms: Knowledge and information. In this plethora of terms, the knowledgeable intellects of yester years go listless in the face of IT informed smarties! In this Ganga–Yamuna confluence, wisdom disappears subliminally as river Saraswathi. In this melee of modern jargons, again thanks to IT revolution, who can take up the task of telling our rural fraternity that many of them can rate themselves among the intellectuals in the world.[1]

PROPERTY

For the majority of India's population living in the villages with agricultural way of life, land is almost the only property they know of–and this is immovable. The only "movable" property they know of are the domesticated animals, besides which, the precious ornaments that their women-folk possess–to whatever extent they could afford. The villagers have the scarest idea–and they will scarcely believe even they are told–that almost anything they possess in the form of ideas, practices or products could be listed as property!

RIGHTS

The concept of Rights could reveal and project the saddest story of the three terms referred to so far. For one thing, most are simply unaware of their rights of any kind. If they do know, they are hopeless. Individually therefore, awareness is likely to make one only more miserable "I wish I didn't know I had the right kind of feeling". In a sense, 'ignorance is bliss' seems to be hard truth with respect to awareness of rights.

DOWN THE IVORY TOWER

The Ivory tower of higher education in India over the decades has created such an unmistakable notion in rural minds that it is seen as what is relevant to urban life. So much so a rural father running head over heels to educate his son seems more than convinced that his son should use the degree as a passport to escape from the harsh realities of his village. And this son may ultimately join a university and even conduct rural research and earn more degrees! After all, one has to publish to avoid perishing in the academic world!

Naïve and gullible rural people in India do not know that the urban academics know about villages a lot more than villagers themselves. An average village in India is totally unaware as to how much of research work has been published in its name and how much money has been spent over the years in the name of its development. The ultimate answer lies in the hands of academics who must now climb down from their ivory towers and involve themselves in rural extension work intensively and extensively.

PARTICIPATORY RURAL APPRAISAL (PRA)[2]

Thanks to the policy of Gandhigram Rural Institute to have rural extension as the vital third dimension in it higher education system. This author had the opportunity of involving in extension almost from day one of his service spanning over a quarter century. He also got trained as master Trainer in PRA and has been able to see for himself now "PRA Works" in reality.

With the PRA experience of over a decade-and-a-half on a variety of issues in Tamil Nadu villages and those of Madhya Pradesh (where he spent a year on deputation), this author is more than convinced that this approach has the vitality in it to bring about the knowledge–information empowerment among the villagers in India that could lay the foundation for an IPR Movement. There is the need for a participatory assessment/ appraisal of the bio–diversity and indigenous knowledge abundant in villages. The next obvious step is digital documentation.

CYBRARIANS, NOT LIBRARIANS[3]

INFLIBNET has rendered even the doctorates in information science belonging to the period earlier that late 1990s outdated. The triple 'W' has made the word a single web. But then, internet and cyber cafés have allowed too many spiders to log on to the web round the clock. LPG (due apologies to the infamous Iraq war): Liberalisation, Privatisation and Globalisation have complicated the triple 'W' so badly, it is difficult to say or catch an individual on the internet for 'stealing'–nay copying nor merely having access'[4]

The other serious fall–out of the above trends is that web makes the world smaller but IPR laws and rules that are localized enough create distances in tracking down the culprits of misuse. Modern digital documentation calls for smart cybrarians more than faithful librarians.

JUST ONE EXAMPLE

It is well know to rural extension people that the pride of selecting and preserving quality seeds from every harvest has been the domain of women in Indian villages. What with the patented 'terminal' seeds[5], will be the future role of Indian women in agriculture? Will her pride be lost for nothing?

IN SUM

LPG has opened the flood gates. The naive rural people in the developing countries do not know what will be in spate around nor what will be their fate. There is no defense available in their armoury, except resigning themselves to destiny as they have always done. Academics of to-day in India can not keep aloof because only they know what is possible under the circumstances. Time to act is now.

NOTES AND REFERENCES

1. Halkar, Giriraj, G and Sangita Gupta "Knowledge Management: A Challenge for the 21st Century" University News Vol. 42, No. 28, July 12-18, 2004 , pp. 4.
2. Narayanasamy, N., Dwaraki B.R, & Boraian, M.P (Eds) "Solving Community Problems: Tentacles of PRA Methodology, New Delhi, Himalaya 2000.
3. Halkar, Giriraj G and Sangita. ibid.
4. Suryavanshi, Harish "Intellectual Property and information Technology: Raids and prospects "University News Vol. 42, No. 27, July 05-11, 2004, pp. 10.
5. Ramesh "Pateut Illiteracy: A threat to Economic Growth" University News Vol. 42, No. 28, July 12-18, 2004 pp. 10.

25

CONSERVATION OF MEDICINAL PLANTS

S. Ganesh, M.Sundaramari & G.S. Kannan

Sustainable management of natural resources has globally become a key issue for the survival of the planet earth. Conservation of nature and natural resources is on the priority agenda throughout the world. The biological diversity and issues related to its conservation have been put on the highest priority. Medicinal plants constitute a segment of the flora. India, the second most populous country in the world is the eleventh mega biodiversity centre in the world and the third in Asia with a share of about 11% of the total floral resources. Conservation of the country's medicinal flora will not only serve national interest but also serve global needs since there is a growing demand world wide for natural medicine.

DISTRIBUTION

The analysis of distribution pattern shows that medicinal plants are distributed across diverse habitats and landscape. Around 70 % of India's medicinal plants are found in the tropical zone, mostly in the forests of Western and Eastern ghats, the Vindhayas, Chotta Nagpur plateau, Aravalis, the Terai region in the foot hills of the Himalays and the North East. Less than 30% of these medicinal plants are confined to the temperate and high altitudes (S.Thamburaj, 2003). A small number of medicinal plants are also found in aquatic habitats and mangroves. Studies by various groups reveal that large percentage of the known medicinal plants occurs in the dry and moist deciduous vegetation as compared to the evergreen or temperate habitats. The Western Himalayas and Western Ghats are especially known for their diversity of medicinal plants. In terms of life forms, medicinal plants are equally distributed across various habits-trees, shrubs and herbs. About two-third belongs to herbs, epiphytes, grasses and climbers. Majority of medicinal plants are higher flowering plants.

PRESENT STATUS

The World Health Organization (WHO) has estimated that about 80% of the population of developing countries relies on traditional medicines, mostly plant drugs for their primary health needs. More over, the modern medicines contain about 25% drugs derived from plants. According to WHO over 21,000 plant species are useful in the preparation of medicines. It is reported the more than 8000 plants available in our country are having medicinal value. These medicinal plants are used by the different systems of medicine like Ayurveda (1769), Folk medicine (4671), Homoeopathy (482), Siddha (1121), Tibetan (279) and Unani (751) in India according to FRLHT, Bangalore. An estimated 800 species are currently used in industry for large scale production of herbal formulations. Presently 15-20% are commercially cultivated and the rest are collected from the wild, mostly from forests.

Over 4000 species of vascular plants are found in South India, out of which nearly 2000 are used in Indian Systems of Medicine (ISM). Millions of rural households use medicinal plants in self-help mode. Over one and half million practitioners of ISM use medicinal plants in preventive, promotive and curative applications. Today there are about six lakhs licensed and registered traditional physicians in India. There are more than 5000 drug manufacturing units existing in India which produce herbal products with an annual turn over of around Rs. 2000 crores per year, which is likely to reach Rs.8000 crores in the near future (K.Ved, and U.G. Geetha, 2000).

UTILIZATION PATTERN

India is one of the 12 mega biodiversity centres in the world with 63.72 million ha. of forest area. In India, out of 50,000 plant species, 9500 plant species are used by tribals for several purposes as mentioned below:

Sl. No.	Particulars	No. of Plant species
1.	Medicinal	7500
2.	Edible	3900
3.	Other materials and cultural requirements	700
4.	Fibre and cordage	525
5.	Fodder	400
6.	Pesticides	300
7.	Gum, resins and dye	300
8.	Incense and perfumes	100

The medicinal plant parts used are listed out below:

Rhizomes	4.4 %
Roots	29.6 %
Leaves	5.5 %
Flower	5.2 %
Fruit	10.3 %
Seeds	6.6 %
Stems	5.5 %
Bark	13.5 %
Wood	2.8 %
Whole plant	16.3 %

(Camp Report, FRLHT, 1997)

Medicinal plants used by traditional practitioners in Vellimalai tribal block (Kalrayan hills) are as follows:

Trees	153
Shrubs/herbs	187
Climbers/Creepers	74
Grasses	8
Epiphytes/Lower plants	5
Total	427

The maximum number of medicinal plants is utilized by the folk traditions, followed by Ayurveda, Siddham Unani, Homoeopathy, Tibetan and Modern respectively.

Several species of plants overlap the system as seen in the Table below:

It is not uncommon to see several "hundred" application of a particular plant used or in various formulations for different purposes. This can be illustrated by the example of a very common plant called "Amla" (*Emblica officinalis*). There are nearly 180 formulations of Amla. These formulations are used in a wide range of disorders.

Sl. No		Usage of medicinal plants across medicinal systems						
		Ayurveda	Folk	Homoeopathy	Modern	Siddha	Tibetan	Unani
1.	Ayurveda	1769	731	164	55	743	271	653
2.	Folk	731	4671	147	56	635	201	486
3.	Homoeopathy	164	147	482	60	142	70	155
4.	Modern	55	56	60	105	41	17	50
5.	Siddha	743	635	142	41	1121	227	486
6.	Tibetan	271	201	70	17	227	279	224
7.	Unani	653	486	155	50	486	224	751

(Pipla pitiya R. 1996).

Examples of Ethno-medicinal plants with 10 and more uses reported across ethnic communities in Vellimalai tribal block of Kalrayan hills are given below:

Sl. No.	Plant Name	Reported uses
1.	Aristolochia indica	24
2.	Hemidesmus indicus	14
3.	Centella asiatica	29
4.	Anacardium occidentale	12
5.	Trianthema portulacastrum	16
6.	Terminalia chebula	15
7.	Bassia latifolia	13
8.	Adenanthera paronia	17
9.	Alstonia scholaris	18
10.	Catharanthus roseus	13
11.	Feronia limonia	16
12.	Adhatoda vasica	18
13.	Aegle marmelos	15
14.	Cassia auriculata	16
15.	Terminalia arjuna	21

For thousands of years, the medicinal properties of herbs are known to Indians and this knowledge is carried out traditionally.

Traditional carrier	Subject/usage	No. of uses
House wives and elders	Home remedies, food and nutrition	Millions
Traditional birth attendants	Normal deliveries	7 lakhs
Herbal healers	Common ailments	3 lakhs
Bone setters	Orthopaedics	60,000
Visha Vaidyas	Natural poisons	60,000
Specialists	Eye, skin, respiratory, dental, arthritis, liver, wounds, fistule, piles	1000 in each area

NEED FOR CONSERVATION OF MEDICINAL PLANTS

The various aspects discussed in the utilization pattern clearly reveals that more than 70 % of the plants from destructive harvesting from the wild because of the use of parts like roots, rhizomes, bark, wood, stem and the whole plants. Further, it is also clear that the maximum numbers of medicinal plants are utilized by the folk traditions, those who mainly depend upon wild source through destructive harvests. It is also a known fact that most of the medicinal plants have wide range of utility which again leads to injudicious harvest.

This poses a definite threat to the genetic stocks and to the diversity of medicinal plants. Many species have become endangered and threatened because of indiscriminate over exploitation. In the present context of "back to nature" in health care, it is relevant that those valuable medicinal plants are not only to be presented but also to be conserved to meet the ever increasing demand.

Some important medicinal plants of India which are endangered are:

Sl. No.	Common name	Botanical name
1.	Indian Belladona	Atropa acuminata
2.	Indian Aconite	Aconitum deinorrhizum
3.	"Kuth" of commerce	Saussurea lappa
4.	Red sandal wood	Pterocarpus santalinus
5.	Blue poppy	Meconopsis betonicifolia
6.	Jatamansi	Nardostachys grandiflora
7.	Sarpa gandha	Rauvolfia serpentina

(Ayensu E.S., 1982).

THREATENED PLANTS OF INDIA

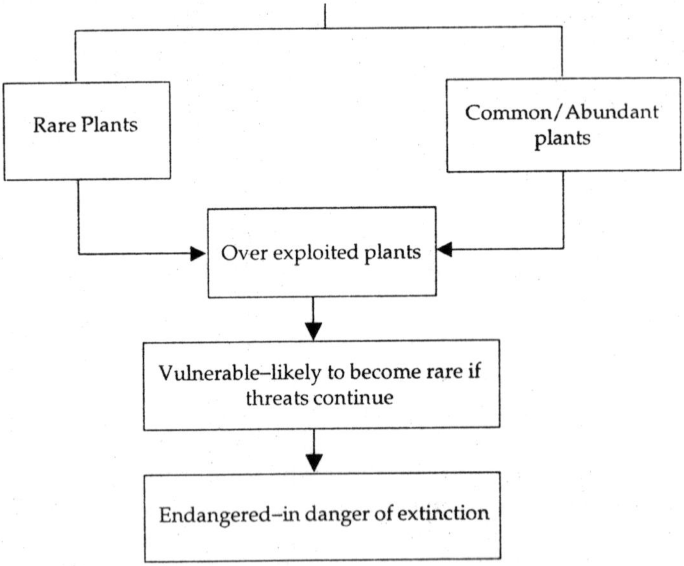

Strategies for Medicinal Plant Conservation

Recent times it is understood that the conservation of medicinal plants is an essential aspect of preventing the danger of extinction of valuable medicinal plants due to over exploitation.

The following are some of the strategies to be implemented to ensure medicinal plants conservation.

Conservation can be classified into two major categories 'in situ' and 'ex situ'.

In situ Conservation

It means conserving plants in their natural habitats (on site) through the establishment of nature or biosphere reserves, national parks, sanctuaries, reserve forests, or by special legislation to protect endangered or threatened species. In this system, wild species and the associated natural eco system are preserved together to maintain the genetic integrity of the population and to allow natural evolution. The in situ conservation approach is not suitable for cultivated farms as there are no natural eco systems to support them.

EX SITU CONSERVATION

It is defined as conservation of plants away from their areas of natural occurrence (off site). The following are the methods of ex situ conservation.

(i) Long term seed storage (Gene banks)

(ii) Mass reservoirs of composites

(iii) Field conservation

(iv) Cold storage freeze preservation of vegetative parts.

(v) In vitro conservation

(i) Seed Gene Banks

The most practical and the cheapest method of conservation of genetic resources of species producing orthodox seeds is through long term cold storage of seeds. Orthodox seeds are those which tolerate a decrease in moisture content under low temperature. In case of those species which produce recalcitrant seeds, the seeds can not be stored in gene banks, because recalcitrant seeds do not stand drying below relatively high moisture content without a serious loss of viability (Roberts, 1973) such as, in the case of cocoa, mango, durian and several other tropical fruits. Among species bearing orthodox seeds, seeds of Cassia, Trifolium and Lupinus species could be cold stored for over 100 years.

(ii) Mass Reservoirs of Composites

Botanic gardens and arboreta are repositories of valuable genetic material and these were fore runners of today's evolution of crops for their productivity. A national policy on conservation of medicinal plants should promote the creation of a network of regional and sub-regional ethno medicinal plant gardens which should contain all the medicinal plants known to various ethnic communities in different regions of India.

(iii) Field Conservation (Field banks)

Cultivation of medicinal plants for sustainable utilization has not emerged yet, as the traditional medicine industry finds it easier and cheaper to procure raw materials from the wild source. Also, there is a lack of knowledge on cultivation, propagation and breeding techniques for many of the forest dwelling species. By controlling the indiscriminate and destructive collection of medicinal plants from the wild, the industry's participation in cultivation of medicinal plants will be made possible. For medicinal plants, organic farming systems and poly culture models could be encouraged instead of synthetic and mono culture models in Agriculture.

The most urgent and primary task to ensure immediate availability of plants and planting materials to various user groups like farmers, industries etc. is to promote a nation-wide network of medicinal plant nurseries which will multiply all the region specific plants. The forest department, agricultural extension agencies, village panchayats, SHGs, NGOs and other private agencies should be encouraged in this direction.

(iv) Cold Storage Freeze Preservation of Vegetative Parts

Various vegetative parts like rhizomes, bulbs, tubers, stolens, suckers etc. of medicinal plants could be stored under this method. DNBA and cells can also be stored. The institutions like IBPGR, NBPGR, CIMAP, FRLHT etc have already involved in this type of conservation.

(v) In Vitro Conservation

Several plant species, including a few commercial species, produce recalcitrant seeds and thus are difficult to be conserved through seeds. Further, some species are shy seed bearers and even fail to produce seeds. In addition, living collections of clonally propagated perennial crops face the problems of maintenance of heterozygous and heterogeneous populations, long life cycle and large space required and high possibility of exposure to the threats of pests and diseases and other biotic and abiotic stresses. To overcome these difficulties, in vitro conservation of vegetatively propagated and recalcitrant seed producing species is being increasingly adopted.

Orchid germ plasm is routinely maintained in vitro in India, Philippines and Thailand. With assistance from the Dept. of Bio-technology, the National Bureau of Plant Genetic Resources (NBPGR) India has established extensive in vitro storage facilities and is already storing germ plasm collections of certain root and tuber crop species and a few fruit species. The same facility may also be extended to medicinal plants.

Activities Associated with Conservation of Plant Genetic Resources

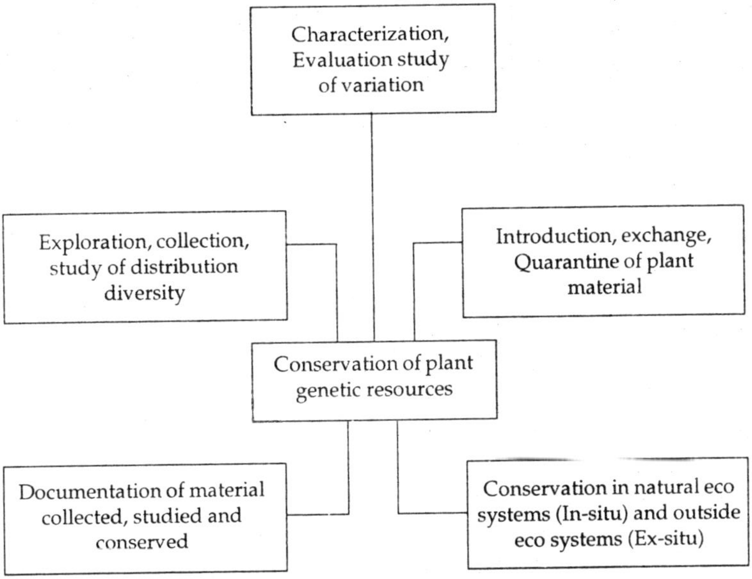

CONCLUSION

Many of the institutions (Government and NGOs) have been taking preventive, remedial measures for conserving medicinal plants. Still we need more awareness and stringent policy, rules and regulations of medicinal plants otherwise we can not see the medicinal plants in natural habitat but for in photographs. It is time to take both preventive and remedial measures for the conservation of our valuable wealth of medicinal plants.

REFERENCES

Anonymous (1997), Camp Report, FRLHT, Bangalore.

Ayensu, E.S. (1982), The World's Diminishing Plant Resources. In: Conservation of Tropical Plant Resources (eds.) Jain S.K and Mehra, R.L., Botanical Survey of India.

Pilapitiya, R. (1996), Traditional Medicine. W.H.O. Regional Health Forum, 1: 51-52.

Roberts, E.H. (1973), Predicting the Storage Life of Seeds. Seed Science and Technology, 1:419-514.

Thamburaj, S. (2003), Production and Utilization of Medicinal Plants. In: Abstract of the National Seminar on Production and Utilization of Medicinal Plants Organized by Dept. of Horticulture, Annamlai University on 13-14 March, 2003, p. 1.

Ved, K. and U.G. Geetha (2000), A Green Pharmacy. In: The Hindu Folio Oct. 2004. p. 14.

26

IMPACT OF TRIPS ON ECONOMIC DEVELOPMENT OF INDIA

Mohd. Shamim

INTRODUCTION

The advent of globalization and digital technologies has changed the engine of economic development from manual and mechanical force to intellectual prowess. This has significantly increased the importance of intellectual property rights (IPR) in the developmental process. However, the general perception is that IPRs play a significant role not only in the case of globalizes Indian economy and has no worthwhile place in the area of rural development. In this paper I have make an attempt to look what are the places of IPRs in rural development in the India context 1.

Intellectual property is intangible unlike movable property such as a car and immovable property such as a house. It is a creation of human intellect. An example is music. The distinctive feature of intellectual property is that it relates to information, which can be used by several persons at the same time, unlike immovable or movable tangible property. There is a variation as to the set of rights forming the basket of intellectual property rights. The agreements on Trade Related aspects of Intellectual Property Rights (TRIPS) includes the following within the scope of IPR:

- Copy rights and related rights.
- Trademarks.
- Geographical Indications.

- Patents
- Lay-out Designs (Topographies) of integrated circuits
- Protection of undisclosed information
- Control of anti-Competitive Practices in Contractual licenses.[1]

Intellectual property (IP) law definition–Intellectual Property is any product of human intellect that is unique and un-obvious with some value in the marketplace.

Intellectual property laws cover ideas, inventions, literary creations, unique names, business models, industrial processes, computer program code, and more.

The TRIPS agreement is composed of seven parts and seventy three articles which includes specific standards concerning several instruments of IPRs protection and guidelines for control of anti competitive practices in licensing IPRs, guidelines for the enforcement of IPRs. Procedure, formalities, criteria for transparency, transitional arrangements for it implements, institutional arrangements and final provisions for its executions.[2]

The speed and scope of IPRs now a days is so much that a person engaged in economic activities, be he a farmer or an entrepreneur, has to take all·precautions to ensure the even inadvertently he does not infringe any IPR and, thereby incur heavy damage. This is particularly so in the case of retailers and petty shoppers which abound in the rural areas.

They have to be very careful about the goods they are storing for sale and watch out for pirated dealing in such illegal goods or even displaying them for sale can, if caught, ruin the entire business of the person nabbed.

WHAT CAN BE PATENTED?

Article 27 of the TRIPS Agreement provides that WTO member states shall provide patents for any invention, either a product or a process for creating a product, "provided that they are new, involve an inventive step, and are capable of industrial application." In other words, to be patentable, an invention must be novel, useful, and nonobvious. A prerequisite to patentability is that the invention must be capable of some practical application. This emphasizes the importance the patent system puts on usefulness. Although this principle remains constant, the phraseology used within the legislation of particular countries varies; for example, in the United States, patentable subject matter must be "useful," whereas in the United Kingdom it must be capable of "industrial application."

The invention must be new—that is, the subject matter of the invention is not or cannot be inferred to be part of what is already known. This is commonly referred to as the "novelty" requirement. New or novel in this context means "new to the public." Therefore, something that has previously been used or known but has not been made available to the public (for instance, if it has been kept a secret) is not a bar to patentability.

The invention must also be nonobvious. This prevents someone from taking advantage of the patent system and obtaining protection for something that is a mere extension or trivial variation of what is known. Generally the test for inventiveness, or "nonobviousness," is based on what a reasonable person skilled in the field to which the invention pertains, at the time the invention was made, would consider to be nonobvious. The TRIPS Agreement provides a transitional period for developing economies that do not currently provide product patent protection in the areas of agro-chemicals or pharmaceuticals. In fact, most already do because of the development benefits to the biotechnology sector from full patent protection. Process patent protection does not encourage investment because of the difficulty of enforcing a process patent. It is particularly difficult to enforce a process patent because the burden of proof to show that the patent has been infringed is on the patent owner. The patent owner must prove that a particular manufacturing process (that is, the process covered by the patent) was used to manufacture the particular chemical. This can be very difficult to show where there are many possible process variants and where access to the potential infringes facility is not available. In practice, this is done by looking for trace impurities that are characteristic of the manufacturing process. One can imagine how complex the issues can become if, for instance, a patent protects a pharmaceutical that is made in a country where there is no protection for pharmaceuticals and then is exported to a second country that provides protection only for manufacturing processes.

Over the past 15 years or so, many countries have changed from "process" to "product" patenting, and we expect all WTO members to upgrade their patent laws within the next few years because, under the WTO's TRIPS Agreement, member states must provide full product patent protection no later than January 1, 2005.

Not only are the utilitarian aspects of new and useful inventions patentable, but also many countries extend patent protection to novel, ornamental industrial designs. In the United States, this form of protection is known as a design patent, while in many European countries, the property right in an industrial design is referred to as a design model.

In addition to such usual subjects of patent protection as devices, chemical compositions, and processes, some countries provide patent protection for living matter. For example, asexually reproduced varieties of plants, excluding bacteria, uncultured plants, and tuber propagated plants, can be protected, as can sexually reproduced plants (by seed), excluding bacterial, fungi, and first-generation hybrids. The TRIPS Agreement does not require protection for new living matter or plant varieties, but WTO members may join the International Union for the Protection of New Varieties of Plants, or UPOV.

Impact of Economic Reforms Process on Indian Agricultural Sector: Agricultural sector is the mainstay of the rural Indian economy around which socio-economic privileges and deprivations revolve, and any change in its structure is likely to have a corresponding impact on the existing pattern of social equality. No strategy of economic reform can succeed without sustained and broad based agricultural development, which is critical for:

- Raising living standards,
- Alleviating poverty,
- Assuring food security,
- Generating buoyant market for expansion of industry and services, and
- Making substantial contribution to the national economic growth.

Studies also show that the economic liberalization and reforms process have impacted on agricultural and rural sectors very much.

Of the three sectors of economy in India, the tertiary sector has diversified the fastest, the secondary sector the second fastest, while the primary sector, taken as whole, has scarcely diversified at all. Since agriculture continues to be a tradable sector, this economic liberalization and reform policy has far reaching effects on (i) agricultural exports and imports, (ii) investment in new technologies and on rural infrastructure (iii) patterns of agricultural growth, (iv) agriculture income and employment, (v) agricultural prices and (vi) Food security.

STRATEGIES

1. The competitive position of Indian Companies in pharmaceuticals and chemical must be fully protected in the home market and not undermined through the patent mechanism. India is entitled to and must claim a waiver in respect of several provisions of the WTO's TRIPS agreement and protect consumer and the drug industry in India.
2. It is the time that India should assert its sovereign status and rights, without any equivocation and false notions of precedence for international over national interests and obligations. In the case of intellectual property rights, the grant of exclusive marketing rights in the Indian market to the patented products of foreign multinational pharmaceutical corporations has actually laid the basis for a totally invidious public health policy.
3. Intellectual Property Laws could be used judiciously for drawing maximum benefits the resources available in rural areas. Many times lack of awareness results in people not claiming Intellectual Property Rights over their inventions, handicraft, designs and literary and artistic expressions thereby losing valuable financial gains for the creators. Inadequate knowledge of the Intellectual Property Rights and the commercial potential of the traditional knowledge and folklore often lead to the holders of them giving away their cultural patrimony to shrewd business people.
4. We are emerging in BPO industry and substantially dominating the world in outsourcing business because of number of factors. There is a large hue and cry in USA and other develop countries to impose anti outsourcing laws, so that their companies could not use outsourcing from India. The time has come; we should also protect our companies by innovating IPR in BPO to give boost to our economy.

As was the case with China, India too showed signs of resistance to quick enforcement of international intellectual property right (IPR) protection laws as demanded by the developed countries, particularly the US. China could get away on grounds that it is not a member of the World Trade Organization (WTO), but India was required to comply. Under the terms of the WTO, India is required to implement WTO-standard IPR protection laws by 2005. It must be acknowledged that there has been remarkable progress in IPR protection the field of software and cinema products.[4]

India's general argument was that it does acknowledge in principle the case for strict IPR protection, but this can be done only in phases suited by its own ground reality. The reality is that absence of international IPR protection for some decades has spawned employment for millions, so an overnight clampdown on IPR violators would foment social unrest.

CONCLUSION

In this globalised regime, the IPR plays an important role in economic development. India is in the transition stage and making substantial growth. The wheel of the growth vehicle is Intellectual property right, therefore we need to look into how best to utilize the same for development, particularly rural development. While the importance of IPRs in national and global economies has received much attention, not enough focus has been given to the importance of IPRs in rural development. The government should come forward to protect our different industries in different sector and their innovation and innovations through IPR otherwise outsiders will reap the maximum benefits of globalization.

NOTES AND REFERENCES

1. James, T.C., "Intellectual property Rights and Rural Development", Kurukshetra, *A Journal on Rural Development*, New Delhi, Pg. 12, April 2004.
2. Rao, M.B., WTO and International Trade, Vikas Publishing House, New Delhi, Pg. 207, 2001.
3. Leading Articles," Patent Law Amendment-Another Contentious Issue", Monthly Commentary, Vol. 541, New Delhi, Pg. 7, August 2004.
4. www.indiaonestop.com/markets-intellectual-prop-rights.htm-19k.

27

INTEGRATION OF INDIGENOUS TECHNICAL KNOWLEDGE FOR IPR

Suman Pandurang Yesane

INTRODUCTION

The farmers in the world have a tradition of experimentation and developing indigenous Knowledge for solution to many of their agricultural problems in harmony with nature. However, some such indigenous Knowledge in the post was often not made use of because of one or the other reason. Of late, the researchers, policy-makers and development professionals have begun recognizing the value of such knowledge. The Key features of such indigenous knowledge are reducing risks, affordability, compatibility with current practices, visible results within a reasonable amount of time and overall satisfying multiple needs. More and more documentation of such indigenous knowledge resources will provide a base to the agricultural researchers and extensionists for appropriate blending with the research information.

Traditional value, which are sustainable in nature, need to be compared with the values of modern systems. The modern agricultural science is different and even contradictory to the traditional agricultural knowledge. The traditional practices of agriculture may disappear unless their values are promoted. For destruction of vast storage of traditional agricultural practices, modern patterns are solely responsible. As long as we shall certainly be in danger. Even our future generation can not escape. Now, it is the time that we have to think about farmers' right and Dunkel's draft. There is a need to disseminate the traditional agricultural wisdom and to give it due encouragement. So that farmers could use the peers knowledge. And all of this can not be done without having the concept of what traditional knowledge or indigenous knowledge is?

WHAT IS INDIGENOUS KNOWLEDGE(TK)?

Indigenous knowledge (TK) is local knowledge. Knowledge that is unique to a given culture or society. It differs from the international knowledge system generated by universities, research institutions and private firms. TK is the basis for local level decision-making in agriculture, health care, food preparation, education, natural resource management and a host of other activities in rural communities.

According to Farrington and Martin (1988). Indigenous Technological Knowledge can be defined as basis for knowledge, beliefs and customs which are internally consistent and logical to those bolding them but at odds with the objectively deduced findings of formal science. So, it is important for scientists to build upon the components or ITK which are not consistent with scientific knowledge seeking to change overtime may potentially counter productive practices associated with local belief system.

Another group of researchers (Reijntjes et.al.,1992) define 'Indigenous Knowledge' as knowledge of the people living in a certain area, generated by their own and their ancestor's experiences and including knowledge originating from elsewhere which has been internalized by the local people.

Traditional agriculture is normally thought to be that collection of practices, which are centuries old and used till modern agriculture began displacing it with its scientific basis. But 'traditional agriculture' is not a universal package of practices, which can be implemented anywhere and any time . What is sustainable at one time and place may not be sustainable in another. There are no universal traditional agricultural systems as there is a western one. Traditional agriculture is also a product of a way of thinking , a way of living and a culture. Traditional farming went beyond boundaries, being integrated with the rest of the village farms, pasture and forest. It depends wholly on the careful and efficient use of available renewable resources and on the maintenance, improvement and even innovations in nutrient cycles. There was no 'waste' with nearly all that was grown being used for on farm or off farm purposes and finally recycled as manure. Its aim was the satisfaction of the basic needs of the surrounding community, not the luxuriant wants of distant regions. The integration of livestock and trees was essential for sustainability (Pereira,1995).

To conclude it might be said that, the local people with their own experiences and experimental to meet their needs generate traditional agricultural knowledge and which is sustainable. This knowledge is tightly interwoven with their beliefs, norms and culture so that it could maintain its identify.

WHY SHOULD WE DOCUMENT TRADITIONAL/ INDIGENOUS KNOWLEDGE?

The majority of the population in most developing countries is small-scale farmers. In most cities, the knowledge system of these farmers have never been recorded systematically in written form, hence, they are not easily assessable to agriculture researchers, extension workers and development parishioners. They have remained invisible to the development community as the myriad of indigenous organization operating in every rural community for the identification and search for solutions to community problems (Warren,1993).

In recent years, interest about TK has grown, alongside recognition of its value for both aboriginal and the industrialized world Preserving TK is vital to the survival of the communities of aboriginal people and local farmers who acquired and protected this knowledge over generations.

Many of the older farming traditions and the knowledge stored within them are being lost. Foreign technology, education, regions and values, the fragmentation of holdings and neglect of agriculture and other factors have led to the marginalization of farmer's knowledge and way of spreading it. With the loss of TK, indigenous practices, crop species, breeds, tools etc. are also lost. But the other way round, when for example certain genetic resources become extinct, knowledge about how to use them is also lost.

Gupta (1990) recognized the causes for documenting traditional wisdom of farmers which are as follows;

- Climate, soil, crop and other variability's at short distance in humid and arid risky environments compel the cultivators to evolve location specific farming practices.

- Science underlying many of these practices still remains to be properly understood with the result that some of the innovative practices are considered traditional and sign of backwardness of the peasants.
- It is possible to generate lateral learning among farmers by sharing innovative practices found suitable in one region with the farmers in another similar region after on farm testing trails if necessary. This will speed up the process of technological change in regions where formal technology generation system has not been any successful. Even in less developed regions, it can not be assumed that an innovative technology will diffuse on its own just because it has been evolved by some farmers in a village.
- Some of these innovations will help extend the frontier of knowledge by providing basis of developing new concepts or adding value by grafting or bedding available formal biological science knowledge to the farmers own knowledge.
- Inclusion of these innovative practices in the graduate and post-graduate curriculum will help instill pride among young minds in their own heritage, make them more humble and respectful towards farmers.
- By sharing this accumulated knowledge with the farmers, their pride in their own innovativeness is restored.
- Agricultural scientists working in Agricultural University, development departments and extension agencies will find an opportunity for recasting their research and action agenda wherever felt necessary. It is not argued that farmers can develop technologies for all situations entirely through their own efforts. Plant introductions and technology transfer across continents has gone for centuries.
- Innovations like any other aspect of knowledge are embedded in a cultural setting.

Besides these, the old and wise persons who were specialists in farming are gradually leaving this world. There is a common property in African Society that 'When a Knowledgeable old person dies, a whole library disappears'. Thus, there is an urgent need to safeguard and reaffirm traditional knowledge. Yet much work must be done to locate, document and disseminate development. Unless we make urgent and quicker efforts to track this valuable knowledge, it will be lost soon, not to be regained in future at any cost.

THE NEED FOR INTEGRATION OF ITKS INTO AGRICULTURE KNOWLEDGE INFORMATION SYSTEMS (AKIS)

Scoones (1989) pointed out that understanding of farmers' knowledge allowed a frame of reference for posing technical and scientific questions in research and provided the basis for evolving technological options.

Warren (1991) reported that it was important to recognize TK and organizational capacity as national resources as they facilitated national development. Farmers had been actively involved in identifying and prioritizing agricultural problems and extending information. He added that farmers continued with their own research and extension agenda outside the public and private sector institutes' set up of a nation to provide them some function.

Fujisaka (1992) pointed out that the farmers and researchers needed to contribute to the development of improved and adaptable upland rice. He remarked that the farmers could contribute to selection criteria about which researchers currently knew little such as deterioration of taste over time, hardening of cooked left over or expansion when cooked. On the other hand, researchers could continue to investigate such things as nutrient uptake dynamics. Mechanics of drought resistance and different strategies for seeking blast resistance.

Reijntjes et al., (1992) reported that indigenous farming systems had following principles and processes in common.

1. *Holistic world view:* It stated that farming was not merely production. It was a way of life. They did not separate farming from their special process.
2. *Community based farming:* Community played an important role in upholding the local culture and knowledge, organized labour, designed and controlled land use and managed change.
3. *Optional use of local resources:* The farming community managed to support itself without external technical support or inputs.
4. *Reliance on genetic and physical diversity:* A wide variety of resources (crops, livestock, trees etc.) were used primarily in

ways that suite the ecological conditions, rather than trying to make major changes in the environment to permit the growth of otherwise unadapted plants and animals.

5. *Soil protection and recycling natural nutrients:* Much emphasis was given to following and recycling plant and animal waste.
6. *Risk minimization:* Greater importance was attached to reducing of risk than maximizing production.
7. *Location specific techniques:* Each farming community has developed different techniques to suit the specific local conditions.

Slikkerveer (1992) observed that in Kenya, many Western technologies, that were aimed at reducing the storage of stable food, had failed, this was partly because agriculture and rural development programmes had ignored the local culture which included the knowledge and perceptions of practices and skill that was evolved over centuries to enable survival.

Tabor (1993) pointed out that indigenous system had an advantage that they were widely known by the people of the region and could easily improve communication between farmers, extension agents and scientists.

From the above reports, it is understood that indigenous agricultural practices are cost effective, time tested, eco-friendly and they serve to sustain the agricultural development. Integration of such practical into AKIS through scientific validation would certainly boost the sustainability of farming.

SOME OF THE INDIGENOUS CROP PRACTICES THAT COULD BE INTEGRATED INTO AKIS

In gram, fewer pre-sowing ploughings result in more clods and provide the required aeration as well as help in checking the unwanted vegetative growth of the crop (Gupta,1985).

The traditional practice of Rab for raising rice nurseries in Ratnagiri district in soils near the sea coast involves covering of seed bed area by about 3-5 inches layer of thick dry refuse, set fire to it in April-May on the eastern end of the area, preferably in the evening so as to allow it to burn slowly. In soils away from sea coast, farmers covered seed bed area by about 3-5″ thick layer of dry leaves, grasses and one inch thin layer of fine soil followed by sprinkling of water. Then dry cattle-dung or other dry refuse was kept over it. This material was set on fire in April-May on the eastern end of the area (Anonymous, 2000).

For in situ manuring, weeds were allowed to grow on rice fields and then trampled at appropriate time. In a larger part of Madras, the spreading of wild shrub such as wild indigo (Wrightia tinctoriao) and the sheets and leaves of Pongumia pinnata and other trees was much used on 'wet' lands, principally on rice fields. The shrubs and leaves were spread green on the fields and then trodden in by feet (Randhawa, 1983).

It was also reported that farmers using Velvet bean (Mucina prunes) for the first time, planted the legume one or two months after planting corn in the beginning of January in Central America. Later, when the corn was harvested, its stalks were bent over and left on the fields. Velvet-bean grew covering these stalks and soon the legume took over the whole cornfield. By December, the large amounts of velvet bean foliage varying from 50-70 mt/ha began to dry out until it finally ended on top of the ground providing a cover, that could be up to 20cm. Thick. This meant that the next corn crop was planted directly through the mulch. The mulch suppressed the weed while allowing adequate establishment of the corn. During the second year, velvet bean seeds would sprout from the previous year's remants and the cycle continued with the planting of a new crop of corn (Flores, 1989).

The practice of removing water from fields of paddy in Andhra Pradesh after 2-3 weeks of plantation was quite valid and needed further testing, in the opinion of the scientists (Gupta, 1988).

In rice fields, application of neem cake as basal manure helped to protect the rice crop from brown plant hopper at the latter stage (Balasubramanian,1998).

In chena village of Sri Lanka whenever a leaf eating caterpillar damage was observed a round section of young plantation stem used to be fixed on to a stick driven into mud, forming a small receptacle or platform about 6″ in diameter. Cool rice, pulses, flowers and a lighted wick dipped in coconut oil were placed at a few spots distributed over the affected and adjoining area. Pest damage was controlled within two days in this method. The birds got attracted by light, tried to eat food on the unstable platform, the whole thing collapsed and the birds picked the food spread on the field and also the leaf eating caterpillars (Upawasa, 1998).

The tribals as an insect repellent used leaves of tulsi (Ocimum sanctum L.) especially at the time of collection of honey (Chaudhuri and Pal, 1997).

Berthold (1989) mentioned a 'bucket trap' for controlling rat damage. A twenty-liter open-mouthed container was set in the ground, so that top edge came in level with the surface. The container was then half filled with water. I t was covered with some tiny sticks and grass and attractant was sprinkled in the centre of that cover. With this method, six rats per container per night were caught.

Leaves of Neem (Ameha xadirachta) or nigadi (1) or teak (Teclona grandis) or fruits of Kubhali or triphala (Zanthozylum rhesta) or gelkand were mixed in the grains by the farmers in Ratnagiri district, Maharashtra and the grain storing kangis were plastered on all sides by cow dung to keep away the storage insects.

Similarly, farmers stored paddy grains in wooden bins or boxes locally called as kothars/hadapa or tattya or kangas (bamboo mats made into hollow cylinders). Kanger was plastered on both sides with cow dung and its bottom was sunk in the ground to a depth of nine inches. In the house or verandah. After thoroughly cleaning it from inside, grains were filled in the kanga. The opening of kanga was secured by light plastering or by stitching with gunny cloth.

Farmers in Sierra Leone practice a combination of different techniques for preventing soil erosion. The most common one was stick and stone bunds which acted as dams to trap the soil being washed down slopes. They were similar to contour bunks and were called stick bunds, when constructed with wood , stone and rocks (Millingtan,1987).

CONCLUSION

Indigenous Knowledge is important activities to be successful. If it has not been recorded, it remains largely inaccessible to development workers and researchers. Indigenous Knowledge is the basis for self sufficiency and self-determination for at least two reasons i.e. (1) People are familiar with indigenous practices and technologies. They can understand, handle and maintain them better than introduced practices and technologies and (2) Indigenous Knowledge draws on local resources. People are less dependent on outside supplies which can be costly, scarce and available only irregularly. Therefore, every effort should be made to document and validate such knowledge, which is useful for development purpose. The indigenous Knowledge of the farmers from a particular zone can be documented and such knowledge should be fed to research system in order to develop low cost and effective technologies for the benefit of the farming community.

REFERENCES

Anonymous (2000), Documentation of Indigenous Technical Knowledge (Unpublished Report), Konkan Krishi Vidyapeeth, Dapoli, Dist. Ratnagiri.

Balsubramanian, A. (1998), Traditional Plant Protection Methods in Tamil Nadu 'Biological Methods of Pest Control–Proceedings of the Southern Regional Seminar'. Ed. K. Vijayalaxmi, PPAST Foundation, Madfas, pp. 35-37.

Berthold, S. (1989), Natural crop protection pest control. Presbyterian Rural Training Centre, Mfonts. Bamenda, Cameroon, p. 14.

Chaudhari, H.N. and Pal (1997), Plants in Folk Relation and Mythology Contribution to Indian Ethnobotany, 3rd Edition. Ed. S.K. Jain Scientific Publishers, Jodhpur, p. 19.

28

RESEARCH AREAS IN IPRs

P. Selvaraj

INTRODUCTION

I think it will not be an exaggeration to say we are living in a terminology era. The subject of intellectual property rights has contributed and continues to add to a board spectrum of terminologies to the already overflowing pool of technical terms. Recently I was traveling by bus from Tirchy to Tuticorin and saw some where on national highway a signboard showing an "Institute of Driving Technology". I don't know what that means as I am a novice in knowing whether house hold cooking comes under the purview of food technology. The taste of a dish varies from kitchen to kitchen and no two housewives need to prepare it in the same fashion anyway. The possibility of bringing such "Technologies" under IPR baffles me and may be, you too.

RESEARCH SURVEY

Defining IPR for a product or technology itself is a complex task. Services like education would only make it all the more complex. A lot of research has to be carried out before operational definitions could be evolved for practical use. I would like to suggest in this context a research project that can be taken up employing survey method. The responses of teachers, students and educators to the segments of a survey schedule structured for such an investigation might be of use in this regard. I have given below a draft schedule with an indication that pre-testing would help improve the same making it adequate for the said purpose.

SURVEY SCHEDULE IPR RESEARCH AREAS

I. Teachers

A. General:

1. Name:
2. Address:
3. Qualification:
4. Responsibility:
5. Experience:

B. Preference:

Would you like to be a:

1. Teacher
2. Teacher–cum-Researcher
3. Teacher–cum-Extensionist
4. Teacher–cum–Researcher–cum-Extensionist

C. Questions:

a. Who should be given copyright for the following teaching resource materials and in which ratios?

1. Course content
2. Courseware
3. Lecture Notes
4. Text-books
5. Monographs

b. What would be your suggestion if the above resource materials are

1. Authored
2. Jointly Authored
3. Inter-disciplinary
4. Multi-disciplinary

c. Do you think students could contribute to them

D. *Constraints*

a. What are the constraints in implementing IPR for the above or other teaching resource materials including multi-media.

1. Need not felt
2. Intra-department issues
3. Inter-department issues
4. Faculty issues
5. Lack of knowledge of IPR
6. Plagiarism

b. Do you think it is necessary to include IPR in the curricula?

II. Researchers

A. *General:*

1. Name:
2. Address:
3. Qualification:
4. Responsibility :
5. Experience:

B. *Questions*

Who should be given IPR for the following outcomes of research and in which ratios?

1. Research reports
2. Research papers published in-house
3. Research papers published in journals
4. A new product
5. A new methodology or procedure

C. As in I D

III. Extensionists

A. *General:*

1. Name :
2. Address :

3. Qualification :
4. Responsibility :
5. Experience :

B. Questions

Who should be given copyright for the following extension resource materials and in which ratios?

1. Extension Literature
2. New Extension Method
3. Scripts Written
4. Creative Arts
5. New Multimedia Applications.

C. As in I D

CONCLUSION

I am indeed aware that the above schedule is too short and too broad and too general. It can be elaborated after administering it in a pilot survey that would generate details.To minimize respondent –bias the size of sample should be large enough and stratified sampling followed. The responses could be discussed threadbare, one by one, in a brainstorming. In my opinion a survey method similar to RRA or PRA or QUERI could save time and costs. The results of analysis of responses could be corroborated with IPR discussed in the literature that is fast building up in the field.

CASES

Williams V. Weisser: Unauthorized commercial sale and distribution of notes taken at a UCLA anthropology professor's lectures.

Abernethy V. Huthchinson: Lectures delivered on own notes at a London Hospital published by "The Lancet".

Carid V. Sime: Defendant published pamphlets of plaintiff professor's lectures based on notes taken at the lecture.

Sherrill V. Grieves: Plaintiff professor wrote a book in conjunction with the course he was teaching in a school.

Weinstein V. University of Illinois: Ownership of artide when the document constitutes a work-for-hire

(Source: *http://mipr.umn.edu/archive/v4n2/townsend.pdf*)*

REFERENCE

Elizabeth Townsend, *Legal and Policy Responses to the Disappearing "Teacher Exception" or Copy right Ownership in the 21st Century University*, Volume 4, Number 2, 2003.

29

INTELLECTUAL PROPERTY RIGHTS REGIME IN INDIA

M. Perumal, Chitra Thennalesswaran & G. Paneer Selvam

INTRODUCTION

On January First, 1995, the most intense and contentious GATT trade round got concluded. This led to the formation of the world's most powerful trade regulating agency namely, the World Trade Organization (WTO). This organization is an umbrella organization responsible for overseeing the implementation of all agreements that have been negotiated just before it came into existence or those that would be negotiated in future. It is supposed to be a forum wherein further negotiations and discussions on the matters covered by the agreements as well as the issues that crop-up while negotiations and discussions are on. Moreover it will be responsible for periodic review of the trade policies of the world trading community.

IPR REGIME IN INDIA VIS-A-VIS THE NEW REGIME

India has a long history of protection of intellectual property rights through legislative enactments. The judiciary too has contributed a lot on its part in extending the protection to the owners or licensees of the trade mark who used to seek remedy under different enactments like IPC 1860; Special Relief ACT 1877 (replaced by Specific Relief Act 1963) for protection of their rights.

Section 479 to 489 of the IPC 1860 provide for penal provisions for the protection of the trademarks. Since thse provisions were inadequate in view of the growing industrialization and the economic development, the Trade Marks Act 1940, was subsequently replaced by the Trade and Merchandise Marks Act 1958, the latter served the purpose for over four decades. In view of the development in the trading practices, globalization of the trade and industry, the need to encourage investment flows and transfer of technology, need for simplification and harmonization of trade and to fulfill the obligations of the agreements related to the intellectual property under the Uruguay round of GATT negotiations. The Indian Parliament enacted the Trademarks ACT, 1999 repealing the 1958 act. The act of 1999 amends and consolidates the law relating to trademarks for goods and services and prevention of the use of the fraudulent marks. The most significant change that the new act has brought is to provide for the registration of the trademarks for service of any description that is made available to potential users and includes provision of services in connection with trade or business of any industrial or commercial matters such as banking, communication, education, financing, insurance, chit funds, real estate, transport, storage, material treatment, processing, supply of electrical and other energy, boarding and lodging, entertainment, telecommunications, amusement, construction, repairs, conveying of news of information and advertising.

THE PATENTS ACT

India's Patent policy dates back to 1856, but much of the attention was received only after the independence. The Patent Enquiry Committee (1948-50) and the Ayyangar Committee (1957-59) were important in shaping the current patent act of 1970. The former felt that the patent system failed to encourage and stimulate the inventions among the Indians, while the latter noted that India is deprived of getting, in many cades, goods at cheaper prices from alternative sources because of the patent protection granted in India.

Since 1970, the Indian Patents Act, 1970 has continued to govern the patents part of the IP regime in India over the past three decades except for the recent amendments bringing in exclusive marked rights in tune with the India's obligations under the WTO's

TRIPS agreement. India joined the Pairs Convention and the Patent Co-operation Treaty in 1999. India has a ten years transition to provide product patents from the process patents by the end of 2004. By now it is well known fact that Indian industry, especially the chemicals and pharmaceuticals, have benefited out of a soft patent regime under the 1970 Act (Fikket, 1993; Haskar 1995; Nageshkumar and Sakib, 1996). The rapid evolution of the Indian Pharmaecuticals industry since the mid –70s highlights the fact that weak Intellectual Property Rights Regime could be instrumental in building up local capabilities even in a poor country like India. It is in the light of flourished pharmaceuticals and chemical industry that the pressure on India persisted for being signatory to the IPR agreement. A brief comparison between the IPA 1970 and the TRIPs agreement can be outlined as below.

IPA Act, 1970	*TRIPs*
(a) Only process patents not product in food medicines and chemicals.	(a) Process and Product patents in almost all fields of Technology.
(b) Term of patents fourteen years; five to seven years in chemicals and drugs.	(b) Terms of patents twenty years.
(c) Compulsory liensing and license of right.	(c) Limited compulsory licensing.
(d) Several areas excluded from patents (method of agriculture and process for medical surgical or other similar treatment of animals and plants to render them free of disease or increase economic value of products.	(d) Almost all fields of technology patentable. Plant varieties excluded form patent protection but confusion exists on protection in some areas of agriculture and bio-techno.
(e) Government allowed to use patented inventions to prevent scarcity.	(e) Very limited scope for government to use patented inventions.

Source: Adapted from the Patent office technical society; IPA 1970; Rules 1991; GATT Agreements, WTO 1995.

Moreover, the Patents (amendment) Act, 1999 provides for exclusive marketing rights for marketing. This enables his product firm the date of filing the applications for the grant of patent without going through the procedure laid down in the Patents Act for the grant of the patent. The Exclusive Marketing Rights can be granted before the grant of patents in the country where the research has its origin. In such case were would not be able to insist on the production of the article. The patent holder in India would be possessing the right to distribute and market the product by importing the same form any other country. This may be at high or prohibitive process. In many cases is it left to the discretion of the patent holder to fix the process. The effect of Exclusive Marketing Rights and other changes in the patents act of the 1970 would be enormous on the Indian Economy, especially the agriculture and pharmaceuticals companies.

THE COPYRIGHT ACT

As one of the branches of the intellectual property copyright provides for protection, *inter alia* of the literacy, musical, photographic and audio-visual works and of computer programs. In the field of copyright, creative intellectual activity is encouraged by according to authors as creators of literacy and artistic works, exclusive rights in their works. These rights also provide legal basis for contractual arrangements/agreements between the authors and the producer or the distributor of the expression of the authors ideas. Owners of copyrights in protected works have the right to exclude others from using the work without authorization. These rights are known as exclusive rights. These rights comprise of (a) reproduction rights-copying and reproducing the work; (b) performing rights–performing the work in public; (c) Recording rights making sound recording of the work; (d) motion picture rights; (e) broadcasting rights and (f) translation and adoption rights. These rights are known as economic rights. However countries are exempted from granting non-economic or moral rights.

Till 1994 amendment, the India copyright legislation did not protect the non-economic rights but the amendment in post 1994 brought into the protection of the moral as well as non-economic rights too. Software too is protected in India through copyright legislation. But before 1994 the legislation was not very clear as to whether object code, as opposed to source code should be accorded the protection. International case law was also ambiguous on this. The TRIPS agreement leaves no scope on this count. In line with this requirement, the legislation was amended in 1999 so as to ensure both the source code and object code is protected. The amendment also enlarged the scope protection of computer programmes regardless of whether such a copy of a computer programme has been sold or given on hire on earlier occasion.

THE DESIGNS ACT

The design act 2000 defines the terms 'design' to mean only the feature of shape, configuration, pattern, ornament of composition of lines to colours applied to any articles whether two/three dimensional or in both forms by any industrial process or means whether manual, mechanical or chemical, separate or combined, which in the finished articles appeal to and are judged solely by the eye, but does not include any mode or principle of construction or anything which is in substance a mere mechanical device an does not include any trademark.

The 2000 Act has widened the scope of designs protection in India. The conditions are (a) that the design sought to be registered must be new and original; (b) that it must not be disclosed to public or must not be publicly known by the user or in any other way prior to the date of filing the application for the registration; (c) that must be significantly distinctive from known designs or combinations thereof; and (d) it must not comprise or contain scandalous or obscene matter. These provisions may prove helpful in putting a check on registration of the fraudulent designs. By and large, industrial designs are protected in consumer goods sector like textiles, leather products and automobiles (Vasanth, V. 2002, p. 9).

The Designs Act, 2000 has enhanced the amount of penalty in the case of piracy of the registered design from Rs. 500.00 to Rs. 25,000. In the case the proprietor chooses to claim damages then the amount which may be paid to him has been fixed at Rs. 50,000 instead of Rs. 1000. This provision will prove helpful in decreasing the ratio of infringement of the registered design.

The Designs Act, 1911 contained the following grounds for cancellation of the registration of design (i) the design has been previously registered in India; or (ii) it has been published in India prior to the date of registration; or (iii) the design is not new or original. The amendment has provided two additional grounds for cancellation or registration of the designs. These are : (i) that the design is not design as defined in the clause (d) of the section 2 of the act. These additional grounds will help the interested persons to get a wrongly registered designs cancelled.

THE IMPLICATIONS OF THE NEW REGIME

Pharmaceuticals

This is industry which has benefited the maximum from the patent regime prior to the WTO regime. One of the main provisions of the act was that only process and product patents could be granted in pharmaceuticals, food and chemicals. The research institutes, industry used the regime to develop reverse engineering technologies to build indigenous technologies and disseminate the same in cheaper from to the Indian industry (Jolly 2001). Further the Indian Industry also benefited by replicating the products introduced in the world in a short span of time, while weaning away the benefits accrued to the actual inventors and the researchers. The regime saw a rapid evolution and growth of Indian pharmaceutical industry and the technological capability. This is reflected in terms of rising exports of drugs pharmaceuticals, with their cost effective process innovations. The Indian companies have emerged as competititve suppliers in the world of a large number of generic drugs that are now outside the patent protection. Thus, the industry has evolved from one being highly import dependent to one that generates increasing export surplus for the country. The technological capabilities of the Indian companies have grown to such an extent that some multinationals have started joint ventures with the Indian companies.

Agriculture

The agreement on agriculture in relation to the intellectual property in the Agriculture sector compels the members to protect innovation in all fields including agriculture. It erodes the authority of the government to demand compulsory licensing of the essential goods. Till now India succeeded in keeping the agriculture sector beyond the purview of new Intellectual Property Regime. But now in the new situation the issues are going to be serious.

The Indian agriculture has lost its base of diversity even in the absence of IPR protection, largely due to public sector research institutions, responsible for green revolution besides the market forces and policy measures such as pricing structure, subsidies, credit policies. Thus, grudging only the IPRs or private sector cannot adequately address the problems of sustainability of the Indian Agriculture.

CONCLUSION

There is no doubt that over the years the TRIPs has emerged as one of the most debated agreements of the WTO. The changes insisted would have severe implications for the developing countries, more to when they are struggling with the implementation hurdles of the new regime. The discussion in the earlier sections suggests that the strengthening and harmonization of the IPR Regime in the developing countries like India in a significant manner.

BIBLIOGRAPHY

Abbott, F.M. (2001), "The TRIPs Agreement Access to Mediciness and WTO Doha Ministerial Conference"; Occasional Paper No. 7. United Nations Office; Geneva.

Anand, A.S. Justice (1997), Intellectual Property-Indian Experience, 6 SCC J 1.

Chaudhuri, S. (2002), "TRIPs Agreement and Amendment of Patents Act in India" EPW; Vol. 37 (32); pp. 3354-60.

Cohen, W.M. (1995), Empirical Studies of Innovative Activity" In Paul Stoneman (ed.) Handbook of the Economics on Innovation and Technological Change' Blackwell, pp. 182-264.

Correa, C. (2001), "Patent Law, TRIPs, and R and D Incentive: A Southern Perspective," CMH Working Paper No. WG: 12; Commission on Macroeconomics and Health; WHO.

Debroy, B. (1998), Intellectual Property Rights, B.R. Publishing Corporation: Delhi-52.

FICCI (1996), "Effects on Industry and Response" Workshop on Patents Amendment Bill 1996; Background Paper. August.

Fikkert, B. (1993), "An Open or Closed Technology Policy? The Effects of Technology Licensing Foreign Direct Investment and Technology Spill over on R & D in Indian Industrial Sector Firms".

30

PROTECTION OF BIO-DIVERSITY AND INDIGENOUS KNOWLEDGE

S. Ramakrishnan

INTRODUCTION

Biological diversity means the variability among living organisms from all sources including terrestrial, marine and other aquatic eco systems and the ecological complexes. Living things as they evolved on the earth, have produced a be wildering diversity. There are millions of species of plants and animals but even within a species there exists enormous diversity. This massive diversity or "Gene Pool" is a common heritage of all human beings. It is also their insurance for future survival. Increasingly as new varieties of plants and animals useful to humanbeings are bread this massive gene bank provided by nature become important.

Bio Diversity assessments need to be made at the community and landscape levels if we are to predict changes over time. It is primarily the loss to habitats that leads to both genetic and species diversity.

India is one of the top 12 mega diversity countries. Diversity in genes , species and ecosystems provides the raw materials with which human communities adopt to change. Thus, the loss of each additional species gene and eco system reduces the ability of nature and people to adopt to the changing environment.

The Food and Agricultural organisation (FAO) of the United nations has defined the sustainable development in forestry, wild life, agriculture, fishery is to conserves land, water, plant and animal genetic resources. It is environmentally non degrading, technically appropriate, economically viable and socially accepted". This four biological pillars of the global economy are crop plants, grasslands, forests, and fisheries. They continue to give valuable substances for human life. The main approaches have been used to determine the value of biological resources namely consumptive use, productive use, social, ethical, aesthetic and option values.

THREATS TO BIODIVERSITY

India has 2.5% of the earth's surface and one seventh of its population. An estimated 20% of the population lives in town and cities and approximately 80% in the rural areas. In proportion to the population India uses only a small fraction of the world's resources. In India's problems revolve around high population density, low available and utilisation of natural resources, poor standard of living, high percentage of illiteracy and low levels of environmental awareness.

India's population density of inhabited areas is 178 persons per sq.km. and at places it reaches 2,738 persons per sq.km. It is one of the highest in the world. Although the pattern of rural-urban population we remained atmost steady during the last 100 years, the density of the population has increased tremendously, particularly in the last few decades. About 3000 million litters of sewage flows out of the cities and towns of India every day. These kinds of change that man has done and is doing to his environment are some of the ways in which the diminishing of environmental quality threatens the existence of earth's organism.

India has uniquely rich diversity of plant and animal life, which constitute in no small measure to the human economy. Expanding human population resulted in the expanding needs of man. With scientific progress and technological development men started utilisation, natural resources at a much larger scale. This paper now would consider each of the natural resources and the possible ways of its conservation particularly in Indian context. They are as follows:

(i) Deforestation (Forest destruction)

(ii) Desertification

(iii) Urbanisation

(iv) River Valley Projects

(v) Minings
(vi) Industrialisation
(vii) Genetic diversity

INTERNATIONAL PROGRAMMES AND CONVENTIONS

India participates with many international agreements and programmes concerned with aspects of nature, conservation and sustainable development. These range from legal instruments such as the convention on biological diversity, which place obligations on those nations which become contracting parties to scientific programmes such as the UNESCO, Man and the biosphere Programme, a global programme of international scientific cooperation. Examples of agreements and programmes with which India is collaborating are as follows.

CONVENTION ON INTERNATIONAL TRADE IN ENDANGERED SPECIES (CITES)

Since India became a party to CITES on 18th October 1976 it has provided data annually to the CITES secretariat on the trade of endangered species through its CITES management authority. The text of the CITES convention along with the CITES appendix are provided.

WORLD HERITAGE CONVENTION

India ratified the world heritage convention in 1977 and since then five natural sites have been inscribed as areas of outstanding universal value. These sites are:

(i) Kaziranga National Park
(ii) Keoladeo National Park
(iii) Manas National Park
(iv) Sundarbans National Park
(v) Nanda Devi National Park

CONVENTION ON BIOLOGICAL DIVERSITY

India signed the convention on Biological diversity on 5th June 1992, ratified it on 18th February 1994 and brought it into force on 19th March 1994. This convention will provide a frame work for the sustainable management and conservation of India's natural resources.

RAMSAR (WETLANDS)CONVENTION

India has been a contracted party to the Ramsar convention since 1st February 1982. India has now six sites covering some 1,92,973 hectares of important wetland. These sites are:

(i) Chilka Lake

(ii) Keoladeo National Park

(iii) Wular lake

(iv) Harike lake

(v) Loktak lake

(vi) Sambhar lake

BIO DIVERSITY AT LOCAL LEVEL

In India, nearly 200 sanctuaries and 19 National Parks have been established for wild life management. Sanctuaries are placed where the killing or capturing of any animal is prohibited except under orders of the authorities concerned. They provide protection and optimum living conditions to wild animals. National Parks are set up for preserving flora, fauna, landscapes and historic objects of an area. Some well known wild life sanctuaries and National parks of Tamilnadu are as follows.

VEDANTHANGAL BIRD SANCTUARY

It covers an area of 0.30 sq.km. over a lake about 85 km south of Chennai. It is a bird sanctuary. Many migratory birds regularly visits this area during October and November. When the summer starts , the lake becomes empty because the birds migrate to their homelands. Ibis, Spon bills, Open bulled stork, egrete, cormorant darter, grey heron, Pebican and Dab chinch are some of the birds that visit this sanctuary.

MUDUMALAI SANCTUARY

This sanctuary is situated in Nilgris district. It was established in 1940. It covers an area of 321sq. km. It is characterised by dense forest and diversity of fauna. The common wild animals of this sanctuary are as follows.

Wild elephant, Bison, Sambhar, Chital, Parking deer, mouse deer, Tiger, Panther, Bonnet Monkey, Giant squirrel, Flying squirrel, wild dog, Jackal, Wild cat, Porcupine, Pangolia, Flying lizard, Phython, Ratsnake etc.

MUNDANTHURAI SANCTUARY

It is situated in Thirunelveli Dist at Pabanasam hills. The Tamiraparani river passes through this sanctuary. It was established in 1962. It encloses an area of 520 sq.km. It is formed of thick forest. The wild animals here include Tiger, Panther, sambhar, and Chital.

ANAMALAI SANCTUARY

This sanctuary is located in Coimbatore district. It was established in 1972. It covers an area of 968 sq.km. The wild animals of this sanctuary include elephants, bison, Sambhar, Spotted deer, Chital, Barking deer, Nilgiri Tahr, lion tailed monkey, tiger, Panther, Sloth bear, langur, Porcupine, Pangolin etc.

POINT CALIMERE

This sanctuary is situated in Tanjore Dist. It covers an area of 17sq.km. The back water of this sanctuary is inhabited by flocks of flamingoes and Pelicans in water. The nearby Vedaranyam forests are inhabited by a large number of block bucks, chital, wild boars etc.

MUNTRADAIPPU SANCTUARY

This sanctuary is situated along the national Highway between Nagercoil and Tirunelveli. This sanctuary is inhabited by many migratory birds.

GUINDY DEER PARK

It is situated near Chennai and has mainly Chitals and black bucks. A few albinos of black buck are also found here.

THE PALANI HILLS

The Palani hills conservation council was formed in 1985 an organisation devoted to Promoting sustainable development. This consists of ecologists, environmentalist, Botanists etc. The Palani hills is basically the eastern spur of the western ghats range in the south India state of Tamilnadu. The hills start at 220m sea level and raise upto 2300 mtrs. The wet temperate forests of these hills are known as "Sholas" in the meaning Natural Prime forests.

KODAIKANAL

Kodaikanal, one of the most beautiful hill town is situated in the Palani hills. It is an important eco town threatened at the sometime by two potential issues of entrophication of the lake and pollution by tourists. The lake situated at Kodaikanal town at 2200 mtrs. above sea level is the main source of drinking water to many towns, the Pilgirm town of Palani in the plains. The lake is spread over an area of 22 Hectare and is fed by natural springs through marsh.

CONSERVATION OF BIODIVERSITY

Conservation strategies currently in voque or the new methods and technologies being integrated mainly keep in view the holistic approach of biodiversity conservation and attempt of the continuance survival and perpectuation of reservoir of variation for discovering new genes or gene recombination required for plant breeding and crop improvement. The needs are further accentuated on account of finding new resources of wider ecological situations and stress conditions. Currently different strategies employed the world over include both in-situ and ex-situ conservation methods.

IN-SITU CONSERVATION

In-situ conservation primarily deals with wild and weedy species, their survival, perpectuation and evaluvation in their natural habitats without their displacement. It involves preservation of eco habitates which permit uninterrupted speciation through gene exchange introgression and through the forces of natural selection such as disruptive selection which might occur overtime and space. Thus the equilibrium and its dynamism continues to function due to energy flow which sustains the environmental balance meeting the requirement of its dependents.

The following table gives details of in-situ conservation (Ecosystem conservation) Programmes in India.

The appreciation of the concept is just not enough in any country even identification area and its demarcation on map will not having any tangible results unless we have the machinery expertise adequate monitory funding, critical scientific back up, governmental and social support, peoples participation, motivation and involvement of tribal, folk, human urge and strong public movement to sustain the movement of conservation of biodiversity.

In-situ Conservation Programmes In India

Sl. No.	*Nature of eco-system*	*State*	*Location*	*Area sq. km*
1.	Himalayan Highlands	U.P.	Nandadevi	1560
2.	North-eastern sub tropical hills	Meghalaya	Nokvek	80
3.	Noth-eastern tropical	Assam	Manas	2837
4.	Eastern rain forest region	West Bengal	Sundarbhans	9630
5.	South eastern costal eco system	Tamilnadu	Gulf of Mannar	535
6.	Malabar region (tropical rain forest)	Karnataka, Kerala & Tamilnadu	Nilgiri Hills	5520
7.	Andaman and Nicobar Islands ecosystem	Nicobar	Great Nicobar Island	885

EX-SITU CONSERVATION

Ex-Situ conservation strategy involves maintenance of germplasm, elite strains, trees, clones in the field, Orchards, Plantations, botanical and herbal gardens, clonal repositories in the gene banks (seed banks) or in plant tissue culture repositories. In the past, in several countries, botanical gardens have played a very conspicuous and predominant role in the introduction and dissemination of new plant species, accessions from one region to another. This process has significantly contributed to the world economy and all nations have derived enormous benefits. The famous botanical gardens such as Kew Botanical gardens, London, Shivpur botanical garden, Kolkatta, Bogar Botanical garden, Zakarta or Peredenia Botanical garden, Columbo and several others in europe and America provide illustrious examples.

The concept of germ plasm diversity could not be fulfilled through botanical garden as this had a limited scope because only limited seeds could be planted which represented only a fraction of Gene Pool or only a few individuals could be established. This brought in the very sound methods of germ plasm conservation through seed storage gene banks.

GENE BANKS

During the past 3 decades, about 100 small medium gene banks have been developed in several countries of the world. Conservation of seed producing agri, horticulture, crop plants have been made possible through seed gene banks where seeds after appropriate moisture reduction can be preserved at a very low temperature of 18^0 C to 20^0C for the period ranging from 10 to 50 years depending upon species. The process reduced the risk of genetic erosion through genetic drift mechanical mixing due to errors or due to natural vagaries. Besides, considerable reduction in cost of field, maintenance and regeneration could be achieved and gem plasm could be safely preserved overtime. Indian gene bank already holds over 1,50,000 accessions.

TISSUE CULTURE REPOSITORY

In vitro clonal repository also provides considerable scope for the conservation of diversity in those species which are predominantly vegetatively propagated or where multiplication rate is slow, limited, tedious and species genomic architecture is complex. India has again taken the lead in this direction and the first national plant. Tissue culture repository established through the financial support of the department of biotechnology (DBT) has demonstrated this feasibility in banana, citrus, garbic, other wild allium species, sweet potato, Yams, Ginger, turmeric and Pepper. Besies several endangered plant species of medicinal and aromatic value have been conserved. Cryopreservational technology also appears quite feasible for the long term conservation of seeds Pollan and in vitro culture systems, animal embryos etc.

CONCLUSION

Now a days living organisms of all sources are terribly hard to survive due to various activities of man for development and application of advanced technology in all fields of life steps. Governments and all organisation of human welfare are interested to protect various biodiversities of living organism. This paper analysed various steps taken by local, state and central government and in international level. It also revealed various strategies taken in all over the world. From that this paper has therefore come to realise that it is urgent and most challenging one to protect the national and international wealth of bio-diversity.

31

INTELLECTUAL PROPERTY RIGHTS AND PUBLIC HEALTH: AN EVALUATION

R. Annapoorani

The advent of globalisation has changed the engine of economic development from manual and mechanical force to intellectual process and this has brought out the significance of intellectual property rights. Intellectual property rights relates to information which can be incorporated in tangible objects and can be used by several persons at the same time, unlike immovable or movable tangible property. Intellectual property rights refer to the assurance given by the Government to reward the innovations by granting monopoly over production and marketing (Subbarao and Thiyagarajan, 1998).

The international environment with respect to intellectual property rights has changed considerably with the conclusion of the TRIPs agreement in the Uruguay round. The TRIPs agreement accommodates the demands of the industralised countries for higher international standard of protection by mandating the extension of patent ability to virtually all field of technology, by prolonging the patent protection for a uniform term of 20 years and by providing legal recognition of the patentee's exclusive right to import the patented products.

There are different aspects of intellectual property rights. They are copyright and related rights, trade marks, geographical indicators, industrial designs, patents, layout designs of integrated circuits, protection of undisclosed information, control of Anticompetive practices in contractual licenses.

With regard to intellectual property rights India differs from other developing countries. It recognizes only process patent, and not product patent. It allows process patents in the area of pharmaceuticals, food products and chemicals.

At the international level, on 31st December, 2002, dead line was proposed for signing of the proposed agreement on TRIPs and public health in the Doha mandate that recognizes the supremacy of public health over intellectual property rights.

The implementation of TRIPS has raised concern about the impact on public health and prices and availability of essential medicines. It is widely believed that prices will go up upon introduction of product patents and have stimulated welfare losses for consumers. Some studies in India found that the increase in pharmaceutical prices could be either in the range between 26 percent to 242 percent or in the range between 182 to 225 percent, with the introduction of product patents on 22 existing pharmaceutical products. A study finds the welfare losses to six developing countries (Argentina, Brazil, India, Mexico, Korea and Taiwan) from introduction of product patents to be US $ 3.5 billion to $ 10.8 billions. The gains to the patent owners would range between $ 2.9 billion to $ 14.4 billion. The huge difference between prices of HIV/AIDS drugs sold by patent holders in South Africa and their generic substitute provides an evidence to the potential of price increase following the introduction of product patents.

Many of the new medical researches are targeting the developed counties with promising profit for medicines for life style diseases, whereas developing countries are still in need of basic health care. Almost 80 per cent of the Indian population will be deprived of the latest life saving drugs as the multinational companies invade the markets of the developing world with self dictated prices and monopoly in marketing.

The Indian drug industry feels that it is under potential threat since the prices of the potential medicines may go up when royalty would have to be paid to the patentee for using the technology.

One of the argument in favour of a stronger intellectual property regime is based on the premise that stringent IPR protection was deemed to be a necessary condition for sustaining the pace of innovation in the global economy. But the empirical literature showed that tightening of IPRs is likely to affect innovative activity adversely by obstructing the spillovers. Further, the research priorities are determined by the purchasing power and very little research and development is done on tropical diseases.

The provision of product patents on chemical and pharmaceutical products would adversely affect the process of innovative activity of the developing country enterprises in the manufacture of chemicals covered by patents. The development of new chemical compounds is beyond the capability of most developing country enterprises in view of the huge resources involved. Therefore, they focus attention on process innovations for the known chemicals and bulk drugs. Above all, the patent system grants temporary monopoly to the firms that introduce innovation.

To reduce the adverse impact of intellectual property rights, the Government of India need to formulate some measures. To protect the poor masses from price increase following the introduction of product patents, Government may impose regulation of prices of essential drugs. There is also a need for defining conditions, norms and practices for facilitating transfer of technology for production of essential drugs. Under the changing circumstances Indian drug industry need to make considerable investment in research and development with a focus in new chemical molecules which can be used for treatment of diseases predominant in India due to its tropical climate.

India can expect a positive effect of IPR on public health, since on 2nd October 2004, Health Canada released regulations that would enable the exports of low cost generic varieties of patented drugs to developing countries.

BIBLIOGRAPHY

General studies manual, (1997), Tata McGraw, Hill Publishing Company Ltd, New Delhi, p. 56.

James.T.C., (2004), 'Intellectual Property Rights and Rural Development', Kurukshetra, April, pp.12-21.

Journal of Intellectual Property Rights, Vol. 9, November 2004, pp. 492-502.

Journal of Intellectual Property Rights, Vol. 9, November 2004, pp. 591-605.

Sudan K. Falendra (2003), 'WTO, IPRs and Indian Agriculture', in Indian Economy under Globalisation Process ed by Sham Bhat, Serials publications, New Delhi, pp. 1-7.

Suresh .A. and Chand Puran (2004), 'Trade related aspects of intellectual property rights', Kurukshetra, April, pp. 21-24.

World Trade and Development Report, (2003), Academic Foundation, New Delhi, pp. 87-98.

32

INTELLECTUAL PROPERTY RIGHTS AND DEVELOPMENT OF TECHNICAL INNOVATIONS IN KENYA'S JUA KALI (SERVICE) SECTOR: AN ANALYSIS

Samwel Kakuko Lopoyetum &
Eric Ndemo Okoyo

INTRODUCTION

The service sector in Kenya which is called Jua Kali Sector in local dialect is historically anchored into the larger informal sector where a majority of the youth engage themselves as a source of self–employment when they fell out of the main stream of education and formal sector due to a variety of socio-economic problems. Initially, this informal sector provided two major basic needs. Firstly, it provided alternative employment and reasonable income to those that could not have the qualifications required for employment in the formal sector. Secondly, it provided alternative goods and services so that section of society that would not afford the costly goods and services rendered by the modern sector of the economy (ILO, 1972).

Today, the Jua Kali sector is recognised and bestowed upon as the main work place for tomorrow's surplus labour force. The sector has moved from providing the basic goods to the next level of quality goods and services. As the government and a large section of the population focus on this sector, it is no longer just expected to provide any job or cheaper products of lower quality but it is expected to absorb the main stream of the population and therefore leading to the New Demands for the Jua Kali Sector.

ORIGINAL MEANING IN JUA KALI

Jua Kali literally means "HOT SUN", it refers to the toiling and sweltering in the open air workshop, using rough equipments and machines in most cases the garages where many Kenyans work in various ways to earn a living. More often involving use of physique and stamina coupled with the problem of poor standard of work measurements and standardization process are not taken into consideration.

Jua Kali was started by people who were known as roadside mechanics and entrepreneurs. They used to help motorists who happened to be in need of mechanical services when the main garages or workshops were closed during weekends. These people proved to be quite useful. At times, they were known as back street mechanics and they operated illegally; they were not licensed although they were known to be carrying out their illegal work by the state. Craftsmen made products such as charcoal stoves, knives, hoes, etc. They repaired sauce pans and a variety of many home appliances. Infact quite a lot of people earned a living in this way in mobile workshops.

Later on in mid-eighties, the government recognised this informal open air industry as a possible way of creating employment and generating sizeable income for a large number of people; especially the youths who left school every year. They can be deployed to work in the Jua Kali sector instead of keeping themselves in the streets in search of employment. Some of these youths were even graduates of polytechnics; others had just no skill at all, but picked up as soon as they entered the Jua Kali traded business.

The first step, the Kenyan government took in encouraging this industry (JUA KALI) was to build open shades in NAIROBI, KISUMU and other Kenyan main towns for the craftsmen, so that they would work in a more organized atmosphere and also to reduce the scorching (hot) sun and even rain which reduce their production persurances. Consequently, a lot of youths have taken up the Jua Kali industry very seriously. Literate youths have the tendency of attaching themselves to skilled or experienced craftsmen and motor mechanics as apprentices. There after and initiate their own Jua Kali enterprises. Those who gain the necessary minimum skills usually continue to work there or can start their own independent workshops in the long-run.

TREND AND GROWTH OF TECHNICAL INNOVATIONS DEVELOPMENT IN KENYA'S JUA KALI SECTOR

(i) Protection and Development: The trend and growth of technological innovations development in Kenya has, historically, not been different from the western experience. It has grown mainly by trial and error subject to the requirements of consumers, customers, economic growth and market demand guided by the application of the growing technical knowledge. Such innovations and technological developments are not centrally planned but rather grow randomly (Abdel-Rahmanann, 1979).

However, in the course of time, technological research institutions such as those of Kenya Industrial Research and Development Institute (KIRDI) and others, training facilities, legislation aims at protecting technical innovation process and even the private institutions are geared towards financing research and development in the future. Infact, the collaboration between the public and private sector would ensure the necessary components of a pragmatically functioning technological system in the long-run. Hence, there is imperative need to sensitize the community through intellectual education and creation of awareness in the future environment.

This is evident in the government's involvement by creating the Ministry of Technical Training and Applied Technology, an Industrial Property Protection Unit in the Ministry of Research, Science and Technology and in proliferation of technical training institutions and research institutes in the country.

(ii) The Innovations and creativity process: The Kenya's innovative capacity in the Jua Kali sector has grown to such an extent that one cannot accurately and sufficiently cover all the upcoming technical innovations currently under way. In this paper, the authors have only shown example that several technical innovations already exist and that their further growth and development and wider dissemination of the IPR issues shall remain as the major challenge now. The technical innovations which spread across products and

services include the following range of products including the traditional and modern forms of products such as, Kiondo (Traditional Multi-purpose basket), Kenya ceramic *Jiko* (Charcoal Stove), Kuni Mbili, sisal fiber roofing tiles, car rims, chaff cutters, wood working machines and tools, building blocks making machine, flour mills, fish flies, dyes, furniture (such as the multipurpose chair), auto body repair, battery servicing etc. Moreover, advanced technologies are coming up targeted at specific consumer needs and requirements such as energy saving, domestic products–furniture, agricultural equipments and implements, metal works, construction materials and tools and other industrial applications tools and equipments.

These innovations, however, seem to reach a point where they can no longer be improved upon and in some cases loose the market for newer products. This has resulted in technological innovations being abandoned or pirated by foreign interested parties. This can be carried forward by strengthening and promoting the IPR education and awareness among the entrepreneurs/innovators.

(iii) *The Need for Protection of Jua Kali innovations through IPR system*: The Right Technological Choice Protection and Transfer shall be the dictum of Jua Kali Sector in the 21st century in developed nations they have developed strong foundations for IPR education systems, over time, strong patent laws and licence agreements to protect their inventions and innovation have been in existence. They have now moved to the protection of "intellectual property". This deals with the full proof protection of high level knowledge and know-how in certain production processes. But in the developing countries such as *India* and *Kenya* are still vulnerable in their technological pursuits because the bulk of its scientists and technologists are still fighting for survival in the world of scientific and technological i.e., meeting their basic needs. Any new knowledge or scientific know-how could easily be given to a third party for a token fee rather than protecting its knowledge fund of the experience. In fact, without some concise and deliberate government intervention, developing countries are less likely to evolve viable scientific and technical industrial bases in the 21st century.

Even, very good leading examples do exist such as those of Japan, South Korea, Mexico, India and Brazil where strong government intervention has accelerated industrial growth

(UNIDO, 1979) and taken suitable measures to protect their products by adopting the IPR and creating awareness among the innovators and intellectual community at large.

(iv) The Scope and Significant Role of Government: The government, therefore, is in a better position to influence technological acquisition within a prescribed, appropriate technological framework because:

(a) An individual company's aim is to maximize profit, hence, concern with technological appropriateness may not be a priority.

(b) Quite often an individual company may not be able to:

   (i) Offer sufficient business to interest the licensor of technology and/or

   (ii) Evaluate properly the technology offered due to lack of expertise and experience in that area of innovations.

(c) A multiplicity of technologies may be imported by entrepreneurs at the same time from he same source without adding significantly to the technical capability of a country.

(v) The Scope and Significant Role of Private Firms: While the government policy will guide the selection of appropriate technologies to meet national needs, it is individual entrepreneurs and private firms that must select and adapt a wide range of technologies available to suit their level of enterprises. Quite often, private firms experience large number of problems when they undertake purchase or operate new technologies under licence.

Therefore, before a company opt and introduces a new technology, it must carefully evaluate many areas such as:

(i) The availability of resources in terms of technical experience and expertise.

(ii) The manpower need and requirements (planning, demand, supply).

(iii) Availability of raw materials within and outside the country.

(iv) The parts components and stores.

(v) Machines and equipments facilities.

(vi) The organizational structure and management process.

(vii) The market acceptance and changing economic environment.

(viii) The prevailing competition and impact on the open market environment.

(ix) The Product Life Circle (PLC) Management and Administration.

(x) The availability of funds (finance) and at all times the working capital requirements.

(xi) The climatic conditions etc: The above considerations must be given due emphasis if any given company wishes to operate profitably on licensed technologies.

In Kenya, there is imperative need for protecting the emerging innovations more now than ever before to protect and strengthen fledgling technologies flowing into the Jua Kali sector. Private firms and organizations cannot protect these technologies due to high costs involved and the ultimate profit marginalisation goals from the technologies. At the individual level, socio-economic pressures override the meticulous attention required of innovation to break new challenging ground.

To cite few instance, it is sad to note that, Kenya has lost some of her Juha Kali innovations and most original inventions such as the world famous kiondo and the recent Kenya ceramic charcoal stove *(Jiko)* both of which are now patented outside Kenya. There is need to challenge the matter in the IPR courts and initiate urgent appeal so that we regain the innovative rights and the famous JIKO product this must be done very quickly. The Japanese are now producing synthetic and more durable kiondos. It might not be long before KCJs are mainly produced and packaged for a worldwide market. It must be protected immediately and notification dispatched to the Japanese Government.

(vi) Technology Licensing and Agreements: The terms of license agreements including legal and commercial consideration are published by the United Nations Industrial Development Organisation (UNIDO) in a monograph in the Development and Transfer of Technology, series No.1 entitled "National Approaches to the Acquisition of Technology" (New York: UNIDO, 1977). These terms and conditions should be studied carefully by those nationals who wish to enter into such negotiations in order to strengthen their positions.

It can be noted for example, that in India, the technology available in the country cannot be imported and that where importing is permissible, the importer of technology is compulsorily associated with one of the national research and development institutions so that at the end of the period of the license agreement, the country may be self-reliant with respect to that particular technology.

In the Republic of Korea, one of the reasons for effective technology transfer has been to stimulate import substitution to meet the great demand for consumer goods. In some cases the government has imposed a total embargo or high tariffs on goods that can be produced locally.

The goals of Mexican policy on technology transfer are: to find a more efficient process for adapting imported technology, to develop gradually local technologies and to encourage domestic productive units to acquire technologies appropriate for the local requirements. Mexico therefore gives great attention in assisting the local entrepreneurs to develop negotiation skills designed to obtain better contractual terms. The lessons and experiences obtained from India, Korea, and Mexico can be borrowed by the Kenyan Government to enhance scientific and technological innovations for self reliance and preferences in the 21st century.

(vii) Technology Development: An investigation into the current technological developments in the Jua Kali sector reveals a considerable number of products and projects already condemned for their industrial wastes, because no further developments were effected beyond the innovation and the entrepreneurial spirit which was vibrant in the beginning. The sector is characterized by crude but functional tools, equipment and at times a good deal of products truly symbolizing the Jua Kali type of character. In some cases some artisans and craftsmen have been known to retort to Jua Kali products as the only way out because of the value put on its functionality rather than on the inherent aesthetics, etc. A more realistic excuse for the Jua Kali artlook is the one of limited finance forcing the artisan to economically use the available resources. This more than often leads to hidden gaps and for quality of the products such as the furniture joints are very weak, tack welds that stand out on a joint, usage of unseasoned timber which later crack on warming, thin paints that can easily crack under the Hot Sun and several other flaws one could come up with in production process. In order to stimulate technological growth in the Jua Kali sector, it is necessary therefore to address some basic key areas. And

followed by need for patenting the products. Hence, for this to success, it is highly essential to provide IPR education and creation of awareness among the entrepreneurs of the community at large.

(viii) Identification and Definition of Technologies: There is a need to identify and document these technologies that have greater potential for wider usage and utilization. In such a process, the technology should be defined and its characteristics analyzed. For example, indigenous dyes for the textile industry should be defined in terms of:

(a) the raw materials (i.e. plants, additives etc),

(b) the process of extraction processing and preservation and

(c) the nature of packaging and marketing system.

For example, the metal technologies could be identified as product, analyzed in terms of its characteristics i.e. type of metal used and work conditions, and in terms of designs and manufacturing processes.

Eventually, such analysis would be helpful in determining the quality control system, measures, system, strategies, operations and tailoring production to capabilities and needs of the market environment.

(ix) Need for urgent Provision for Research and Development: After identification and analysis, there is a need for the technologies to be researched and subjected to efficiency, efficacy and performance tests, through both regional, national and private research and development institutions. This process will enhance the technology's marketability and capability in the long-run. Quite often, we come across frameworks of tools, machinery, equipments and materials which are useful but do not conform to any standard specification; regional and international they have rough finishing and most of them dare not standardize their innovative products. Consequently, they cannot be mass reproduced and may not be patented in the long-run. Hence, there is imperative need for IPR education and training system.

(x) Need for Market Research and Development: It is not enough to have products and services that merely serve an immediate need, e.g. turning table stands or stools (wooden or metal) because some customer has ordered them. There is a need for the Jua Kali artisans to move into the next stage of the process of automation modernization, upgradation and standardization on mass

production. This will undoubtedly reduce production costs and subsequently lead to higher sales and attract more customers and hence a large turnover in the business. The Jua Kali Entrepreneurs should aggressively market their merchandise and products. They should survey their markets, determine the needs of their customers and specialize in their production, system, thus greatly enhancing their quality, productivity, profitability, and sustainability in the Twenty First Century.

(xi) The Qualify of Products: As part of initiations taken in the areas such as innovation, diversification, scientific innovations and improvement in all segments of Jua Kali industry, artisans and craftsmen, it is imperative to look seriously into the future quality of these products. It is essential that, the quality of products has to be standardized by every entrepreneurs/producer and produce good quality of products. This may mean that, a metal worker must consider the quality of metal to be used for his craft to produce the desired and designed level of quality of products.

Take an example of manufacturing of a bread knife, it is used for cutting bread and food materials. How could anyone like a knife made of rusting metal? What about a charcoal stove or a metal box made from the bodywork of a car that once caught fire? This situation is happening in some sections of Jua Kali Sector. It is also difficult to tell the consumer how long such articles can last and how efficiently they can serve their purposes. Hence, i.e customers and users there is need for improving the *"source development of the raw materials"* for manufacturing the Jua Kali products in the future.

In Kenya, there exists the famous KENYA BUREAU OF STANDARDS (KBS) to gauge the standards of all products in the country. Several companies are producing products which are manufactured locally have registered with the organization. The products of high quality and standard are usually marked with symbol KBS. These are supposed to be made to KBS specification and standardization. However, Jua Kali craftsmen, many of whom work either individually or in small groups have not thought of producing standard goods, which can have a standardized quality similar to that required by KBS. Hence unable to capture international and external markets for their own products. Therefore, It is felt that with the diversification of various types of products, there should be some measure of standard quality as well. If there is a serious venture to sell Jua Kali products outside Kenya, only those goods that meet the KBS standards and patent rights will be able to enter into foreign market.

The need of the hour is to improve the Jua Kali industry by introducing some competitive approach in manufacturing goods with high quality and sustain them beyond Kenyan markets. It is necessary for craftsmen and women to develop scientific oriented technology and to infuse some aesthetic characteristics in their products range. There is a tendency to emphasize functional values in all hand made articles e.g. pottery, leather goods, metal and fibre based products etc. All these products should look extremely attractive to the users or market environment as well as being of durable nature having higher and functional value to the customers/consumers.

It is essential that, most of these products need to have well design based ideas–original and not imitative of the existing prototype. And a such, these design ideas could be introduced into pottery or ceramics–e.g. flower pots, water pots, metal. In metal ware, even a metal dust bring must be quite functional and designed to look attractive and beautiful. So articles produced by artisan A may not look identical with those of artisan B and all of them must be short-listed for patenting and meet IPR rules and regulations.

(xii) Branding/Labeling and Packaging: Another important factor which should be introduced into the Jua Kali Technology is the use of proper branding labeling and packaging of the products. Most of the imported products from say Japan, India, China, Hong Kong, Italy etc. are branded or printed on the country of origin. The brands on swords (pangas), stoves, knives etc. are quite familiar. It is also the same on the packaging materials meant for exports purposes. It is the highest time, that Kenyans need to infuse an amount of national pride in their own products by labeling as "Made in Kenya". In fact, this is a form of national patriotism. It is also a form of accountability for what is done in developing its own technology. Moreover, the Products which bear no identity of the maker producer and where they are made, showing no brand at all, possess a quality of being sham. Therefore, Branding a product with a selected brand name/or trademark may enable the consumer to contact the producer in case of advice, complaint, or consultation regarding the products. It also helps to protect every

work done by Jua Kali workmanship using their own technology and invention methods.

(xiii) Scope and Patentality for technical Innovations: Kenya is a developing country as far as technology is concerned. In the current economic environment, citizens are given as much opportunity and wider scope as possible by the state to innovate and diversify their skills in making products using locally available raw materials and facilities under the umbrella of Jua Kali. It is not only to create employment but also to open a way to scientific rather than folk art activities. It is a challenge to the Kenyans to develop and adopt modern technology as much as possible. The maintenance of the status quo of traditional techniques that can help man and the environment to survive, for example, designing and making fuel effective charcoal stove (jikos) and gadgets that can ensure the economical utilization of available renewable energy. Such original gadgets which have been certified by Kenya Bureau of Standards (KBS) should be for Juha Kali enterprise and copyrights can be reserved. Wasteful traditional practices have to be modified through Jua Kali technology system.

CONTRIBUTIONS OF UNIVERSITIES IN INTELLECTUAL PROPERTY EDUCATION, PROTECTION AND PROMOTION OF THE JUA KALI SECTOR: AN OVERVIEW

The main function of any public universities and institution of higher learning in Kenya is to provide university education, which can include technological, scientific and professional education, so as to produce mature and conscientious graduates possessing the requisite skills, technical knowledge, ability and desire to contribute to the growth and development of the nation. They are expected to contribute and enhance the livelihood and well being of the community. Another major function of the universities is to participate in the discovery, innovation, creation, protection and preservation of all fund of knowledge through viable research programmes and process. They are expected to process, transmit and disseminate such fund of knowledge so as to stimulate the intellectual life and cultural development of the country. Every university has the task of identifying the best means and ways of serving the nation and contribute effectively to the national development. It invariably depend on the university's caliber of staff, motivation and the type of manpower resources available within the community system and its disposal.

Infact, the training of engineers and technologists in Kenya is being undertaken by all the public universities. The graduate engineers from these universities are mainly absorbed into the public and private sectors. They are mainly offering services in such places as the manufacturing sector and processing industries, mechanical and electrical engineering service industries, agricultural industries and in the overall building and construction of the industries in the country. The majority of Jua Kali activities have a strong technological flavour. Yet, the Jua Kali sector hardly absorbs any university graduates with a technology or engineering background. This trend can be revised by encouraging the use of modern technology by the Jua Kali sector.

The Jua Kali sector contributes significantly to the national development of Kenya. In an informal sector, Jua Kali artisans manufacture a variety of leisure goods, consumer and industrial products and provide a wide range of services like the repair of motor vehicles, agricultural machinery and creation of employment.

The main objective of this paper is to discuss the contributions of the Universities in the promotion of intellectual property rights education, protection and promotion of the Jua Kali Sector, with reference to the government, private sector and the public universities.

EXPANSION AND EXTENSION OF APPLIED RESEARCH BY UNIVERSITIES

Many university lecturers and professors carry out applied research with the object of making their results or findings available to interested organizations and industries who may further develop and utilize the findings more effectively. Traditionally, those who make use of such research findings are large organizations and heavy industries, thus leaving the informal industries, small entrepreneur (Jua Kali Sector) with little or no benefit from university research programmes in terms of intellectual property rights (IPR), dissemination of innovative techniques, IPR education, etc.

Development of Prototype Design and University Contribution towards Technical Innovations

The Jua Kali artisans are usually semi-skilled and sufficiently equipped to produce certain range of goods and products.

Therefore such artisans can continuously be encouraged to diversify by producing items which have been designed by technical and teaching staff at various universities in the country.

Infact, faculties of engineering and technology could mobilize their technical staff into designing and producing prototypes with such designs which are protected according to the immediate needs which would be made available for mass production at the Jua Kali level. Such prototypes could be range or assortment of goods and products such as agricultural equipments and implements, machinery for small-scale industries, domestic appliances, tools, machine components and spare parts. If that approach is followed, there would be greatly expansion of Jua Kali activities in Kenya. Other than their flexible designs, the products should be tested by the university laboratory and send to Kenya Bureau of Standards (KBS) before being protected as *Juha Kali products from the Republic of Kenya.* Eventually, it must be patented and IPR processing shall commence as soon as preliminaries are finalized.

In developing such prototypes designs the universities will need to take into consideration the local availability of raw materials, the level of technology required to produce such items, the market potential of the products and the social and environmental impact of the products. The use of alternative energy resources could also be incorporated in the prototype design so that the potential for solar energy, wind power and biogas can be recognized better even at the Jua Kali level. The Department of Production Technology at Moi University is already working on various proposal to produce prototypes for a range of machinery and tools which can be massively produced by medium scale and small scale Jua Kali type of industries. The Faculty of Engineering at Jomo Kenyatta University College of Agriculture and Technology has produced prototypes for a range of laboratory equipments and farm machinery some of which could be made available to the Jua Kali sector for continued production system.

The Department of Agricultural Engineering at Egerton University has developed prototypes of seed oil processing machines which are meant to be mass produced by local medium scale industries and Jua Kali artisans. The Department is also in consultation with the local farmers to ensure that the machines/ equipments are affordable and convenient for their use. This means, the Department also maintains links with the Jua Kali artisans who are involved in production so that the quality of the machines are frequently maintained and operated with less difficulties. These few examples demonstrate that, the public Universities (mentioned above) are already engaged in activities which help to promote the Jua Kali sector. It is true, however, that universities have taken a very low profile in such activities. The authors of this paper, have felt that the time has come for the Kenyan universities to diversify their technical innovation and research activities which would involve the Jua Kali artisan at some stage. All the technical innovations must be protected under IPR rules and regulations from time to time.

SIGNIFICANCE OF SEMINARS AND SHORT COURSES

One very apt advantage is that, most universities have an element of continuing education and faculty improvement (development) programmes in which staff members organize seminars, improve their knowledge and short courses for both University staff and personnel from Government and private organizations and even the manufacturing industries. Many such seminars, conferences colloquium, workshops, brain storming, are organized at all levels. It is essential for the universities to organize seminars, workshop and short courses aimed at attracting technicians, artisans and other Jua Kali Entrepreneurs to educate and create awareness on the importance of protecting their manufacturing secrets and obtain IPR in the long-run.

All technical Seminars and short courses could be based on a number of innovative topics. The pattern of Jua Kali may include aspects of technology, entrepreneurship, marketing, economics, quality control art and design. As an example, the Department of Production Technology at Moi University can organize a seminar on foundry technology. The main aspects of discussion will be pattern making, core making and quality control of castings and pattern rights protection. The technical seminar will be of immense interest to the local foundry technicians even at the Jua Kali level.

The Department of Agricultural Engineering at Egerton University has been running short term training courses and seminars every year to train and educate manufacturers and service technicians dealing with agricultural implements and processing machines on different aspects of quality control and productivity. Such seminars and short training courses have been organized by

Kenyatta University and the University of Nairobi on a variety of topics with an intention of creating the awareness on protecting all the copy rights and patent rights. The Jua Kali artisan should always be invited to some of the technical seminars in as much as the seminars have some relevance to the Jua Kali sector.

SUGGESTIONS FOR PROMOTING INTELLECTUAL PROPERTY RIGHTS EDUCATION AND TECHNICAL INNOVATIONS

Each university is likely to come up with its own plan of action for implementing the proposed activities. Some will however find it useful to have a central body which would coordinate all technical and research activities in the University that would eventually help to promote the Jua Kali Sector. This may involve the establishment of Intermediate Technology Centers or Appropriate Technology Centers similar to the one already existing at Kenyatta University. Before any pattern to Jua Kali is done, the following role should be enacted by the University.

1. All the public universities in Kenya have at some stage engaged some of their staff in activities which have helped to promote the Jua Kali sector. However, universities have always taken a low profile in such activities licensing and copyrights and IPR issues.
2. The following examples have been cited as areas in which universities have been active or should be actively by promoted in order to the promote growth and development of Jua Kali sector.
   (a) Expansion and Extension of applied research by universities.
   (b) Undertaking Feasibility studies and market surveys from time to time.
   (c) Prototype design by university staff.
   (d) Conducting Technical Seminar and short training courses/ programmes.
   (e) Manufacture of machinery and machine tools and equipments for Jua Kali artisans.
3. It must be noted that, the Jua Kali sector plays a significant role in the socio-economic development of the nation. It is

therefore proposed that the public universities should consider adopting and adapting a *Jua Kali-friendly policy* which will enable their staff to enhance their roles in the promotion of patent and IPR rights in the Jua Kali sector. One way of implementing the policy would be to set up "Intermediate Technology Centres and innovation cells with complete IPR processes and Equipments" which would coordinate the proposed activities of Jua Kali Sector in the long-run.

(a) To work in close liaison and collaboration with all the relevant organizations involved in the promotion of the Jua Kali sector.

(b) To disseminate technological information and knowledge to the Jua Kali artisans through seminars and short training courses.

(c) To create the awareness of the importance of quality control and help to test raw materials and products of the Jua Kali industry subject to patenting and IPR rules and regulations.

(d) To study Jua Kali methods of production and suggest methods of improving efficiency in production, manpower utilization and energy efficiency components.

(e) To advise Jua Kali artisans on all matters of safety and security.

(f) To conduct feasibility studies and work studies and initiate Jua Kali artisans into newer or better methods of production and help them to diversify their range of products by supplying them with newer prototypes and designs.

(g) To make available to the Jua Kali artisans tools and machinery which would improve productivity, profitability and capacity utilization in the long-run.

CONCLUSION

To sum up, Kenya's Jua Kali Sector has over the past fifteen years grown tremendously. It is now perceived by both Government, Quasi-Governmental and Private Organizations as holding the highest potential for creating employment opportunities and developing an industrial base in Kenya. Despite this reputation, the sector still continues to experience huge problems in meeting the now sharpened (growing) demands for its products by the public. It is further riddled with obsolescence in terms of emerging advance technologies and further more some of its best ideas now stands higher risk to be pirated to other places in the world (global) market. Hence, there is imperative need to completely sensitize up the entrepreneurs, Jua Kali members, university innovators, academic, researchers, policy makers and public in all matters pertaining to the intellectual property right, copy rights, trade marks and others.

There is a need, therefore to protect such technologies through appropriate legislation, use of IPR rules and regulations and at the same time increase research and development activities on potential scientific and innovative technologies. Ultimately, all these technologies will have to be widely marketed to ensure handsome returns (benefits) for the entrepreneurs in the long-run. Only then Kenya will be on the technological development track for eventual revolutionary industrial base in East and Central Africa. It is time to go with scientific technological innovations, advancement of science and technology through IPR, copy righting as required by World bodies such as, World Intellectual Property Organization (WIPO) African Regional Industrial Property Organization (ARIPO), UNO and WTO in the 21st century.

REFERENCES

Abdul Rehmann, I.H. (1970), Operational Policy Choice Technology and Industrialization in Developing Countries. "In Conceptual and Policy Frame-work for Appropriate Industrial Technology", UNIDO Monograph 1, New York, UN, pp. 44-49.

Achoka Awoni (1991), "Indigenous Knowledge Myth or Reality". In Resource: Journal of Sustainable Development in Africa Vol. 1, No.1.

Arthur Raphael Miller, Michael H. Davis (2000), Intellectual Property: Patents, Trademarks, and Copyright, West Wadsworth; 3rd Edition.

Carr, M. (1982), "Women and Appropriate Technology: Two Essays." Occasional Paper, IDS, University of Nairobi.

Congdon, K.J.Ed. (1977), Introduction to Appropriate Technology. Towards a Simpler Life Style. Rodale Press Emmos.

Daily Nation News Paper, June 15, 1991.

Daily nation, News Paper, June 12, 1991.

Darrow, K. and Sexenian, M. (1996), Appropriate Technology Sourcebook: A Guide to Practical Books for Village and Small Community Technology Volunteers in Asia (VIA) Press.

Food and Agricultural Organisation (1991), "Sustainable Agricultural and Rural Development" in sub-sahanan Africa Regional Document No. 1, FAO/Netherlands Conference, on Agricultural and the Environment Hentogenbosch, Netherlands 15-19 April.

Fransman, M. and King, K. (Editors) (1989), Technological Capability in the Third World, Hong Kong.

Gamser, MS. Application, H and Carter (1990), Tinker, Tiler, Technical Change, Intermediate Technology Development Publications, U.K.

Government of Kenya, Ministry of Technical Training and Applied Technology, A Report on the proceedings of the Central Province, Jua Kali Exhibition, November, 1991.

International Labour Office Employment Incomes and Equality. Astrology for Increasing Productive Employment in Kenya, Geneva, ILO, 1972.

International Wonen's Tribune Centre and Intermediate Technology (1986). The Technology and Tools Book: A Guide to Technologies Women are Using Worldwide.

Jones, Andrew (1991), Setbacks to Technology Development in Kenya, Resource, Vol. 2, 1, 19-22–1991.

Kapiyo, R.J. (ed.), "African Regional Workshop on Curriculum and Social-cultural Issues in Approptiate technology Education." 19-23 February, 1990, Nairobi, Kenya.

Lane de Moll and Gigi, Coe eds (1979), Stepping Stones: Appropriate Technology and Beyond? Marion Boyas, London.

Mamadzigo, M. (1991), The Interaction of Research Institutes with Industry and Development Institute, D.Phil Research Proposal, Science Policy Research Unit, University of Sussex, UK.

Mburugu, K.G. (1991), "Appropriate Technology: Overview." A Paper Presented to Inservice Training for Home Economics Extemsion at the Hotel Kunste, Nakuru, November, 1991.

Michael Perelman (2002), Steal this idea: Intellectual property Rights and the Corporate Confiscation of Creativity, Palgrave Macmillan, (a Critical Discussion of some of the Social, Scientific and Cultural Impacts of Recent Intellectual Property Developments, 2002).

N. Ngethe and G. Ndua, A Study on Carpentary and Metal–work in the Eastland's of Nairobi, Kenyan Institute for Development Studies University of Nairobi, 105 occasional paper No. 33.

GLOSSARY OF INTELLECTUAL PROPERTY TERMS*

ASSIGNMENT [patent-trademark-copyright]. A transfer of rights in intellectual property. An assignment of a patent, for example, is a transfer of sufficient rights so that the recipient has title to the patent. The assignment can be a transfer of all rights of exclusivity in the patent, of an undivided portion (for example, a 50 percent interest), or of all rights within a specified location (for example, a certain area of the United States). Transfer of anything less is considered to be a "license." (See LICENSE, GOODWILL).

AUDIOVISUAL WORK [copyright]. A copyrightable work consisting of images that are related, presented in a series, and intended to be shown by use of a machine, as well as any sound accompanying a work. A common example of an audiovisual work is a slide show, such as that used in a sales presentation, a lecture, or an introduction to a museum.

AUTHOR [copyright]. Either the person who creates a copyrightable work or the employer of a person who creates a copyrightable work within the scope of employment. "Author" in copyright law includes not only writers of novels, plays, and treatises, but also those who create computer programs, arrange data in telephone books, choreograph dances, take photographs, sculpt stone, paint murals, write songs, record sounds, and translate books from one language to another. (See WORK MADE FOR HIRE, JOINT AUTHORS).

BERNE CONVENTION [copyright-international]. The major multilateral copyright treaty, signed in Berne, Switzerland, in 1886. The Berne Convention, whose members form the Berne Union, is adhered to by more than 75 nations. The World Intellectual Property Organization (WIPO) is the administering agency for the Berne Union.

BEST MODE [patent]. A condition for the grant of a patent. An inventor must describe the best method he or she knows for carrying out the invention.

COMMUNITY TRADE MARK (CTM) [trademark-international] A trademark registration granted by the European Community Trademark Office and enforceable throughout EC member nations.

COMPILATION [copyright]. A copyrightable work consisting of an assembly of preexisting material. The assembly must exhibit at least minimal originality in the selection, organization, and arrangement of the material without making any internal changes in it.

CONTRIBUTORY INFRINGEMENT [patent-trademark-copyright]. Indirect infringement of intellectual property rights in which one person contributes to the direct act of infringement of another. Contributory infringement of a trademark, for example, occurs when a manufacturer of goods aids or encourages its distributors to pass off its goods as those of another manufacturer.

COPIES [copyright]. As a noun, the material objects that store or fix copyrightable information other than sounds; as a verb, the act of copying.

COPYING [copyright-patent-trademark]. In copyright law, "copying" denotes two separate but interrelated concepts. To constitute an infringement of copyright, a work must be a "copy" in the sense that it is substantially similar to a copyrighted work, and it must have been copied from the copyrighted workas opposed to being the result of coincidental, independent production or from being taken from the same source as the copyrighted work. Legal standards for infringement of copyright differ from those for patents and trademarks; the latter do not require proof of copying.

COPYRIGHT [copyright]. An exclusive right conferred by the government on the creator of a work to exclude others from reproducing it, adapting it, distributing it to the public, performing it in public, or displaying it in public. Copyright does not protect an abstract idea; it protects only the concrete expression of an idea. To be valid, a copyrighted work must have originality and some modicum of creativity.

COUNTERFEITING [trademark]. The act of producing or selling a product containing an intentional and calculated reproduction of a genuine trademark. A "counterfeit mark" is identical to or substantially indistinguishable from a genuine mark. Often, counterfeit goods are made to imitate a popular product in construction and appearance so as to deceive customers into thinking they are purchasing the genuine merchandise.

DEPENDENT CLAIM [patent]. A claim in a patent that refers back to a previous claim and defines an invention that is narrower in scope than that in the previous claim. A dependent claim is written so as to be more restricted than the technology defined in the previous claim.

DERIVATIVE WORK [copyright]. A work based on a preexisting work that is changed, condensed, or embellished in some way.

DESCRIPTIVE MARK [trademark]. A word, picture, or other symbol that describes something about the goods or services in connection with which it is used, such as their purpose, their size and color, the class of users, or the end effect on users. A descriptive term is not considered to be inherently distinctive; to establish validity for registration or protection in court, it needs proof of acquired distinctiveness, known as "secondary meaning." (See SECONDARY MEANING, SUGGESTIVE MARK)

DESIGN PATENT [patent]. A government grant of exclusive rights in a novel, nonobvious, and ornamental industrial design. A design patent confers the right to exclude others from making, using, or selling designs that closely resemble the patented design. A design patent covers the ornamental aspects of a design; its functional aspects are covered by a utility patent. A design patent and a utility patent can cover different aspects of the same article, such as an automobile or a lamp.

DILUTION [trademark]. A type of infringement of a trademark in which the defendant's use, while not causing likelihood of confusion, tarnishes the image or blurs the distinctiveness of the owner's mark. To possess the selling power and recognition protected by antidilution statutes, a mark must be relatively strong and famous, at least within a certain group of people, product line, or territory.

DISTRIBUTION RIGHT [copyright]. Exclusive right of a copyright owner to distribute copies or phonorecords of his or her work to the public by sale, lease, or rental. Unlike the other rights of copyright, the distribution right is infringed merely by a transfer of copies of a work, whether those copies were made lawfully or unlawfully, except under the "First Sale Doctrine." (See FIRST SALE DOCTRINE)

DOMAIN NAMES [trademark]. The names and words that companies designate for their registered Internet Web site addresses, such as the "Forbes" magazine name in the URL http://www.forbes.com. Trademark disputes arise when more than one company tries to use the same domain name, or one company appropriates another company's brand or product name for its URL.

DURATION [patent-trademark-copyright-trade secret]. The term or length of time that an intellectual property right lasts. A U.S. patent on an invention, for example, has a duration of 20 years from the date on which the patent application was filed, as does a plant patent. The basic duration of a U.S. copyright is the life of the author plus 70 years. Protection of information as a trade secret lasts as long as the information remains secret.

EQUIVALENTS, DOCTRINE OF [patent]. A rule of claim interpretation under which a product or process, although not a literal infringement, is an infringement if it performs substantially the same function in substantially the same way to obtain substantially the same result as a patented product or process.

FAIR USE [copyright-trademark]. A defense to a charge of copyright or trademark infringement. For copyrights, U.S. courts consider four factors in determining if a fair use defense exists: the purpose and character of the disputed use; the nature of the copyrighted work; the importance of the portion used in relation to the work as a whole; and the effect of the use on the market for or value of the copyrighted work. For trademarks, the secondary user must show that he or she is not using a descriptive, geographically descriptive, or personal name mark in a trademark sense but only to describe his or her goods or services or their geographic origin, or to name the person running the business.

FIELD OF USE RESTRICTION [general intellectual property-antitrust]. A provision in an intellectual property license restricting the licensee to use the licensed property only in a defined product or service market.

FIRST SALE DOCTRINE [copyright]. An exception to the exclusive right of a copyright owner to distribute copies or phonorecords of a copyrighted work. Under this principle, the copyright owner has the right to sell a copy of a book but not the right to control subsequent sales of that copy. (See DISTRIBUTION RIGHT).

FIRST TO FILE [patent-trademark]. A rule under which, for patents, priority is determined by which inventor was the first to file a patent application, rather than by who was first to invent. This rule is followed by almost every nation in the world except the United States. For trademarks, priority between conflicting applications to register a trademark is handled by publishing the application with the earliest filing date for possible opposition by the applicant with a later filing date. In the United States, ownership of a trademark is determined by who was first to use it, not by who was first to file an application for registration. However, under the new intent-to-use system, an application for registration can be filed prior to actual use of a mark. (See INTENT-TO-USE APPLICATION).

FIRST TO INVENT [patent]. A rule under which patent priority is determined by which inventor was the first to actually invent, rather than by who was the first to file a patent application. This is the rule followed in the United States.

FUNCTIONALITY [patent-trademark-copyright]. That aspect of design that makes a product work better for its intended purpose, as opposed to making the product look better or to identifying its commercial source.

GENERIC NAME [trademark]. A word used by most people to name a class or category of product or service, such as "personal computer" or "cellular phone." No one person may have trademark rights to a generic name.

GOODWILL [trademark]. The value of a business or of a line of goods or services, beyond its tangible assets, that reflects its commercial reputation. A business with a well-established goodwill could have all its tangible assets destroyed yet still own its reputation—its goodwill. Since a trademark or service mark is a symbol of a business's goodwill, trademark infringement is a form of theft of goodwill.

IDEA-EXPRESSION DICHOTOMY [copyright]. A fundamental rule of law that copyright does not protect an idea: copyright protects only specific expressions of an idea.

INFRINGEMENT [general intellectual property]. An invasion of an exclusive right of intellectual property. Infringement of a utility patent involves making, using, or selling a patented product or process without permission. Infringement of a design patent involves fabrication of a design that, to the ordinary observer, is substantially the same as an existing design, where the resemblance is intended to induce the observer to purchase one thing supposing it to be another. Infringement of a trademark consists of the unauthorized use or imitation of a mark that is the property of another in order to deceive, confuse, or mislead others. Infringement of a copyright involves reproducing, adapting, distributing, performing in public, or displaying in public the copyrighted work of someone else.

INTELLECTUAL PROPERTY [patent-trademark-unfair competition-copyright-trade secret-moral rights]. Creative ideas and expressions of the human mind that have commercial value and receive the legal protection of a property right. The major legal mechanisms for protecting intellectual property rights are copyrights, patents, and trademarks. Intellectual property rights enable owners to select who may access and use their property and to protect it from unauthorized use.

INTENT-TO-USE APPLICATION [trademark]. Since 1989 in the United States, an optional method of applying for federal registration of a trademark based on a declared intention to use the mark on specific goods or services.

INVENTION [patent]. The creation of a new technical idea and of the physical means to accomplish or embody it. To be patentable, an invention must be novel, have utility, and differ from what skilled users might expect.

JOINT AUTHORS [copyright]. The creators of a copyrightable work who merge their separate contributions to the work. If there is joint authorship, then it follows that there is joint ownership of copyright in the work created. Co-owners of a copyright are treated as "tenants in common," with each co-owner having an independent right to license the use of a work, subject to accounting to the other co-owners for any profits.

JOINT INVENTORS [patent]. Two or more inventors of a single invention who work together in the inventive process.

KNOCK-OFF [patent-trademark-copyright]. An identical copy of a work or product that is protected by patent, trademark, trade dress, or copyright.

KNOW-HOW [trade secret]. Information that enables a person to accomplish a particular task or to operate a particular device or process.

LICENSE [patent-trademark-copyright]. A permission to use an intellectual property right within a defined time, context, market line, or territory. In intellectual property law, there are important distinctions between "exclusive licenses" and "nonexclusive licenses." An exclusive license is "exclusive" as to a defined scope; it is not the one and only license granted by a licensor. In giving an exclusive license, the licensor promises that he or she will not grant other licenses of the same rights within the same scope or field covered by the exclusive license. However, the owner of rights may grant any number of nonexclusive licenses of the same rights. In a nonexclusive license, title remains with the licensor. A patent license is a transfer of rights that does not amount to an assignment of the patent. A trademark or service mark can be validly licensed only if the licensor controls the nature and quality of the goods or services sold by the licensee under the licensed mark. Under copyright law, an exclusive licensee is the owner of a particular right of copyright, and he or she may sue for infringement of the licensed right. There is never more than a single copyright in a work regardless of the owner's exclusive license of various rights to different persons.

MISAPPROPRIATION [unfair competition]. A common law form of unfair competition in which an individual or firm copies or appropriates some creation of another that is not protected by patent, copyright, or trademark law, or any other traditional theory of exclusive rights.

MORAL RIGHTS [copyright-author's rights]. Certain rights of authors, beyond those recognized in copyright law, as recognized by the legal systems of some European and other countries. Moral rights generally fall into three categories: the right of an author to receive credit as the author of a work, to prevent others from falsely being named author, and to prevent use of his or her name for works he or she did not create; the right of an author to prevent mutilation of a work; and the right of an author to withdraw a work from distribution if it no longer represents his or her views.

MUSICAL WORK [copyright]. A category of copyrightable work expressed in notation for sounds. A musical work can be fixed in physical objects that are classified as either "copies" (e.g., sheet music) or "phonorecords" (e.g., compact discs or tapes). A composer's song is covered by a musical work copyright, but a recording of the song is covered by a sound recording copyright.

NOTICE [patent-copyright-trademark]. A formal sign or notification attached to items that embody or reproduce an intellectual property right—for example, placing the word "patent" or its abbreviation, "pat.," together with the patent number, on a patented article made by a patent holder or his/her licensees. The formal statutory notice of U.S. trademark registration is the letter R in a circle symbol -®, "Reg. U.S. Pat. & Tm. Off.," or "Registered in U.S. Patent and Trademark Office." Many firms use informal trademark notices, such as "Brand," "TM," "Trademark," "SM," or "Service Mark," adjacent to words or other symbols considered to be protectable marks. Notice of copyright consists of the letter C in a circle symbol - © or the word "Copr." or "Copyright," the copyright owner's name, and the year of first publication.

NOVELTY [patent]. One of three conditions an invention must meet to be patentable. Novelty is present if every element of an invention is not disclosed in a single piece of prior art.

OBVIOUSNESS [patent]. A condition in which an invention cannot receive a valid patent because a person with ordinary skill in that technology can readily deduce it from publicly available information (prior art).

ON SALE [patent]. The situation in which an inventor cannot obtain a patent if he or she waits for more than one year to file a patent application after a product embodying the invention has been placed "on sale."

ORDINARY SKILL IN THE ART [patent]. The level of technical knowledge, experience, and expertise possessed by the ordinary engineer, scientist, or designer in a technology that is relevant to an invention.

PASSING OFF [trademark]. (1) The substitution of one brand of goods for another. (2) Trademark infringement in which the infringer intentionally means to mislead or deceive purchasers. (3) Trademark infringement in which there is no proof of intent to deceive but likelihood of confusion can be proven. (4) In British-law countries, acts illegal under the common law, apart from registered trademark law, involving the misrepresentation of one's goods or services as those of a competitor, usually by using a similar mark.

PATENT [patent]. A grant by the federal government to an inventor of the right to exclude others from making, using, or selling his or her invention. There are three kinds of patents in the United States: a utility patent on the functional aspects of products and processes; a design patent on the ornamental design of useful objects; and a plant patent on a new variety of a living plant. Patents do not protect ideas, only structures and methods that apply technological concepts. Each type of patent confers the right to exclude others from a precisely defined scope of technology, industrial design, or plant variety. In return for the right to exclude, an inventor must fully disclose the details of the invention to the public so that others can understand it and use it to further develop the technology. Once the patent expires, the public is entitled to make and use the invention and is entitled to a full and complete disclosure of how to do so.

PERFORMANCE [copyright]. To recite, render, play, dance, or act a copyrighted work, including the radio or television broadcast of a performance and the reception of such a broadcast. The right to perform a copyrighted work publicly is granted to all types of copyrighted works except for pictorial and sculptural works and sound recordings.

PHONORECORD [copyright]. The material object that stores or fixes copyrightable sounds, such as audiotapes, compact discs, computer chips that store sounds, and the like, other than the sound track of a motion picture.

PRIOR ART [patent]. The existing body of technological information against which an invention is judged to determine if it is novel and nonobvious and can thus be patented.

PROCESS CLAIM [patent]. A claim of a patent that covers the method by which an invention is performed by defining the steps to be followed, in contrast to a product claim or an apparatus claim, which covers the structure of a product.

PRODUCT-BY-PROCESS CLAIM [patent]. A patent claim in which a product is claimed by defining the process by which it is made. The product-by-process form of claim is most often used to define new chemical compounds, since many new chemicals, drugs, and pharmaceuticals can practicably be defined only by describing the process of making them.

PRODUCT CLAIM [patent]. A claim of a patent that covers the structure, apparatus, or composition of a product, in contrast to a process claim, which covers a method or process.

PUBLICATION [copyright]. The distribution of copies or phonorecords of a work to the public.

PUBLIC DOMAIN [general intellectual property]. The status of an invention, creative work, commercial symbol, or any other creation that is not protected by some form of intellectual property. Items that have been determined to be in the public domain are available for copying and use by anyone. The copying of such items is not only tolerated but encouraged as part of the competitive process. (See COPYING, INTELLECTUAL PROPERTY.)

REDUCTION TO PRACTICE [patent]. The physical part of the inventive process that completes and ends the process of invention. After a reduction to practice, the invention is complete for patent law purposes.

RENEWAL [trademark-copyright]. The extension of a registration of a trademark or the extension of a copyright.

REVERSE ENGINEERING [trade secret]. A method of obtaining technical information by starting with a publicly available product and determining what it is made of, what makes it work, and how it was produced. This method goes in the reverse direction of usual engineering efforts, which start with technical data and use them to produce a product. If the product or other material that is the subject of reverse engineering was properly obtained, the process is legitimate and legal.

RIGHT OF PUBLICITY [general intellectual property]. The inherent right of every human being to control the commercial use of his or her identity.

SECONDARY MEANING [trademark]. A meaning for a trademark or service mark that customers associate with a particular brand of products or services. For trade symbols that are not inherently distinctive, distinctiveness must be acquired in order to be protected by a trademark or service mark. This acquired distinctiveness is known as "secondary meaning" because it is acquired second in time to the primary meaning of a word. A word such as "best" for milk is regarded as descriptive and not inherently distinctive. The primary meaning is that milk thus described is purported to be the best. To achieve exclusive trademark rights for a product called "Best Milk," a seller using this word must use it so that it achieves a secondary meaning denoting that all milk marked "best" comes from a single commercial source.

SERVICE MARK [trademark]. A word, slogan, design, picture, or any other symbol used to identify and distinguish a service (hotel and restaurant services, sales services, investment services, and the like) as opposed to a product.

SKILL IN THE ART [patent]. An ordinary level of proficiency in the particular technology in which an invention is made. (See OBVIOUSNESS.)

SOUND RECORDING [copyright]. A category of copyrightable work consisting of the sounds that are recorded on a phonorecord.

SUBSTANTIAL SIMILARITY [copyright]. The degree of resemblance between a copyrighted work and a second work that is sufficient to constitute copyright infringement by the second work. Exact word-for-word or line-for-line identity is not necessary for copyright infringement. Rather, U.S. courts have chosen the phrase "substantial similarity" to define the level of similarity that, together with proof of validity and copying, constitutes copyright infringement.

SUGGESTIVE MARK [trademark]. A word, picture, or other symbol that suggests, but does not directly describe, something about a good or service in connection with which it is used as a mark. For example, "goliath" for wood pencils suggests, but does not literally describe, large size. A suggestive term is regarded as being inherently distinctive and needs no proof of secondary meaning for registration or protection in court. (See DESCRIPTIVE MARK.)

SUPPLEMENTAL REGISTER [trademark]. A register of words, symbols, package trade dress, product or container shapes, or slogans that do not qualify for registrable trademark status but can achieve trademark status once they acquire secondary meaning. (See SECONDARY MEANING.)

TRADE DRESS [trademark]. The totality of elements in which a product or service is packaged, such as the shape and appearance of a product or container, the cover of a book or magazine, and the distinctive and recognizable shape of an automobile. These elements combine to create the visual image presented to customers and can acquire exclusive legal rights as a type of trademark or identifying symbol of origin.

TRADEMARK [trademark]. 1. A word, slogan, design, picture, or other symbol used to identify and distinguish goods. 2. Any identifying symbol, including a word, design, or shape of a product or container, that qualifies for legal status as a trademark, service mark, collective mark, certification mark, trade name, or trade dress. Trademarks identify one seller's goods and distinguish them from goods sold by others. They signify that all goods bearing the mark come from or are controlled by a single source and are of an equal level of quality. And they advertise, promote, and generally assist in selling goods. A trademark is infringed by another if the second use causes confusion of source, affiliation, connection, or sponsorship.

TRADE NAME [trademark]. A symbol used to identify and distinguish companies, partnerships, and businesses, as opposed to marks used to identify and distinguish goods or services.

TRADE SECRET [trade secret]. Business information that is the subject of reasonable efforts to preserve confidentiality and has value because it is not generally known in the trade. Such confidential information is protected against those who gain access to it through improper methods or by a breach of confidence. Infringement of a trade secret is a type of unfair competition. (See UNFAIR COMPETITION).

UNFAIR COMPETITION [general intellectual property]. Commercial conduct that the law views as unjust, giving a civil claim against a person who has been injured by the conduct. Trademark infringement has long been considered to be unfair competition. Other recognized legal categories of unfair competition are false advertising, trade libel, infringement of a trade secret, infringement of the right of publicity, and misappropriation.

UTILITY [patent]. The usefulness of a patented invention. To be patentable, an invention must operate and be capable of use, and it must perform some "useful" function for society.

WORLD INTELLECTUAL PROPERTY ORGANIZATION (WIPO) [international]. One of the 16 specialized agencies of the United Nations system. WIPO, located in Geneva, Switzerland, was created in 1967 and is responsible for promoting the protection of intellectual property throughout the world. It fulfills this responsibility by promoting cooperation among nations in intellectual property matters, administering various "unions" and other treaty organizations founded on multilateral treaties, and creating model laws for adoption by developing nations.

WORK MADE FOR HIRE [copyright]. A work prepared by an employee within the scope of his or her employment or a commissioned work that the parties agree in writing to treat as a work made for hire. The real person, partnership, or corporation for which the work is prepared is considered to be both the author and the owner of copyright from the moment of creation of the work.

WORLD TRADE ORGANIZATION (WTO) [international trade-intellectual property]. An international body dealing with the rules of trade between nations. At its heart are agreements negotiated and signed by the bulk of the world's trading nations. These documents provide the legal ground rules for international commerce. The three main purposes of the WTO are to help trade flow as freely as possible, to serve as a forum for trade negotiations, and to provide for settlement of disputes.

* *The information provided here was excerpted from McCarthy's Desk Encyclopedia of Intellectual Property, Second Edition, written by J. Thomas McCarthy as quoted by Benjamin Oelsner.*

INDEX